LATINO LIBRARIANSHIP

LATINO LIBRARIANSHIP
A Handbook for Professionals

Salvador Güereña
Editor

McFARLAND & COMPANY, INC., PUBLISHERS
Jefferson, North Carolina, and London

The selected, annotated bibliography of titles in Spanish by and for American writers, from *Booklist*, May 15, 1986, is reprinted by permission of the American Library Association.

The "RASD Guidelines for Library Services to Hispanics," by the Reference and Adult Services Division's Committee on Library Service to the Spanish Speaking, adopted June 1988, is reprinted by permission of the American Library Association.

The Queens Library's Hispanic Committee's *"Say Si" Manual*, September 1988, is reprinted by permission of the Queens Borough Public Library.

The Santa Barbara, California, Public Library bilingual interview questionnaire, n.d., is reprinted by permission of that library.

The "Spanish Language Reference In-Take Form ("¿Habla usted Español? ¿Tiene usted una Pregunta?"), n.d., is reprinted by permission of CORE, California Opportunities for Reference Excellence.

British Library Cataloguing-in-Publication data are available

Library of Congress Cataloguing-in-Publication Data

Latino librarianship : a handbook for professionals / [edited by]
  Salvador Güereña.
    p.   cm.
  [Includes index.]
  Includes bibliographical references.
  ISBN 0-89950-532-5 (lib bdg. : 50# alk. paper) ∞
  1. Libraries—Special collections—Hispanic Americans.
2. Hispanic Americans—Bibliography—Methodology.   3. Hispanic
Americans—Information services.   4. Hispanic Americans—Archival
resources.   5. Hispanic Americans—Library resources.   6. Hispanic
Americans—Data bases.   7. Hispanic Americans and libraries.
I. Güereña, Salvador.
Z688.H57L38   1990
027.6′3089′68—dc20   90-52571
                                                      CIP

Manufactured in the United States of America

McFarland & Company, Inc., Publishers
  Box 611, Jefferson, North Carolina 28640

to my son
Davíd Tonatiuh

ACKNOWLEDGMENTS

First and foremost, I want to thank the authors for their fine contributions and their welcomed cooperation; I appreciate the thoughtful attention they each gave their respective articles despite their very busy schedules. I have been enriched by their collegiality and friendship. I also wish to thank Raquel Quiroz González for her invaluable assistance with the manuscript, and to offer a word of appreciation to Sarah Capitelli, Michelle Hayner, and Ilia Rodriguez for their keyboarding assistance.

I would like to acknowledge the University Library of the University of California at Santa Barbara, whose support of my work has made this, and many other projects, a reality, in the interest of service to the Latino community. Acknowledgment is also due the Center for Chicano Studies on the Santa Barbara campus, for its support.

TABLE OF CONTENTS

Appendices

INTRODUCTION

This handbook was prepared to give guidance to librarians who are either presently involved in serving Latino communities, or for whom this will be a new responsibility. *Latino Librarianship* will be useful to library administrators who are concerned with planning and providing library services to Latinos. Also, given the increasing interest in this field of study, library school students should find this an excellent introduction. The chapters in this book were selected to cover diverse aspects of the field. In addition to providing background, they help to inform about issues, strategies, and resources involving this population group. It is hoped that the handbook will contribute to a better understanding of Latino librarianship, not only by those within the ranks of librarianship, but by those outside the profession as well.

Latino Librarianship, by design, does not address children's issues. There are several recent publications which offer an excellent orientation to children's services and can aid in developing children's collections. These are Adela Artola Allen's *Library Services for Hispanic Children: A Guide for Public and School Librarians* (Oryx Press, 1987) and Isabel Schon's *Books in Spanish for Children and Young Adults: An Annotated Guide* (Scarecrow Press, 1989).

Collectively, the authors of the present work call attention to the great diversity that exists among the Latino population, and it is with this in mind that the reader is introduced to the various dimensions involved in delivering effective services. For example, Eugene Estrada, in his thought-provoking chapter on the challenges of the changing Latino demographics, not only gives us a profile about the Latino population and its needs, but also suggests a blueprint for action by libraries. In my own article on community analysis, librarians are introduced to the process by which they may study a Latino community and assess its needs, a prerequisite to planning and developing services.

Albert J. Milo describes the characteristics of Spanish reference service within the context of California's public libraries, but there are many parallels with patterns of service involving libraries outside that state. Moreover, his recommendations for improved reference services will be as pertinent and timely to a library in Illinois or North Carolina as they would be to one in East Los Angeles. Richard Chabrán, in his bibliographic essay on Latino reference sources, has prepared an excellent survey of the many available tools with which to serve users. Even a cursory examination of his list of reference sources will discover evidence that these indeed "reflect a growing sophistication and specialization." Ron Rodríguez's piece on Latino online databases and CD-ROMs yields some critical perspectives about the status of online services, and his discussion of emerging products informs us about new information systems and their implications for improved Latino reference services.

The next three chapters involve collection development concerns. Linda Chávez's chapter on building Spanish language collections defines what are the appropriate criteria for book evaluation and selection and gives very practical advice on the use of selection aids, and on identifying appropriate vendors and distributors. In the chapter that follows, Robert G. Trujillo and Chávez team up to discuss comprehensively the nature of collection development on the Mexican-American experience. They thoughtfully review the various bibliographic aids and acquisitions strategies, and present guidelines for evaluation and selection of materials in the different formats. Danilo Figueredo's chapter involves a very different approach in his coverage of Cuban-American authors and resources. His emphasis is on imparting knowledge about the various genres of Cuban-American literature in relation to its major writers. His panoramic literary analysis is meant to give librarians a better understanding of the available materials with which to build collections. The book titles in his selected, annotated bibliography are recommended for medium-sized libraries interested in reaching the Latino community, regardless of the number of its Cuban-American constituents.

The next two chapters cover an overlooked field of Latino librarianship, namely, the development of archival and manuscript collections. César Caballero addresses many of the issues and opportunities involved in documenting and preserving Latino culture and heritage. Nélida Pérez and Amilcar Tirado Aviles, on the other hand, have prepared a very thoughtful and effective case study that speaks to us about the unique and special role played by the Centro de Estudios Puertorriqueños, of Hunter College, in preserving the cultural and historical record of Puerto Ricans in this country and of Puerto Rico itself. All three authors underscore the value of having strong linkages with the community.

The chapter that follows, by Patrick José Dawson, examines the history and role of REFORMA, on the eve of the twentieth anniversary of this national association, which has championed the promotion of library services to the Spanish-speaking in this country. His insightful chronology helps us to better understand this vital and maturing organization.

And finally, I have provided an extensive bibliography on the movement to establish English as the sole official language of the United States in the hope that it will help direct librarians and others to sources of information about this very significant public policy issue.

Inevitably, questions arise concerning the use of the term "Latino" versus "Hispanic" or some other term, and the selection of the most appropriate words to describe individual Latino subgroups. Much discussion could ensue over this issue and, in fact, some of the authors in this anthology do address it. The editor's preference is to use the term "Latino" as a more or less generic and inclusive descriptor which encompasses subgroups of various Latin American origins. Nevertheless, in recognition of the spirit of pluralism, use of the terms preferred by the individual contributors has been retained in each chapter. Within the book as a whole, the term "Spanish-speaking" has mainly been used to describe persons whose first language is Spanish. It is sometimes also used as a term referring to Latinos in general, regardless of language abilities or preferences. This explanation is not meant to further cloud the issue, it is simply an acknowledgment of prevailing practices. Ron Rodríguez does an excellent job of examining the subject in his chapter.

And finally, the reader should note that this book must not be construed as *the* authoritative guide to Latino librarianship. As a handbook, it builds on the work of other publications on this subject. There are many possible topics to explore, and it is conceivable that greater diversity could have been reflected in its pages; it is hoped that other laborers will carry the mission forward.

Salvador Güereña
January 1990

CHANGING LATINO DEMOGRAPHICS AND AMERICAN LIBRARIES

Eugene Estrada

The 1980 federal census heralded a new "Decade of the Hispanic." The results of the census revealed Hispanic population totals to be significantly higher than in the previous census of 1970. Spanish-surnamed totals had increased from just over 9 million in 1970 to more than 14.6 million in 1980, a net increase of 61 percent in the total Hispanic population.[1] Latinos had new hope that these fresh figures would add credence to their arguments for social and economic justice. It was as if a long period of neglect would come to an end by merely reaching a numeric plateau. Surely now we would become significant players in the politics of the nation. Now our needs would be taken seriously, due to the strength of our collective voice.

Unfortunately, this has not been the case. From 1980 to 1988 the Hispanic population is estimated to have increased by 34 percent. This represents an extra 5 million people above 1980 census totals. Now as we stand on the doorstep of the 1990s, officially numbering nearly 20 million, we can clearly see that numbers alone won't do it. The very same problems that have plagued us in the past, that bedevil our present, will surely follow us into the future. The tremendous growth rate has had virtually no positive impact on some of our most pressing economic and social problems. In fact, there are indications that things are getting worse.

Who are we? What does the word Hispanic mean? The Census Bureau defines Hispanic as "persons who reported themselves as Mexican-American, Chicano, Mexican, Puerto Rican, Cuban, Central or South American, or [of] other Hispanic origin." The phrase "other Hispanic origin" in turn is described as applying to "those whose origins are from Spain or persons identifying themselves as Hispanic, Spanish, Spanish-American, Hispano, Latino, etc." Non-Hispanic Americans generally consider Hispanics to be persons of Mexican or Latin American descent, or immigrants from Mexico or Latin America. What we call ourselves at home or within our communities includes quite a number of colloquial terms. The word "Latino" seems to have found favor in some circles. For our purposes I will use Hispanic and Latino interchangeably in the course of this chapter.

First, a brief overview of the demographic situation.

1

Numbers

How many of us are there? As of this writing the official Census Bureau estimate of the March 1988 Current Population Survey stood at 19.4 million.[2] By the time this piece is published the official figure should be in excess of 20 million. The two strongest sources of this population explosion have been the mass migration of people from Mexico, Central America and the Caribbean, and the high birth rates found among native-born United States Latinos. Hispanics are also growing at a faster rate than both blacks and non–Hispanic whites.

Geographic Concentration

Where do we live? While the Spanish surnamed can be found in every state, the vast majority can be easily located in a few key states. Texas and California alone accounted for a whopping 55 percent of all Latinos in 1988, California having more than a third of all American Hispanics with 34 percent of the nation's total. Texas is the state of residence for a little more than 21 percent of United States Latinos. Add in Arizona, Colorado and New Mexico, and the Southwest is home to 63 percent of all Hispanics.[3]

Outside of the Southwest we find 11 percent of the total in New York and 8 percent in Florida. Illinois has 4 percent, and New Jersey has 3 percent. That makes nine states with 89 percent of all United States Hispanics.[4] This geographic concentration tends to limit the awareness of the rest of the country to the issues and concerns of Latinos. Consequently, we have not played a prominent, recognized role in the heritage and tradition of the Eastern Seaboard, the South, or the Midwest. New York has over 2 million Hispanics, mostly Puerto Ricans, and Florida has more than a million, mostly Cuban, Hispanics. We are now and will continue to be, with these significant exceptions, a people whose location will be concentrated in the Sunbelt.

Urban-Based

Within these states we are overwhelmingly an urban people. More than 90 percent of United States Hispanics are found in metropolitan areas.[5] The image of the farmworker notwithstanding, we are not a rural bucolic people. Hispanics are subject to all the pressures and pitfalls of modern, urban America.

Age Characteristics

The age structure of Hispanics is an important and telling component of our demographic profile. The median age for all Hispanics in 1988 was

25.5. For those Americans not of Hispanic origin the number was 32.9.[6] We are as a group younger than most Americans and will continue to be so for many decades to come. In fact, the gap is widening. According to Census Bureau projections, in 2030 the gap in median age between Hispanics and white non–Hispanics could be as much as 10 years (a median age of 33.0 years compared to 43.9).[7]

Fertility Patterns

In addition to being younger we are also more fertile. The fertility rate for Hispanic women in the 1980s has been nearly 50 percent higher than for non–Hispanic women. In 1987 Latinos accounted for 11 percent of all American births, even though they represented only 8 percent of all women 18–44 years of age.[8] This high fertility rate continually adds to the pool of younger age groups. Hispanic women are more likely than non–Hispanic women to have borne children in their lifetime. Generally they also tend to have more children in the course of their lifetime than their non–Hispanic sisters.

Youthful Profile

Immigration from Latin America also helps keep our population young, since most immigrants tend to be young adults. Immigrants in turn have a birth rate even higher than United States Latinos and generally maintain larger families, as was the custom in their native countries. Combine all the aforementioned factors and we are assured of maintaining our youthful age structure well into the future.

The Role of Immigration

Immigration — or, "look out here we come" — continues to be a major source of replenishment for nearly all Hispanic subgroups. The Census Bureau estimates over 2 million Hispanic immigrants have been received by the United States between 1980 and 1988 alone.[9] This figure, according to the Bureau, includes the undocumented as well. Over the years, the accuracy of any estimate of illegal aliens has been subject to dispute.

Immigration accounted for roughly half of Latino population growth in the 1980s. These New Americans heavily influence most aspects of our demography. The challenges that these New Americans represent, not only for Hispanics but for our nation as a whole, are well documented. Younger, less educated, poorer, usually lacking job skills, their presence exacerbates the already serious social and economic problems that exist in our barrios.

And yet the United States economy still has need of this vast, cheap source of labor, and will be increasingly dependent upon it as elements of the nation's native-born workforce continue to shrink. Despite the landmark legislation that the Immigration Act of 1986 represents, these hemispheric neighbors will continue to come.

Schooling

Education is often cited as the primary solution to our collective woes, the surest vehicle out of our socioeconomic depths. Despite this perception, despite the phenomenal increase in Latino school-age children, the number of Latinos 25 years and over, in 1988, who had completed four years or more of high school was 51 percent, more than 25 percentage points lower than those Americans not of Hispanic origin.[10] Half of all Hispanic adults lack a high school diploma. This devastating statistic is somewhat mitigated by the fact that the 51 percent is an improvement, a big improvement, over earlier figures. Consider this: in 1970 the number of Hispanics 25 years old and over with a high school education was 32 percent. In 1980 the figure was 44 percent. Further progress may be noted among those Latinos 25–34 years of age. In 1988, it was found that 62 percent in this group had completed high school.[11]

There is good news and bad news about Latino college graduates as well. The proportion of Hispanics 25 years old and over who had completed four or more years of college in 1988 was 10 percent. This is less than half of the percentage for non–Hispanic college graduates, which was 21 percent.[12] Clearly we have tremendous barriers to surmount, and great strides to make before we can catch up to the educational attainment levels of our fellow Americans.

Economic Characteristics

Poverty, and plenty of it: One in four American families of Hispanic origin lives in poverty. The number of Hispanic families living below the poverty level in 1987 was 25.8 percent.[13] This is two and a half times as high as the figure for non–Hispanic families, which was 9.7 percent.[14] This poverty rate of approximately 25 percent for Hispanic families has remained constant throughout the 1980s. While the percentage has remained the same, the actual number of poor Hispanics has risen by millions.

Family income statistics are yet another way to gauge our shortcomings. The median family income for Hispanic families in 1987 was $20,300. Non-Hispanic families had a median income of $31,600—a full third higher than Latinos. Incredibly, the median family income of United States Hispanics, adjusted for inflation, fell by 8.5 percent during the 1980s.[15]

Work and employment: The unemployment rate for non–Hispanics 16 years old and over was 5.8 percent in 1988. For the Hispanic worker in 1988 the rate was 8.5 percent. But throughout the 1980s the unemployment rate for Latinos has been in double digits: 10.2 percent in 1987, 11.3 percent in 1985, 16.5 percent in 1983. For the non–Hispanic, unemployment reached double digit proportions only once in the eighties. In fact 1988 is the first time in the 1980s that the unemployment rate for Latinos has not been in double digits.[16]

When Hispanics are employed they generally find themselves at the lower end of the pay scale. Their general lack of educational attainment virtually assures that Latinos will be earning far less than non–Hispanic working Americans. Median earnings for Latino men in 1987 was $12,527; for non–Hispanic working men it was $20,496. The median earnings of women was, however, far closer, with non–Hispanic women earning $10,745 and their Latina counterparts earning $8,554.[17]

The occupations held by Latinos also reflect the earnings and educational levels they achieve. Only 13 percent of Latino males were in managerial or professional specialty occupations. Less than half the percentage of non–Hispanic males who totaled 27 percent were employed in that category. The circle of lower educational levels, low-paying jobs, and meager family incomes goes round and round. We can expect to witness more of the same.[18]

In 1987 Latinos made up only 7 percent of total employment in the United States. This figure is rapidly increasing because between 1980 and 1987 we accounted for nearly a fifth of the total increase in new employment. Hispanics are the fastest growing labor force in the nation. Given the relatively high birthrates, the continuing flow of new immigrants, and the increased participation of female Hispanics in the labor force (Hispanic women's employment levels are up almost 50 percent since 1980), we should remain the fastest growing segment of the population for some time to come. The Bureau of Labor Statistics projects the Hispanic civilian labor force will grow by 74 percent by the end of the century.[19]

Family Characteristics

While some things remain unchanged and other conditions change tremendously, some of the modifications we are experiencing lead in painful new directions. The much commented-upon Hispanic family, the ideal from which we derive such comfort, is changing in composition. The evolution of the American family includes the family-oriented Hispanic. Changes in family composition among Latinos parallel the dramatic changes that have occurred in non–Hispanic American family life in recent decades.

The proportion of Hispanic families maintained by married couples was down, from 74 percent in 1982 to 70 percent in 1988. Actually this is a full 10 percent lower than non–Hispanic families, who in 1988 could count just over 80 percent of families maintained by married couples.[20]

The percent of Hispanic families headed by a female householder with no husband present rose to 23.4 percent in 1988. In 1982 it was 21.5 percent. Almost a quarter of all Latino families are headed by a single woman. For non–Hispanics the percent of all families headed by a female householder was only 15.8 percent, far below the percentage for Latinos.[21]

The mythic strength of the Latino family is being sorely tested. The number of births out-of-wedlock for Hispanics was 26 percent. While this was considerably lower than the 55 percent for all black births, it was still more than double the out-of-wedlock rate for white women.[22]

The expanded participation of Latina women in the labor force also spells change for Hispanic family life. Increasingly, both parents in Hispanic families are required to work. Childcare concerns and the latchkey child dilemma are as familiar to Latino families as they are to non–Hispanic Amerian families.

Latino families also tend to be larger than other American families. Average family size for Hispanics was 3.8 person versus 3.1 for non–Hispanics in 1988. This seems fairly close but consider that more than 25 percent of Latino families have five or more persons, while only 13 percent of non–Hispanic families are that large.[23]

The Electorate

Voting: This simple yet profound act may be the single most effective weapon we possess in our battle against the woes which beset us. It is one of the more immediate undertakings available to us to effect change in our system. Unfortunately, here again the evidence points to a dismal record.

We don't vote. At least not in numbers equal to our potential strength. We have the worst voting record of any group in the United States. In the presidential election of November 1988 only 28.8 percent of Hispanics reported voting. This is the lowest voter turnout of any group, anywhere. There is no region, no race, no age group that does not outstrip the Hispanic presence in the voting booth. In 1988 Hispanics couldn't even match their own previous efforts. The Latino turnout for the 1988 presidential election was the lowest recorded turnout for a presidential election since records of Hispanic voting have been available. The Hispanic presidential election turnouts in 1972, 1976, 1980, and 1984 were higher than in 1988. But in those elections as well we maintained the worst record of any race, any age group, any region. The voting record of Latinos in Congressional election years is even more dismal. The Hispanic voter turnout for the 1986 Congressional election was 24.2 percent.[24]

In the presidential election of 1988, 57.4 percent of all voting age

Americans reported voting. This performance itself is the worst of any industrialized nation in the world. How can it be that Hispanics, as a whole, fail to meet even this poor performance? Blacks in the South; young people 18–24; people with elementary school educations; the unemployed—all posted a higher percentage than Latino voters.[25]

As might be expected, Hispanic registration levels are very low as well, a little better than half the national figure at 35.5 percent. This is one of the prime reasons Latinos do not vote. However, once registered, Hispanics are about as likely as non–Hispanics to cast a ballot. Of those Hispanics registered in 1986, 68 percent reported voting.[26]

You cannot register if you are not a citizen. At 37 percent, better than a full third of all voting age Hispanics are not citizens; thus they are effectively dealt out of the political game before it even starts. This, combined with the disadvantages previously mentioned, conspires to keep our political aspirations in abeyance. With new immigrants arriving daily we can expect to keep our poor record intact.

There has been some improvement in the number of Hispanic elected officials. In 1988 there were over 3,300 Latino elected officials according to the National Association of Latino Elected and Appointed Officials. Almost all of these officials are county and municipal office holders or school board members. Realistic representation at the national level and in the statehouse still awaits us.

Hispanic Subgroups

If we examine the major Hispanic subgroups separately we find that broadly applied statistics are misleading. Each group forms a distinct population with a unique culture and an original history.

Cubans or Cuban-Americans account for slightly more than 5 percent of all United States Hispanics at just over 1 million. The highest concentration of Cubans can be found in Florida, the state to which they fled following the rise of Fidel Castro. Cubans are much closer to non–Hispanics in their levels of social and economic achievement. They are an older population with a median age of 38.7. Their educational progress places them on a par with non–Latinos. Their median school years completed is actually above that of Hispanics for the 25- to 34-year-old group. The Cuban median family income is the highest of any Hispanic subgroup. Cubans have the lowest poverty rate among Hispanics at 13.8 percent. The Cuban unemployment rate is extremely low, 3.1 percent of their civilian labor force. This is far lower than their non–Hispanic counterparts. They also fare better than non–Hispanics in the percentage of their labor force employed as managers or professionals. The number of Cuban families headed by a female is almost the same as non–Hispanics. For the United States Hispanic, Cubans are the American success story.[27]

Hispanics of Puerto Rican origin number 2.5 million, or 12.7 percent of the total Hispanic picture. "Borinqueños" can be found throughout the United States but primarily reside in the northeast. The largest concentration of Puerto Ricans is in the Greater New York City area. Puerto Ricans are unique among Hispanics in that they enjoy United States citizenship from birth and face few of the restrictions of immigration. Puerto Ricans are a young population and suffer the usual Hispanic woes. They have high drop-out rates; only half of Puerto Ricans 25 years old and over have completed high school. Their unemployment rates are high and they have a higher percentage of people below the poverty level than any other Hispanic group. Almost 38 percent of all Puerto Rican families live below the poverty level. Compounding this tragedy is the high rate of illegitimacy and single motherhood that exists among Puerto Ricans. A staggering 44 percent of all Puerto Rican families are headed by a female householder with no husband present. There is no more telling and painful statistic in this chapter than this one.[28]

Mexicans, Mexican-Americans or Chicanos are the largest Latino subgroup. At just over 12 million they constitute about 62 percent of all United States Hispanics. Most Mexican-Americans and Mexican immigrants live in five southwestern states: California, Texas, Arizona, New Mexico, and Colorado. Increasingly they can also be found in the Midwest.

Mexicans have consistently been the youngest of the Hispanic subgroups. The Mexican median age in 1988 was 23.9 years, far below the median age of non–Hispanics at 32.2 years.

Mexicans are the least educated of all Latinos in the United States. Only 44.6 percent of Mexican adults 25 years of age and over have completed high school. Only a minuscule 7 percent have completed four years or more of college. The median school years completed for Mexican adults was 10.8 years as late as 1988. The social and economic implications of this mass undereducation are devastating. Even generations of legitimate residency and its attendant acculturation are no guarantee of achievement for Chicanos. Fortunately for younger Mexicans there is a drift toward high levels of educational attainment. Yet even among Hispanic young adults aged 25 to 34 years, Mexicans have a markedly lower level of educational achievement.[29]

As might be expected, the Mexican unemployment rate is the highest of all Hispanic subgroups and they have the smallest percentage of workers in higher paid positions.

The Mexican family is about as stable as the overall United States population, with almost 75 percent comprised of married-couple families. Mexican families continue to be the largest among Latinos with 4 being the mean number of persons per family.[30]

The median family income for Mexicans was $19,969 in 1988.[31] Mexican median family income actually fell by almost 6 percent from 1981 to 1986.[32] As of 1988 one in four Mexican families lived in poverty.[33]

New Immigrant Groups

The Central and South American origin category of Hispanics represents the newest group of United States Latinos. They make up about 12 percent of Hispanics, at 2.2 million. The majority are immigrants. Eighty percent were classified as foreign-born in 1980. These newcomers tend to be clustered in California, the prime destination point for refugees from El Salvador, Guatemala, and Nicaragua. The Eastern seaboard also contains significant communities of Central and South American immigrants. They are generally to be found in metropolitan areas like Boston or Miami.

The economic and social status of these New Americans is on a par with the achievement levels of Hispanic Americans as a whole. Their age structure, educational attainment levels, and family types are about equal to the Hispanic norm. Their numbers below poverty level, median family income, and occupational representation are also similar to total Hispanic figures. One interesting note is the figure for unemployment among this group. Only 4.8 percent of their civilian labor force were listed as unemployed in 1988. This indicated that these New Americans do indeed come to work.[34]

We can expect to hear more from this multinational group, the fastest growing of all Hispanic subgroups. Hispanics and non–Hispanics are expanding their perceptions of what constitutes a Latino in America. No longer are we confined to the tripartite of Mexican, Puerto Rican, and Cuban. Because of the continuing civil wars in Central America and the social unrest in South America, we can expect to see many more immigrants added to this Hispanic population group.

Language Usage

Español and English: Most American Hispanics speak English. The majority of American Latinos are fluent English speakers even if they regularly speak Spanish at home. Yet the use of Spanish in the United States is growing tremendously, mirroring the rise in immigration and the proliferation of the native Spanish-speaking population. As long as our ranks continue to be replenished by migrating Latin-American peoples, the United States will remain one of the largest Spanish-speaking nations in the world. The United States is home to more than 10 million Spanish-speakers, putting it in the middle rank of nations speaking Spanish.

Evidence of this growth can be noted in the rise of media oriented to the Spanish-speaker. Since 1970 the number of Spanish language newspapers in the United States has grown to more than 60. Radio stations devoted to the Spanish language now number more than 200. Television stations serving the Spanish-speaking have dramatically increased nationwide from 12 in 1970 to over 160 in the 1980s.[35]

While the use of Spanish is on the rise, and bilingualism remains a certainty, the number of Hispanics speaking English is also growing. Perhaps as many as 3.5 million younger, native-born Latinos currently speak little or no Spanish.

Projections for the Future

What does the future hold for Hispanics? The 1990 census will reveal new growth and promise. The complete results of this decennial population count won't be available for several years but increases are guaranteed in all categories. Once again our hopes will be raised and our suspicions confirmed.

New numbers, however impressive, will not lead to greater achievement in and of themselves. The gap is widening in the United States today between the haves and the have-not's. Will we move closer to a status resembling the inequality of South Africa? Clear-cut economic and social distinctions exist now. The ranks of the underclass are swelling in America. Latinos can be assured of being well represented in their midst.

Paradoxically, despite the negative drift of the underclass toward deprivation, a healthy middle class of Hispanics does exist and will also continue to grow. Those who are second generation or more, those who have adapted to the more profitable aspects of North American culture, will be the ones most likely to succeed.

United States Census Bureau predictions place the number of Hispanics at over 25 million by the year 2000. That is the middle series figure. The outside projection from the highest series quotes a number in excess of 31 million for the year 2000. By the year 2030 the Bureau expects the population of Hispanics to be about 42 million, and perhaps as many as 68 million.[36]

More Hispanics can simply mean more of the same. Unless profound and fundamental changes occur in American life and in the Hispanic community, we should not expect to see great variations on the current themes. It will take a miracle of major proportions to effect the kind of changes we require. Instead, a realistic appraisal will determine that the evolution of the Hispanic will proceed at a snail's pace for the many, and permanent conditions of deprivation will continue to exist for sizable portions of our population well into the foreseeable future.

Once again immigration can be a wild card. Circumstances can worsen considerably if population increases in Mexico and Latin America exceed predicted levels. The political and economic future of Mexico and Central America will have dramatic effects on life for Hispanics in the United States as well as the rest of America.

In Mexico alone a million new job-seekers enter the labor force each year. If current conditions continue to prevail many of these young people will head north to seek opportunity. Latin America as a whole is predicted to increase in population by approximately 70 million by the year 2000.[37] How many of these people will be drawn to our borders?

Progress in educational attainment for Hispanics will continue to be crucial to any substantial shift in our fortunes in the decades to come. Particular attention must be paid to the retention of students in college and at the high school level. Parental involvement in the scholastic life of young Latino children is of paramount importance. A diligent family partnership can accomplish that which beleaguered school systems and transitory dollars cannot.

Events in the political arena will be interesting to note in the nineties. The results of the 1990 census will mandate a reshaping of political boundaries. States in which Latinos reside stand to gain new seats in the House of Representatives. These same states, rich in electoral votes, will be increasingly important in future presidential elections as well. Early in 1990 California changed its presidential primary from June to March; the votes of Hispanics in that state could have added significance.

In local politics emerging Latino majorities can mean the end of gerrymandering and "at-large" elections as a means of political suppression within county and municipal governments. In large urban areas where we will continue to be a minority, albeit a hefty one, new population gains can mean a larger share of the political pie.

The key to political success for Latinos lies in the ballot box. Unless we can register massive amounts of new voters and motivate them to vote through get-out-vote drives, any future political success will be limited. Higher rates of naturalization and the legal requirements for naturalization in the 1986 law could also add to Latino political participation.

America's ability to compete in international markets and her domestic productivity will depend increasingly on the caliber of her workforce. In the nineties the American workforce will include more Hispanics than ever before. A literate, well trained worker is essential to America's economic well-being. The social and economic improvement of the Latino can translate into a healthier economic future for the United States. And, as has been noted, Hispanics are the fastest growing component of the United States labor force.

Library Services

Latinos and the library: We use the word "library" to mean public and academic institutions and their professionals. What does all this mean to the library? How can the library hope to serve this community? Will it be able to help resolve some of the problems which beset the Hispanics? Is service to the Hispanic really a part of the mission of the library? Is this service incorporated into library policies? These are questions this essay alone cannot answer. The answers lie in the hearts and minds of librarians and library administrators.

The information and recreation needs of the Hispanic patron are basically no different from those of any other kind of patron. Information about jobs, resources for schoolwork, a means of self-improvement, cultural enlightenment, all these traditional areas of library concern apply to Hispanics as well. The Hispanic patron may need material in Spanish. She may not be as academically prepared as another patron to mine the resources of the library. She may come from a culture that is unfamiliar with libraries, especially public libraries. Whatever the real or perceived limitations or shortcomings of the Hispanic patron or potential patrons, the fact remains that this special population has tremendous information needs, needs that are not always being met.

The responsibility of librarians is not lessened because the Hispanic community is underutilizing the library. On the contrary, expanding populations and changing neighborhoods demand an appropriate, effective response to the obligation of service to the Hispanic.

One of the most pressing challenges for the library in the decades to come will be service to ethnic and minority Americans. For many of our libraries this means service to the Hispanic. In San Diego, California, on May 25–27, 1988, a major conference was held to address this challenge. A Rand Corporation report had surveyed the situation in California and its findings were presented to the conference.[38] Convened by the state librarian, librarians, library administrators, politicians and influential people from outside the library met to wrestle with the issues and to develop recommendations. The conference was entitled "A State of Change: California's Ethnic Future and Libraries" and provided conferees with an unprecedented opportunity. Many of the recommendations were obvious, some innovative, but all were aimed directly at the goal of greater service for ethnic Americans. Most of the recommendations had specific applications for Latinos. Very briefly, the issues addressed by the conference were change, community relations, finance, libraries, politics, and the socioethnic perspective.[39] At the end the "Challenge Sessions" in which conferees participated they made recommendations to the State Library, local library jurisdictions and library supporters, library schools and the library community at large. The conferees came up with 135 recommendations. Statewide follow-up forums, attended by hundreds of librarians, supplied an additional 125 recommendations. The recurrent themes running through the recommendations were money, commitment, and involvement. Each recommendation required commitment from the library world. Every recommendation demanded involvement. And money was the support and springboard for all the recommendations.

The following is an overview of some of the possible directions which may be taken in pursuit of conferees' suggestions. The library must change; it has no choice. It has to adapt to serve new populations. The library must pay for new programs and personnel to serve and attract these new patrons. It must be culturally aware and sensitive. The library must become more political. The library needs to mount vigorous public relations compaigns to market its services and to secure the necessary support from the community. Librarians, administrators, and staff must be free of prejudice and be personally committed to provide full service to these new patrons. Library materials and services should reflect the specific needs and wants of ethnically diverse patrons. Certainly all these are splendid goals. One suspects even opponents of equity know full well the courses to follow to achieve results. Will these ideas be acted upon? Can the library take these suggestions and criticisms and forge new strategies of service? Will the California model serve as an example for the rest of the nation? Again, the answers are embedded in the bosom of the profession. Perhaps time will tell.

More than ten years ago, in July of 1978, an article appeared in *Library Journal* by Yolanda Cuesta and Patricia Tarín. It was entitled "Guidelines for Library Services to the Spanish-Speaking."[40] The article, after a brief demographic overview, divided the topics of concern into five areas: planning and evaluation, access, personnel, materials, and services and programs. These areas are further divided into 78 specific "Guidelines." These "Guidelines" are strikingly similar to the recommendations generated by the State of Change Conference. The responses to the various challenges created by demographic change have been available to libraries for some time. Certainly the Latino librarian has been aware of the need for change. What is necessary to follow the "Guidelines" or to implement the recommendations is the will to do it—political and economic will. If this will is lacking in our libraries or their funding bodies, then the Hispanic community itself or their political representatives must supply the necessary will.

How our American institutions respond to the challenges of Hispanics and other minorities will be the measure of our democracy and the worth of our Republic.

Blueprint for Action

Our positive response as professionals can serve as a blueprint for action in the nineties and the century to come. If we fail to live up to our professional responsibilities, if we decline to ally ourselves with Hispanic patrons, then we can expect to be repaid with indifference and hostility. As a profoundly public institution the library must be attuned to the changes taking place in its communities. To do otherwise is to invite inequity.

Finally, a few thoughts for the Latino community. In 1979, in Ann Arbor, Michigan, a group of newly graduated librarians, along with other graduates, heard the Rev. Jesse Jackson speak. As the commencement speaker, Jackson spoke about the failure of blacks, Hispanics, and other disadvantaged peoples, to read and otherwise to educate themselves. Jackson said racism certainly played a part. So did bad nutrition, broken homes, and indifferent teachers. But he also said part of the reason Johnny couldn't read was because Johnny didn't pick up a book. We have a duty to foster amongst ourselves a desire and a commitment to change. The Hispanic patron can grow old and weary waiting for the federal government, the state, the county or the city to do the right thing. If change is necessary then those most needful of change must discover in themselves the will to accomplish it.

In the movie *Stand and Deliver* teacher Jaime Escalante speaks of "ganas" (will, or desire). With "ganas," he implies, you can accomplish virtually anything. If you lack the will, if you are short of "ganas," life is less fulfilling, less interesting, and you are less able to contribute something positive. His Chicano students developed the "ganas" and accomplished amazing things.

A review of the demographic statistics for Hispanics in the last 20 years shows spectacular population growth. And yet positive social and economic gain eludes us. Progress to match this growth is unrealized for many Hispanics. If Latinos want responsive libraries (or schools, or city halls), they must work to make them so. Organized community pressure can force change upon the most recalcitrant of local governments. Mass naturalization and voter registration drives can help generate the votes to elect those who will be responsive to our needs. But if we do not prepare ourselves for power, we will never be able to wield it. The America of the next century will, in all likelihood, be a service economy. But the question is who will be the served and who will be the servers?

NOTES

1. U.S. Bureau of the Census, "1980 Census of Population, General Population Characteristics, United States Summary," p. 21.

2. U.S. Bureau of the Census, "The Hispanic Population in the United States, March 1988," *Current Population Reports*, Series P-20, No. 431, August 1988, p. 1.

3. Ibid., p. 1.

4. Ibid., p. 3.

5. U.S. Bureau of the Census, "The Hispanic Population in the United States: March 1986 and 1987," *Current Population Reports*, Series P-20, No. 434, December 1988, p. 35.

6. U.S. Bureau of the Census, "The Hispanic Population in the United States, March 1988," *Current Population Reports*, Series P-20, No. 431, August 1988, p. 7.

7. U.S. Bureau of the Census, "Projections of the Hispanic Population: 1983–2080," *Current Population Reports*, Series P-25, No. 995, November 1986, p. 11.

8. U.S. Bureau of the Census, "Fertility of American Women: June 1987," *Current Population Reports*, Series P-20, No. 427, May 1988, p. 2.

9. U.S. Bureau of the Census, "The Hispanic Population in the United

States, March 1988," *Current Population Reports,* Series P-20, No. 431, August 1988, p. 1.

10. Ibid., p. 3.

11. Ibid., p. 7.

12. Ibid., p. 3.

13. U.S. Bureau of the Census, "Money Income and Poverty Status in the United States: 1987," *Current Population Reports,* Series P-60, No. 161, August 1988, p. 8.

14. U.S. Bureau of the Census, "The Hispanic Population in the United States, March 1988," *Current Population Reports,* Series P-20, No. 431, August 1988, p. 8.

15. "Bad Economic News for Hispanics," *Los Angeles Herald Examiner,* 25 May 1989, p. A-5.

16. U.S. Bureau of the Census, "The Hispanic Population in the United States, March 1988," *Current Population Reports,* Series P-20, No. 431, August 1988, p. 5.

17. Ibid., p. 11.

18. Ibid., p. 8.

19. Peter Cattan, "The Growing Presence of Hispanics in the U.S. Work Force," *Monthly Labor Review,* August 1988, pp. 9–14.

20. U.S. Bureau of the Census, "The Hispanic Population in the United States, March 1988," *Current Population Reports,* Series P-20, No. 431, August 1988, p. 7.

21. Ibid.

22. U.S. Bureau of the Census, "Fertility of American Women: June 1987," *Current Population Reports,* Series P-20, No. 427, May 1988, pp. 3–4.

23. U.S. Bureau of the Census, "The Hispanic Population in the United States, March 1988," *Current Population Reports,* Series P-20, No. 431, August 1988, p. 10.

24. U.S. Bureau of the Census, "Voting and Registration in the Election of November 1988 (Advance Report)," *Current Population Reports,* Series P-20, No. 435, February 1989, p. 1.

25. Ibid., pp. 1–3.

26. U.S. Bureau of the Census, "Voting and Registration in the Election of November 1986," *Current Population Reports,* Series P-20, No. 414, September 1987, p. 7.

27. U.S. Bureau of the Census, "The Hispanic Population in the United States, March 1988," *Current Population Reports,* Series P-20, No. 431, August 1988, pp. 7–8.

28. Ibid.

29. Ibid., p. 7.

30. Ibid.

31. Ibid., p. 8.

32. Joe Schwartz, "Hispanics in the Eighties," *American Demographics,* January 1988, p. 8.

33. U.S. Bureau of the Census, "The Hispanic Population in the United States, March 1988," *Current Population Reports,* Series P-20, No. 431, August 1988, p. 8.

34. Ibid.

35. Rafael Valdivieso and Cary Davis, "U.S. Hispanics: Challenging Issues for the 1990s," *Population Trends and Public Policy,* No. 17 (Washington, D.C.: Population Reference Bureau, December 1988), p. 9.

36. U.S. Bureau of the Census, "Projections of the Hispanic Population: 1983 to 2080," *Current Population Reports,* Series P-25, No. 995, November 1986, p. 4.

37. Rafael Valdivieso and Cary Davis, "U.S. Hispanics: Challenging Issues for

the 1990s," *Population Trends and Public Policy*, No. 17 (Washington, D.C.: Population Reference Bureau, December 1988), p. 9.

38. Judith Payne, *Public Libraries Face California's Ethnic and Racial Diversity* (Santa Monica, Calif.: RAND Corporation, 1988).

39. California State Library Foundation, *A State of Change: California's Ethnic Future and Libraries, Conference and Awareness Forum Proceedings* (Stanford, Calif.: Planning Group for the "State of Change" Project, 1988).

40. Yolanda Cuesta and Patricia Tarín, "Guidelines for Library Service to the Spanish Speaking," *Library Journal* 103 (July 1978); 1354–1355.

COMMUNITY ANALYSIS AND NEEDS ASSESSMENT

Salvador Güereña

Gaining an understanding of the community to be served is basic to the library planning process. This involves describing the characteristics of the people and the environment in which they live, and assessing their needs for library information services. While one of the traditionally held goals of public libraries has been to provide access to library resources and services which can meet the needs of all segments of the community, the fact remains that outside the library's more traditional clientele there is often a lack of reliable and culturally sensitive patterns of service which are truly responsive to the needs of the Spanish-speaking. In this article the term "Spanish-speaking" is used in its broadest sense. While it encompasses a population group of largely Mexican origin, people of other Latin American origins are also included, and language proficiencies range from the monolingual Spanish-speaker to the English-speaking bicultural person.

As it relates to this group or any other group, a community study should include constituent-based data to support library service development. This will provide the basis for both short and long range planning, and for the formulation of library policy. This must proceed from broad-based quantitative as well as qualitative information. Clearly, attitudes and opinions, whether advanced solely by visible and vocal members of the community or by library decision-makers, constitute a shaky basis for building an effective library program. In developing library service to the Spanish-speaking, community analysis which includes constituent-based data will produce the comprehensive information needed in the decision-making process to thereby provide the appropriate content and direction for library service. Basic to this process is the use of community analysis, which involves gathering data about the community, and needs assessment, which requires obtaining data directly from the community. These two elements are precursors to planning; they are necessary in order to describe, assess, and analyze library and information needs. The end result facilitates the linkage of present and potential clientele with the information resources, services, and facilities of libraries.

Community analysis basically involves systematic data collection, organization, and analysis in order to describe a community as a whole

17

through its component parts. Data are obtained from two types of sources. The first consists of primary data which come directly from individuals through the use of a community survey, by neighborhood reconnaissance, or by conducting interviews with community agency heads. Secondary data are generally those which have been previously collected and recorded in published or other printed sources. A basic data source is the decennial federal census reports. Among the comprehensive data contained therein are detailed socioeconomic and housing characteristics of the population and ethnic or racial data. Beginning in 1980 the federal census identifies people of Hispanic group origin or descent. Other sources include data reports of governmental planning agencies or groups at various jurisdictional levels. It can be especially helpful to consult special county or local census reports and planning department documents on community demographics. Various nongovernment sources also exist, such as business and industry surveys and marketing studies. Local chambers of commerce would be appropriate contacts. Lastly, the news media occasionally highlight population trends. The media can be another source of data or can be used for referral to additional sources.

Because libraries must be people-oriented in order to meet their service objectives, community analysis is firmly based in the demographic characteristics of the population to be served. Therefore, valid library services must be geared to the needs of the local community. Patterns of library and information needs in the community are generally a product of local community and population characteristics, and are highly correlative to problems resulting from social and economic factors bearing upon that particular community. Therefore, demographic and socioeconomic characteristics of an area must be studied carefully, be it urban, suburban, or rural.

Community analysis will assess variables such as the number of potential users, age characteristics, and the levels of educational attainment. Education, for example, is an important factor since it correlates with library use and will influence the way in which information will be presented. The implications of lower educational attainment underscores the need for outreach and other nontraditional access systems, materials at lower literacy levels, and nonprint resources. Ethnicity and language characteristics must be assessed as factors which will affect library usage. Since there may be any number of Hispanic subgroups in a given community, it will be important to identify which groups there are, their density, and distribution. The number and types of non–English resources and services must be ascertained. Occupational and income data must also be compiled, including the relative proportion of people in major occupational categories. One must account for possible changes in employment patterns. Income is a significant variable which usually correlates with education and therefore these two statistics may profitably be used with each other.

Another aspect of community analysis lies in assessing the community environment — the library's overall service area. To be examined are growth and development, library-government jurisdictional relationships, and business and industrial activity. Communication and transportation systems must be accounted for inasmuch as they relate to the convenience of access to libraries. The available range of educational and cultural facilities and programs should be assessed as they will have an impact on library services. Identifying other community information programs and resources can pave the way for cooperative arrangements and reduce duplication. An appraisal of community organizations and groups is important as they will shed further light on particular aspects of the community and its library needs. These can also serve as conduits through which to reach under-served segments of the community such as the Spanish-speaking. Furthermore, not only should the library look outwardly, but it must also be introspective. Questions to ask include: What is the existing nature and scope of its collections? its services? its personnel? In particular, in what way do these relate to the Spanish-speaking? To anticipate near and long-term needs, an analysis of the current status of library resources and services will provide further insight into how the groups identified in the community analysis process are being served by libraries. It will also provide the foundation for the development of short and long range goals and objectives for service. This will form the basis for establishing greater contact between the library and the Spanish-speaking community.

To date, a number of libraries have engaged in community analysis–related projects, some of which have been directed specifically to Spanish-speaking communities. The findings of such studies have also served as precursors for extramurally funded demonstration projects whose success led their sponsoring libraries to make them permanent programs. In California alone such projects have included the Biblioteca Latino Americano in San Jose, the Chicano Resources Sharing Project of the Inland Library System, the Latino Services Project of the Serra Cooperative Library System, and Proyecto Ideal of the North Bay Cooperative Library System. Another type of study, as conducted in Santa Barbara, incorporated an analysis of the Spanish-speaking as a major subset of its ethnic minority population at large. An outcome was the establishment of the Ethnic Services Outreach Project, which was a springboard for a long range locally funded program (See Appendix D for a sample bilingual interview questionnaire.) Other studies, such as the Community Analysis Project of the Santiago Library System in Orange County constitute important and comprehensive research on a much larger scale, providing useful models for subsequent community analysis studies.

Documentation efforts may range from largely community-specific studies, such as the El Paso Public Library's community survey of the Clardy Fox Branch area, to more comprehensive studies. Of course, it would not be feasible for every library to conduct an extensive community analysis. Local conditions will largely determine the nature, scope, and structure of a particular community study. Important factors in the planning of a community analysis will include the level of available funding and personnel resources to conduct such a study.

Planning in this area warrants an examination of several pertinent and timely publications which provide guidelines for conducting community analysis and needs assessments. These will help a library to plan more effectively without spending a great deal of time determining how to proceed. Helpful research tools include Vernon E. Palmour's *A Planning Process for Public Libraries*, which was published by the American Library Association in 1980, and a *Guide for Developing Ethnic Library Services*, a 1979 publication of the California Ethnic Services Task Force. While *A Planning Process* features a comprehensive methodology for conducting a systematic study of the community, the *Guide* offers recommended guidelines specifically for conducting an information needs assessment of the ethnic community. Libraries which have used the *Guide* have invariably rated it highly. According to Grace Liu, who was the coordinator for the South Bay (California) Cooperative Library System's "Underserved Community Library Awareness Project," the *Guide* "is a valuable resource which provides innovative ideas as well as practical tips.... [M]any activities suggested in this handbook were experimented with by this project with great success" (see Bibliography immediately following; p. 81).

A brief discussion of these two guides would be appropriate here. Firstly, both approaches stress the need for a community-based effort. Local conditions and needs must be scrutinized and accounted for. Secondly, they also call for a participative approach involving both librarians and community members in the planning process. Thirdly, both are data-based, requiring that concrete, quantitative information be derived about and from the community. Lastly, both view this as a cyclical process. A community study should not be a one-time endeavor. Since communities are never static, continuing study is called for so that changing information needs may be reliably assessed. In addition to these library planning tools, a variety of general survey research handbooks are available from which to choose. A rather thorough manual on survey techniques found helpful to this writer is Charles H. Backstrom's 1964 *Survey Research*. It is filled with practical wisdom and step-by-step procedures relating to random sampling, questionnaire construction, interviewing tips, and more.

While previous library surveys of the Spanish-speaking have tended to follow traditional social science research methods, an analysis of these helps bring to light the exigencies and constraints bearing upon fruitful and statistically valid research concerning the Spanish-speaking community. These studies should be consulted as models for future planning. Furthermore, the data and conclusions documented in these reports may supplement and validate the finding of subsequent studies.

The California Ethnic Services Task Force's *Guide* will be especially useful in that the techniques and approaches of general studies are not specific enough to allow for the unique characteristics and needs in the ethnic community. Language and cultural variables should especially be accounted for. One should consider that information inequity is linked with specific cultural settings which must not be overlooked. As advanced by G. Cochrane, "each significant ethnic group can be thought of as a distinct information constituency. Its distinct values and attitudes act as a filter in the absorption of externally produced information" (see Bibliography following). Aruna Shah, in an article on the various facets of multiethnic service delivery (see Bibliography following), emphasizes the importance of effective staff training, especially accounting for such factors as race and ethnicity. Recruiting staff from the minority community was considered desirable.

Therefore, in this case, the information gathering process needs to grasp the cultural and behavioral dimensions associated with this population group. To help assure this, a community study should involve an advisory committee that includes members from the Spanish-speaking community itself and provides for various types of expertise; it should, further, include representatives from such programs as bilingual and migrant education as well as from concerned community agencies serving the Spanish-speaking. Continuous involvement by this advisory committee is necessary. Furthermore, an attempt should be made to identify sympathetic social researchers in the area to serve in a consulting capacity. A nearby college or university would be the first place to look. Often there is no cost factor involved. The advisory committee, staff, and consultant working together would assure the needed validity and reliability of the needs assessment component and provide legitimacy to the study.

Finally, among the desired outcomes of a community analysis survey project is that it provide an infrastructure for the concrete involvement of the Spanish-speaking community in the library planning process. The measure of the library's success in serving these groups can be predicted by how well disposed it is to learn, understand, and explore with the Spanish-speaking community more responsive, viable, and thus more beneficial means of providing relevant library services to them. Community analysis must produce fruitful results.

Information resulting from this process must not be left to meander through the bureaucratic wilderness. The products of this labor must be visible to the community, in the form of effective near and long-term service strategies and tangible resource development. This will be the only way to win the trust and confidence of the Spanish-speaking in their library.

BIBLIOGRAPHY

American Library Association. Library Community Analysis Project. *Studying the Community.* Chicago: American Library Association, 1960.

Backstrom, Charles H. *Survey Research*. Evanston, Ill.: Northwestern University Press, 1964.

Barenó, Laura. "Survey of Spanish-Speaking Users and Non-Users" (unpublished report). San Diego: San Diego County Library, 1978.

Barrón, Daniel, and Charles Curran. "A Look at Community Analysis: Some Myths and Some Realities." *Public Libraries* 20, 1 (Spring 1981): 29–30.

Burgess, Robert, ed. *Field Research: A Sourcebook and Field Manual*. London: George Allen and Unwin, 1982.

Busha, Charles H., and Stephen P. Harter, eds. *Research Methods in Librarianship: Techniques and Interpretation*. New York: Academic Press, 1980.

California Ethnic Services Task Force. *A Guide for Developing Ethnic Library Services*. 1979.

Clamurro, William. "Community Analysis and the Role of Library Committees." *Community Analysis Studies* 1, 1 (Summer 1980): 14–16.

Cochrane, G., and P. Atherton. "The Cultural Appraisal of Efforts to Alleviate Information Inequity." *Journal of the American Society for Information Science* 41, 4 (July 1980), 283–292.

Dooley, David. *Social Research Methods*. Englewood Cliffs, N.J.: Prentice-Hall, 1984.

Evans, Charles. "A History of Community Analysis in American Librarianship." *Library Trends* 24, 3 (January 1976): 441–457.

Fink, Arlene. *How to Conduct Surveys: A Step by Step Guide*. Beverly Hills, Calif.: Sage Publications, 1985.

Goldhor, Herbert. "Community Analysis for the Public Library." *Illinois Libraries* 62, 4 (April, 1980): 296–302.

Gollattscheck, James F. "Confronting the Complexity of Community Analysis." *Community Services Catalyst* 12, 1 (Winter 1982): 7–11.

González, Michael, et al. "Assessing the Library Needs of the Spanish-Speaking." *Library Journal* 105 (April 1, 1980): 786–789.

_____. "Library Needs Assessment of the Spanish-Speaking" (unpublished report). San Bernardino, Calif.: San Bernardino Public Library, n.d.

Güereña, Salvador. *Santa Barbara Public Library-Ethnic Minority Needs Assessment Project; Preliminary Report*. Santa Barbara, Calif.: Santa Barbara Public Library, 1981.

_____. "Library Survey Analysis and the Spanish-Speaking in California." *Bibliopolitica: Chicano Perspectives on Library Services in the United States*, ed. Francisco García-Ayvens and Richard Chabrán. Berkeley, Calif.: Chicano Studies Library Publication Unit, University of California, 1984.

Haro, Roberto. "How Mexican Americans View Libraries: A One-Man Survey." *Wilson Library Bulletin* 44 (March 1970) 736–742.

_____. "Library Services to Mexican Americans." *El Grito* (Spring 1970) 30–37.

_____. "Community Analysis and Public Libraries." *El Libro Abierto: An Occasional Newsletter About Library and Information Services for Hispanic Origin Americans* 5, 2 (April 1982): 1–3.

Hot, Raymond M. "New Horizons for Arizona Libraries: A Report of the 1978 Library Needs Assessment Survey of Arizona Libraries." November 1978.

"Indiana Community Analysis Project." *Information and Library Manager* 1, 1 (June 1981): 7–8.

Johnstone, James C., et al. "La Biblioteca Latino Americano: User Survey, San Jose Public Library." San Jose: Department of Librarianship, San Jose State University, 1977.

Kunz, Arthur H. "The Use of Data Gathering Instruments in Library Planning." *Library Trends* **24**, 4 (January 1978): 458–472.

Lipsman, Claire K. *The Disadvantaged and Library Effectiveness.* Chicago: American Library Association, 1972.

Liu, Grace. *Promoting Library Awareness in Ethnic Communities.* Santa Clara, Calif.: South Bay Cooperative Library System; Chicago: American Library Association, 1985.

Lotspeich, Margaret L., and John E. Kleymeyer. *How to Gather Data About Your Neighborhood.* Chicago: American Society of Planning, Vol. 1, No. 10, n.d.

Los Angeles (City). Community Analysis and Planning Division. *An Ethnic Trend Analysis of Los Angeles County: 1950–1980.* Los Angeles, 1978.

Luévano, Susan C. "Santiago Library System Population Profile: Orange County Community Analyis Data." Santiago Library System, 1980.

Martin, Lowell. "User Studies in Library Planning." *Library Trends* **24**, 4 (January 1976): 483–496.

Michael, Mary Ellen, and Leticia Encarnación. *An Evaluation of the el Centro de la Causa Library and Information Center: August 1973 to July 1974.* Final Report. (Sponsoring Agency: Chicago Public Library.) Urbana: University of Illinois, Library Research Center, September 1974.

Mueller, John H., et al. *Statistical Reasoning in Sociology.* Boston: Houghton Mifflin, 1970.

National Education Resources Institute, Inc. *A Systems Analysis of Southwestern Spanish-Speaking Users and Non-Users of Library and Information Services Developing Criteria to Design an Optimal Model Concept.* Final Report. Washington, D.C.: The Institute, 1972.

Palmour, Vernon E. *A Planning Process for Public Libraries.* Chicago: American Library Association, 1980.

Robinson, Charles W. "Libraries and the Community." *Public Libraries* **22**, 1 (Spring 1983): 7–13.

Ryan, Kathryn E. "Libraries, Prejudice and the Portuguese." *Current Studies in Librarianship* **9**, 1–2 (Spring/Fall 1985): 59–64.

Shah, Aruna. "The Positive and Negative of Multi-ethnic Provisions." *Library Association Record* **86**, 5 (May 1984): 215, 217.

Simon, Julian L. *Basic Research Methods in Social Science: The Art of Empirical Investigation.* New York: Random House, 1978.

Soltys, Amy. "Planning and Implementing a Community Survey." *Canadian Library Journal* **42**, 5 (October 1985): 245–249.

Sudman, Seymour, and Norman M. Bradburn. *Asking Questions: A Practical Guide to Questionnaire Design.* San Francisco: Jossey-Bass, 1982.

"Third World Populations in California." Sacramento: Office of the Lieutenant Governor, 1977.

Warner, Edward I. *Information Needs of Urban Residents.* Baltimore: Baltimore Regional Planning Council, 1973.

Warren, Roland. *Studying Your Community.* New York: Russel Sage Foundation, 1955.

Weinberg, Eve. *Community Surveys with Local Talent: A Handbook.* Chicago: National Opinion Research Center, University of Chicago, 1971.

Weisberg, Herbert F. *An Introduction to Survey Research.* San Francisco: W.H. Freeman, 1977.

Zweizig, Douglas L. "Community Analysis." In *Local Public Library Administration,* ed. Ellen Altman. Chicago: American Library Association, 1980.

_____. "Measuring Library Use." *Drexel Library Quarterly* **13**, 3 (July 1977) ?–15.

REFERENCE SERVICE
TO THE SPANISH-SPEAKING

Albert J. Milo

This chapter has its origins in a workshop that was cosponsored by the Orange County Chapter of REFORMA (the National Association to Promote Library Service to the Spanish-Speaking) and the Santiago Library System. It was for that workshop, dealing with "Library Services for the Latino Community," that I first prepared a presentation on providing reference service to the Spanish-speaking. My primary purpose will be to describe how the reference needs of the Spanish-speaking community are being met by the public libraries in California, but the information contained in this chapter is applicable to most parts of the United States.

While the terms "Latino" and "Hispanic" will be used interchangeably, it must be pointed out that the term "Spanish-speaking" represents a subset of these two broader terms. For the purposes of this paper, the term "Spanish-speaking" has an even narrower definition in that it refers to those individuals who are exclusively monolingual Spanish speakers. It excludes those Latinos who are monolingual English speakers as well as those who are bilingual in both languages.

California Demographics

According to the *Mexico-United States Report*, "the Latino population in California is projected to reach approximately seven million in the 1990 Census, one-fourth of the state's total."[1] By the year 2000, over 29 percent of the state's 23 million population will be Latino. These figures include both documented and undocumented Latinos residing throughout the state.

It is difficult to determine exactly how many of the state's Latino population is "Spanish-speaking." For one thing, the ability to speak Spanish is not a clear-cut characteristic but is really a matter of degree. At one end of the spectrum there are those Latinos who are exclusively Spanish speakers and who speak little, if any, English. At the other extreme there are Latinos who speak no Spanish at all but are strictly English speakers. Studies have shown that by the third generation, groups that have immigrated to the United States tend to have lost their mother tongue, with most of them becoming monolingual English speakers. Latinos are no exception. The largest number of Latinos fall somewhere in between these two extremes. Many are, in fact, bilingual with English or Spanish being predominant in varying degrees. In some cases "Spanglish," a combination of both languages, is commonly spoken.

In a document published by the Bureau of the Census entitled *Condition of Hispanics in America Today,* the following statistic is cited:

> The 1980 census included a question on language spoken in the home. Of the non–English languages, Spanish was reported most frequently. Over 11 million persons, or 5 percent, reported that they spoke Spanish at home. Of these Spanish speakers, about one-fourth reported that they did not speak English well or at all.[2]

If one uses the statistic that one out of four Latinos can be considered a monolingual Spanish speaker, then in 1990, about 1,750,000 of the state of California's projected 7 million Latinos will be monolingual Spanish speakers.

In his book, *Reaching the Hispanic Market Effectively: The Media, the Market, the Methods,* Antonio Guernica says that "Spanish . . . is used by every one of the twenty Spanish-speaking nationalities comprising the U.S. Hispanic population." He goes on to say that "the use of the Spanish language is not limited to older Hispanics, as is sometimes believed. According to a study conducted by the U.S. Department of Commerce in July 1976, over 64 percent of the Spanish-origin population under 20 years of age prefers [Spanish as their] native tongue." "More recent estimates place the use of Spanish in the homes of the U.S. Spanish-origin population at 80 percent or more."

> The recently released Yankelovich study, *Spanish USA* [subtitled *A Study of the Hispanic Market in the United States*], conducted in 1981 for SIN Spanish International Network], found that 99 percent of the study's self-identified 'Hispanic descent or background' respondents spoke at least 'enough Spanish to get by.' Of the Hispanic-descent respondents, 90 percent spoke Spanish fluently or as a primary language, 47 percent were bilingual, and 23 percent knew Spanish only. Only 1 percent of the Hispanic-descent respondents knew English only.[3]

These figures, which are larger than those of the Census Bureau, are reconfirmed in later book entitled *Hispanic Media, USA.* The author, Ana Veciana-Suárez reports that "in interviews conducted by Strategy Research [Corporation] . . . at least 90 percent of Hispanics surveyed said the first language they learned to speak was Spanish. The same study concluded that more than two-thirds of the population preferred to speak Spanish at home and 18 percent spoke both languages."[4]

If one uses the figure that two-thirds of Latinos prefer to speak Spanish at home, by 1990, 4,690,000 of California's 7 million Latinos should fit into this category.

California's Public Libraries

According to the 1988 edition of *California Library Statistics:*

> [There are] 169 public libraries throughout the state with 3,022 public service outlets. By jurisdictions, there are 43 county, 106 city, 8 combined city-county, and 12 district public libraries.
>
> By level of service, there are 163 main libraries, 601 branch libraries, 371 library stations (a library structure smaller than a branch and providing a lower level of service), and 1,887 mobile library stops (a location visited by a bookmobile or other traveling library). There are 80 mobile libraries in operation.
>
> Combining main, branch and station figures, there are 1,135 fixed public library outlets.[5]

The BPLG/BALIS Study

The state of California has always been a bellwether state with respect to the library profession. This is indeed the case when it comes to serving the reference needs of the state's Spanish-speaking.

In 1987 a very important study was published as a result of a 1986/87 Library Services and Construction Act (LSCA) grant project called "Reference Referral for Spanish-Speakers and Other Spanish Language Users in California." The study itself was entitled *A Study of Reference Referral Service for Spanish Language Library Uses in Northern California* and was cosponsored by Bibliotecas para la Gente (BPLG) and the Bay Area Library Information System (BALIS).[6] Martín Gómez served as the consultant for the BPLG/BALIS study. Its purpose was "to provide essential information to reference planners with responsibility for designing reference services to this underserved population."[7]

As part of the study, 419 reference questions handled by 15 local libraries and the Bay Area Reference Center (BARC) during 1986 were reviewed. Of these 419 inquiries, 305 (73 percent) of them were successfully answered using local library resources. Eighty-three inquiries (19 percent) were referred on to higher reference centers. The remaining 8 percent of inquiries were unanswerable.

Two of the findings of the BPLG/BALIS study were:

First, the discovery of an informal reference network or "invisible college" (separate from the formalized BARC structure) that was used by some public librarians in answering Spanish reference questions. This network, for the most part, consisted of members of BPLG. These individuals, primarily librarians employed at various libraries in the San Francisco Bay Area, were aware of each other's library holdings. Librarians unaware of this informal network, on the other hand, tended to abort reference questions sooner or referred them to BARC for further research. Interestingly enough, BARC staff, who were aware of the existence of the "informal network," would often use it to answer questions sent to them. The fact that this "informal network" should be recognized, formalized, and publicized was one of the recommendations of the study.

Secondly, it was found that, while there were certain questions asked which one could predictably expect to find associated with Spanish-speaking patrons (e.g., English as a second language [ESL] and United States citizenship), most of the questions being asked by the Spanish-speaking could be classified as basic, first-level, reference inquiries. The main reason the questions were considered difficult was that they were asked in Spanish and required Spanish resources for an answer. The questions being asked were as varied as those asked by English speakers. In other words, the Spanish-speaking were not limited to just a few areas of reference needs. In fact, to limit one's collection to ESL and citizenship materials would be stereotyping the needs of the Spanish-speaking.

Some of the major barriers to the reference referral process for Spanish reference questions included lack of Spanish language fluency by library staff dealing with Spanish-speaking patrons; lack of library resources, especially at the local level, including bilingual personnel, Spanish language collections, and bibliographic access to those collections which did exist; and lack of awareness of what other collections, resources, and library personnel existed in other libraries.

In 1987 the grant project published a valuable resource which contained identifications and descriptions of key collections in the San Francisco Bay Area as well as a section in the book called "Descriptive Bibliography of Spanish Language Reference Works."[8] The latter is of value to all public libraries in that it serves as a core list of Spanish reference materials as well as the basis for a revised and expanded new edition.[9]

The Rand Report

In 1988 another important study, entitled *Public Libraries Face California's Ethnic and Racial Diversity*, conducted by Judith E. Payne, reaffirmed previous studies that found that few members of the public use the reference services of public libraries. "Various studies have found that between 2 and 17 percent of the public turn to public libraries to answer questions or solve problems." It went on to describe the use of reference services by minorities. "While Asians were much more likely to use libraries as a source of information for their important questions (20%), Blacks and Hispanics were least likely (3% and 4% respectively)."[10] The report also documented the tremendous demographic changes which California is experiencing. The implication is that unless libraries expand their services to include the needs of minorities, the percentage of the general public using public libraries for reference service will continue to diminish. Traditional methods for reaching minorities may not be sufficient.

To encourage public libraries to address the findings of the Rand Report, the California state librarian, Gary Strong, announced at the 1988 California Library Association Conference in Fresno that $3,000,000 in LSCA funds would be set aside for a special category of grant applications. The first library recipients of this ambitious program, called "Partnerships for Change," were announced in the fall of 1989.

In addition, the State Library is planning to develop several statewide Ethnic Resource Centers (ERCs). In a June 21, 1988, memo addressed to the California library community, Gary Strong states that "the primary purpose of these centers will be to develop creative and innovative library delivery systems to address community-defined needs, and to remove existing barriers, both inside and outside the library, to increase library use by ethnocultural groups."

Initially, four ERCs will be established, one for each of the state's major ethnocultural groups (American Indian, Asian/ Pacific, Black and Latino). While many librarians view the ERCs as signaling progress in addressing some of the needs mentioned in the BPLG/BALIS study, other librarians have cautioned that the establishment of ERCs might give some non–ERC libraries an excuse *not* to develop their own local collections and *not* to hire bilingual personnel.

C.O.R.E.

The California Opportunities for Reference Excellence (CORE) Project was funded by an LSCA grant and was administered by the San Joaquin Valley Library System. It was designed to improve the collections of reference materials and reference skills of library staff in public libraries throughout the state. In some cases, such as with rural and branch libraries, the project provided basic reference materials to those outlets lacking them. The CORE Project targeted the reference needs of the "underserved," including Latinos. Among the Project's accomplishments was the development of a Spanish reference in-take form that can be used by library personnel who do not speak Spanish. The form assumes that a patron can read and write in Spanish. The form can later be referred to an appropriate person or agency to answer. (A copy of the CORE reference in-take form appears as Appendix A.)

Information and Referral

Many reference questions asked by Spanish-speakers often fall into the category of "survival needs." Some examples of these types of questions include:

"Where can I find a Spanish-speaking doctor?"

"Where can I take a class to learn to speak English?"

"Who do I call if the gas has been turned off in my apartment?"

"What do I need to do to get my former landlord to return my rent deposit?"

"Am I eligible for the INS Amnesty Program?"

To answer such questions one of the best methods employed by public libraries is the use of the information and referral (I&R) technique. In the state of California an I&R model is being used successfully by the Los Angeles County Public Library to serve non–English speakers.

> Since 1979, CALL (Community Access Library Line) has served as the Los Angeles County Public Library's telephone multi-lingual information and referral service to the residents of Southern California via a toll-free 800 number. CALL was established by a grant from the . . . Library Services [and Construction] Act, and has been supported by the Library since 1982.
>
> CALL both creates and maintains specialized resources. Its staff includes seven professional librarians and two clerical staff with foreign language skills in Spanish, Chinese, Japanese, and English.
>
> In order to achieve the goal of providing more access, CALL upgraded its computer system and purchased high speed modems and communications software; and during the months of January and February [of 1989], installed the modems at the [four] regional libraries . . . and Library Headquarters.
>
> It may be possible in the near future to link the circulation system, the CD-ROM catalog system, and CALL's community information files so that access will be expanded to all the [Los Angeles County Public Library branch] libraries. And one day, there will even be dial-up access to those with home computers.[11]

Other examples of successful Spanish I&R services offered by public libraries exist outside of California. For example, The Chicago Public Library offers a service called "El Centro de Información," and the District of Columbia Public Library offers a similar service as part of its Community Information Service. Moreover, Spanish I&R services are not always restricted to sponsorship by public libraries. Oftentimes, they are sponsored by social service agencies such as United Way. In Los Angeles County, in addition to CALL, there is a second I&R service called Info-Line. It too offers assistance by telephone in Spanish. However, rather than being in competition with CALL, Info-Line attempts to support and supplement it, the two often making referrals to one another.

Reference Guidelines

Libraries interested in guidelines which might help them in serving the Spanish-speaking should consult two very important documents now available. Both offer a more general perspective than just concentrating on reference library services. However, both contain sections which relate to reference services, in particular those pertaining to the areas of access, personnel, and collection development.

The first document, compiled by Yolanda Cuesta and Patricia Tarín, is entitled "Guidelines for Library Service to the Spanish-Speaking" and was published in *Library Journal*.[12] More recently, the Reference and Adult Services Division (RASD) of the American Library Association published a document entitled "RASD Guidelines for Library Services to Hispanics." The guidelines were compiled by its Committee on Library Services to the Spanish-Speaking and were published in *RQ*.[13] (See Appendix B, where the guidelines are reprinted.)

Future Concerns and Issues

Much has been done in California to address the reference needs of its Spanish-speaking community. Some of the major accomplishments in this arena have herein been described. Still, major concerns and issues remain that will determine whether we will see further strides made in the delivery of public library reference services to the Spanish-speaking.

Funding

Unfortunately, most of these accomplishments have had to depend upon "soft" monies, largely LSCA and CLSA (California Library Services Act) funds. The amount of such funds available to public libraries has been diminishing over recent years. In fact, under the Reagan Administration, LSCA funds were earmarked for zero funding by the President. Fortunately, Congress restored the amounts to the federal budget, albeit at a lower level than in previous years. Twenty-five years after it was first introduced, LSCA is facing another challenge. The Bush Administration is currently seeking to replace LSCA with a new Library Services Improvement Act.[14]

In 1985 the governing Council of the American Library Association endorsed the document, *Equity at Issue: Library Services to the Nation's Major Minority Groups*. One of the document's findings stated that "minority services have historically been funded by 'soft' monies and earmarked for demonstration projects primarily." The document goes on to say that "locally, most directors continue to give . . . service [to minority communities] low budget priority. Services to minority communities cannot succeed without administrative support."[15]

Technology

Another finding mentioned in *Equity at Issue* dealt with the issue of technology. "There is a danger that to cover the cost of new information systems, fees being instituted in libraries will severely limit information access by minorities and the poor.... If in the future information becomes a purchasable commodity in public libraries, minorities and the poor will lose their last meager source for information and the nation as a whole loses one basis for survival and freedom."[16]

Aside from the fee issue, new library technologies also pose the issue of lack of library skills among the Spanish-speaking. Already, most Spanish-speakers are unable to use traditional public library resources, such as the card catalog.

> In a recent assessment of literacy among 21- to 25-year-olds, the [U.S.] Education Department found these alarming statistics:
> Only 60 percent of whites, 40 percent of Hispanics, 25 percent of blacks can find specific information in a news article or almanac.
> Only 25 percent of whites, 7 percent of Hispanics, and 3 percent of blacks can understand a bus schedule.[17]

Will the introduction of new technologies, such as online public catalogs and CD-ROMs only serve to further deny the Spanish-speaking access to public library resources? In a paper presented at a conference entitled "The New Information Technology and Hispanics," Henry T. Ingles states:

> The issue of equitable access to the new information media and technology by Hispanics and other minority groups . . . has far-reaching implications for our nation as a whole. It is a particularly significant issue for minorities because of the majority role envisioned for Hispanics and other minority population groups in society and the future work force. With the existing and continuing spread of the new information technology at work, school, and in the home, we all need to learn more about the technology to assume positions of leadership and expertise in guiding its evolution and service for the best benefit of the society. Numerous scholars and researchers . . . are warning us of the dangers inherent in widening the existing gap between the so-called "information rich" and "information poor" segments of our society unless constructive and systematic intervention approaches are implemented to curb and reorient the current trends.[18]

On the brighter side, technology does hold some promise for improving access to information. For example, California has decided to standardize all records in its Statewide Data Base by adopting OCLC as the database's official bibliographic utility. In an effort to promote resource sharing, public libraries in the state are encouraged to contribute their holdings to the California Statewide Data Base through OCLC. In a September 5, 1986, memo to Data Base participants, the state librarian says:

Seventy-four languages other than English are currently represented in the [California Data Base]. However, materials in Spanish [and] S.E. Asian languages are not represented to the extent that the present and future demography of California would suggest is necessary to satisfy the needs of speakers of these languages.[19]

A collection analysis of the Data Base by language code shows that while 1,294,901 (95.3 percent) of the records in the Database are in the English language, only 39,898 (2.7 percent) of the records are in the Spanish language. A more recent study has found that the latter figure has increased to 3.5 percent.[20] As an added incentive, California public libraries receive partial reimbursement for contributing Spanish language titles to the California Statewide Data Base.

Still another example where technology is helping to improve Spanish reference is evidenced by the availability of a range of new CD-ROM products, e.g. the *Chicano Periodical Index*. Periodical articles (in English and Spanish) not indexed in other standard indexes will now be accessible through a variety of access points to the records.

Politics of Language

The movement to make English the official language of the United States and of the individual states has resulted in some libraries choosing to deliberately ignore the information needs of the Spanish-speaking out of fear of antagonizing local government officials.

When the library board of Monterey Park Public Library in California took a stand to allow the library to purchase Asian language materials, the city council and the city manager attempted to disband the library board altogether. The case was heard by the California Court of Appeal, which ruled in favor of the library board.[21]

It should not be considered a political statement to provide library service to non–English speakers, but given today's political climate it has become just that. This situation is further exacerbated by the growing sentiment against bilingual education and the use of public services by undocumented workers. Local jurisdictions often overlook the fact that the Spanish-speaking are taxpayers too.

Professional Networking

Efforts must be made to interact more frequently with librarians from Spanish-speaking countries, especially nearby Mexico. The Asociación Mexicana de Bibliotecarios (AMBAC) is the Mexican professional organization akin to the American Library Association. In March, 1989, AMBAC held a roundtable discussion on the topic of new Spanish reference books being published by Mexican publishers. Unfortunately, few, if any, librarians from the United States were able to attend. Similarly, few Mexican librarians are able to attend the American Library Association conferences, let alone any state conferences, such as the California Library Association. More exchange programs involving Spanish-speaking librarians need to be supported.

Two binational conferences held in Tijuana and Mexicali were funded and cosponsored by the California State Library. The conferences did much to spark professional interest and dialogues between librarians in California and their counterparts in Mexico. The proceedings of the second Binational Conference have been published and distributed by the California State Library.

Another example is the very successful Feria Internacional del Libro (FIL) or the International Spanish Book Fair held annually in Guadalajara, Mexico. This book fair is also serving the purpose of permitting United States librarians to interact with the major world publishers of Spanish books. Publishers in the United States, through the lobbying efforts of librarians, should also begin to recognize the growing Spanish market in the United States.

Bilingual/Bicultural Reference Librarians

Finally, the most essential ingredient to having a successful library reference program is the librarian. While a strong public service orientation plays an important role in encouraging patrons to use the reference department of a public library, in the future it may not be enough. Libraries wishing to provide effective Spanish reference service will need to aggressively recruit and retain qualified bilingual/bicultural librarians and professional organizations like REFORMA and Bibliotecas para la Gente, will need to make a concerted effort to recruit and train qualified library science students possessing bilingual/bicultural skills.

NOTES

1. *Mexico-United States Report* Vol. 2, no. 9 (June 1989): 4.

2. United States Dept. of Commerce, Bureau of the Census. *Condition of Hispanics in America Today.* Washington, D.C.: U.S. Government Printing Office, September 13, 1983, p. 8.

3. Antonio Guernica, *Reaching the Hispanic Market Effectively: The Media, the Market, the Methods* (New York: McGraw-Hill, 1982), p. 124.

4. Ana Veciana-Suárez, *Hispanic Media, USA: A Narrative Guide to Print and Electronic Hispanic News Media in the United States* (Washington, D.C.: Media Institute, 1988) p. 3.

5. California State Library, Library Development Services Bureau, *California Library Statistics 1988: Fiscal Year 1986–1987 Data from Public, Academic, Special, State Agency and County Law Libraries* (Sacramento: California Office of State Printing, 1988), p. 41.

6. Bibliotecas para la Gente in English means "Libraries for the People" and is an organization based in Northern California interested in library services to the Spanish-speaking. BPLG is a chapter of the California Library Association as well as an affiliate of REFORMA.

7. Bay Area Library and Information System (BALIS, *Reference Referral for Spanish-Speakers and Other Spanish Language Users in California* (1986–87 Library Services & Construction Act Application), p. 2.

8. *Fuentes de Información/Reference Sources: A Guide to Selected Spanish Language Reference Referral Resources in Northern California* (Oakland: BALIS, 1987).

9. Bibliotecas para la Gente, *Spanish-Language Reference Books: An Annotated Bibliography* (Berkeley: University of California, Chicano Studies Publications Unit, 1989).

10. Judith E. Payne. *Public Libraries Face California's Ethnic and Racial Diversity* (prepublication copy) (Santa Monica, Calif.: Rand Corp., May 1988), p. 40–42.

11. Los Angeles County Public Library, *Library Newsletter* 6, 6 (June 1989): 4.

12. Yolanda Cuesta and Patricia Tarín, "Guidelines for Library Service to the Spanish-Speaking," *Library Journal* (July 1978): 1350–1355.

13. "RASD Guidelines for Library Services to Hispanics," *RQ* (Summer 1988): 491–493.

14. "LSCA Reauthorization Goes on Fast Track," *American Libraries* (July/ August 1989): 628.

15. American Library Association, President's Committee on Library Services to Minorities, *Equity at Issue: Library Services to the Nation's Major Minority Groups (1984–85 Council Document #40)* (Chicago: The Association, 1985), p. 14.

16. Ibid., p. 7.

17. Ronald L. Krannich, *Careering and Re-careering for the 1990s: The Complete Guide to Planning Your Future* (Manassas, Va.: Impact Publications, 1989), p. 20.

18. Henry T. Ingle, *Sharpening the Issues and Shaping the Policies: The Role of the New Information Media and Technology Within the U.S. Hispanic Community* (Claremont, Calif.: Tomas Rivera Center, March 1988), p. 19.

19. Gary Strong, "Memo on CLSA Statewide Data Base: A Study of Content and Expansion of Coverage," September 5, 1986, p. 5.

20. Kathleen Low, *CLSA Statewide Data Base: Status Report* (Sacramento: California State Library, Library Development Services, July 1989), p. 4.

21. "Decision Upholds Administrative Trustees in General Law Cities," *California State Library Newsletter* No. 103 (July 1989): 2–3.

LATINO REFERENCE SOURCES: A BIBLIOGRAPHIC ESSAY

Richard Chabrán

Bibliographers have made great strides in documenting the writing on Latinos in the United States. However, because of the historical neglect in this area, much remains to be done. While carrying out research for this essay, I had an opportunity to reflect back to 1972, when I began working in the Chicano Studies Library at the University of California, Berkeley. I remember talking to Raymond Padilla about his "Apuntes," a work that took me about ten years to appreciate. I also recall assisting Guillermo Rojas locate newspapers for his bibliography on literature. At the time, I hardly knew about libraries or Chicano studies. I have come to appreciate the seminal work carried out in those early years of the Chicano movement and marvel at the foresightedness of those Latinos who established Chicano and Puerto Rican studies libraries. So much of what follows could not have been accomplished without these libraries. I have gathered much of the following information from my work as a practicing Chicano librarian and as a teacher of Latino bibliography. This essay is part of a larger work tentatively entitled "Tools for Latino Research."

The following bibliographic essay seeks to document rather than critique selected Latino reference works. Major reference sources in the 1980s and those which are often cited prior to this period are emphasized. For a more comprehensive treatment of bibliography prior to this period the reader is referred to Barbara Robinson's *Mexican Americans: A Critical Guide to Research Aids*. Inasmuch as possible, I have attempted to provide some balance across fields. Even so, such areas as history, social sciences and literature predominate.

The standard categories which one would expect to find, such as bibliographies, indexes, source materials and so on, are included. Also included are key literature reviews which help us situate a field. It is often useful to consult an early review as well as one written recently. Such reviews often reveal the changing areas of emphasis and the growing complexity of a field. In areas where there is a dearth of reference sources, general works are included. Those monographs which are major sources within the field are also included.

The first part of the essay covers source materials. Included here are encyclopedias; fact sources, biographical and genealogical sources; and directories. The second part of the essay covers newspaper and periodical resources as well as major indexes. The third part of the essay covers general bibliographies; subject bibliographies in the areas of education and fine and performing arts; folklore; health and mental health; historical and archival sources; language sources and dictionaries; literacy sources; social science sources; and women's sources.

Fact Sources and Compendia

The 1980s saw the development of many Latino source materials. The *Encyclopedia of American Ethnic Groups* provides information on many Latino populations as well as thematic articles on topics such as language and immigration (Cortés, 1980; Fitzpatrick, 1980; Hendricks, 1980; Orlov, 1980; Pérez, 1980; and Thermstrom, 1980). The *Dictionary of Mexican American History* provides general coverage of Chicano history (Meier, 1981).

The *Borderlands Sourcebook* provides numerous short articles on various aspects of the Mexico–United States border (Stoddard, Ellwyn R. et al., 1983). *Chicanos in America* contains several historical documents of the Chicano Movement and a historical chronology (García, 1977). *Sources for the Study of Puerto Rican Migration* contains historical documents on the Puerto Rican migration to the United States and Hawaii (Centro de Estudios Puertorriqueños, 1982).

There are several statistical sources available. Major sources for national general data are presented in the *Hispanic Population in the United States* (Bean and Tienda, 1988), the *Hispanic Almanac* (Hispanic Policy Development Project, 1984), *The Changing Profile of Mexican America* (Tomás Rivera Center, 1985), *Persons of Spanish Origin* later named *Persons of Hispanic Origin* (U.S. Bureau of the Census, 1974–). Other general statistical sources include: *Cuantos Somos* (Teller, 1977), *The Changing Demography of Spanish Americans* (Jaffe, 1980), and "The Mexican Origin Population in the United States" (Bean, 1985).

Statistical sources which provide valuable statistical information on marketing include the *Hispanic Media and Markets* and the *U.S. Hispanic Market (1987)*. California statistical sources are available through *Projections of Hispanic Population for California* (Center for the Continuing Study of the California Population, 1982), *Statistical Sources on California Hispanic Population* (Loh, 1984), *Online Information on Hispanics & Other Minority Groups* (Medford, 1986), the *Demographics of California's Latinos* (Rose Institute, 1988) and *Burden of Support* (Hayes-Bautista, Schink, Chapa, 1988).

Biographical and Genealogical Sources

A very useful beginning point for work on Latino genealogy is "Hispanic-American Records and Research" (de Platt, 1983). Haigh, 1978, and Robinson, 1980, offer more detailed information. The best Chicano biographical source is the *Dictionary of Mexican American Historical Biography* (Meier, 1988). Other useful Chicano biographical sources are *Mexican Amercians: Movements and Leaders* (Larralde, 1976) and *Mexican Autobiography* (Woods, 1988). Puerto Rican biographical sources include *Mango Mambo* (Maldonado, Adal Alberto, 1988), *Portraits of the Puerto Rican Experience* (Maldonado, Adal Alberto, 1984), and the *Index to Puerto Rican Collective Biography* (Fowlie-Flores, 1987). *Rising Voices* is another source for Latino biography (Martínez, 1974). Martínez, 1979, provides biographical and bibliographic information on Chicano writers. Two related sources are *Spanish Surnames in the Southwestern United States* (Woods, 1978) and *Hispanic First Names* (Woods, 1984).

Directories

While there are literally dozens of directories, most are either out of date or narrow in focus. *Hispanic Resource Directory* (Schorr, 1988) and *Hispanic American Voluntary Organizations* (Gonzáles, 1985) are important general sources which focus on Latino organizations. The forthcoming "Latino Information Directory" (Gale, no date announced) promises to be an important source. The *Chicano Organizations Directory* is an essential source for Chicano organizations (Caballero, 1985). *Who's Who, Chicano Officeholders* (Martínez, 1975–) and the *National Roster of Hispanic Elected Officials* (National Association of Latino Elected and Appointed Officials, 1984–) assist us in identifying elected officials. While dated, *Hispanic Bibliographic Services in the United States* remains useful for identifying Chicano and Puerto Rican collections (Chabrán, 1980), and *Hispanic Media, USA* provides a useful listing of both print and electronic media (Veciana-Suárez, 1987). Mexican and Chicano research which are in progress are listed in the (*International Guide to Research in Mexico*, 1987). There are many regional directories such as *Ethnic Orange County* (García-Ayvens, 1989).

Serials

The Latino press has been and continues to be a major vehicle for documenting Latino serial life. Gutierrez and Schement, 1977, have compiled a bibliography on the press and media. Ríos-C. and Castillo, 1970, and Ríos-C., 1972, have listed Chicano newspapers. Chabrán, 1987, has surveyed the radical labor press among Latinos. Directories of the press have been prepared by Güereña, 1989; Kuhn Al-Bayti, 1977; Soto, 1983–; Marquez, 1985; and Danky, 1978. The most current tool which lists serials is *Hispanic Media and Markets,* a quarterly publication of Standard Rate and Data Service, Inc.

Indexes

Periodical literature constitutes a significant portion of the literature on Latinos. *The Chicano Periodical Index* is the major source for accessing this literature. The early volumes covered only Latino journals, while the more recent ones cover all periodical literature. Its primary arrangement is by subject, with supplementary author and title indexes. While its emphasis is on Chicanos, it covers Puerto Ricans and Cubans (Castillo-Speed, Chabrán, García-Ayvens, 1981–). Recently it has changed its name to the *Chicano Index* (Castillo-Speed, Chabrán, García-Ayvens, 1989–).

Its new coverage includes books, periodical literature, parts of books and dissertations. This work will be complemented by García-Ayvens' forthcoming index to anthologies (García-Ayvens, announced for 1990). The Centro de Estudios Puertorriqueños has produced a series of indexes to periodical newspaper literature (Centro de Estudios Puertorriqueños, 1981, 1981, 1981b). The *Bibliographic Guide to Latin American Studies,* 1967–, is an annual which covers primarily monographic material but also has some periodical literature included. The holdings of the Benson Latin American Collection at the University of Texas are included. The *Hispanic American Periodical Index* (Valk, 1977–) is the major index for Latin American periodicals. While it provides limited coverage for Latino periodicals in the United States, it is especially important for Puerto Rican, Cuban and immigration materials.

The *Handbook for Latin American Studies* (Hispanic Division, Library of Congress, 1935–) is an annual which includes limited information on Latinos but is useful in researching United States–Latin American relations. During the 1970s the Comite de Mexico y Aztlan provided access to newspaper literature in major English southwestern newspapers. *Chicanos in These Times* (García-Ayvens, 1987–) resumed this coverage for the *Los Angeles Times.*

While many mainstream indexes include citations on Latinos, the most important are the *Congressional Information Service Index, Dissertation Abstracts,* the *American Statistical Index, Psychological Abstracts,* the *Current Index to Journals in Education, Resources in Education,* the *Social Science Citation Index,* the *Arts and Humanities Citation Index, America: History and Life,* and the *MLA Bibliography.*

Bibliographies

Bibliographies produced during the 1960s and early 1970s tended to provide general coverage of a particular Latino group. More recent bibliographic products have been on a particular topic. While this kind of specialization is welcome, not all subject areas are equally represented. At the time of the writing of this chapter, there are no current general bibliographies on Latinos.

Bibliographies of historical interest are described in "Apuntes" (Padilla, winter 1971–72). Arno Press reprinted three bibliographies of historical interest in *Mexican American Bibliographies* (Córtes, 1974). Robinson & Robinson (1980) compiled a comprehensive bibliography of bibliographies. This work was partially updated by Julio Martínez (1984). García-Ayvens (1981) has compiled a more selective listing of reference sources.

The major Chicano bibliographies have been compiled by Barrios, 1971; Pino, 1974; Trejo, 1975; and Trujillo, 1987. Major bibliographies on Puerto Ricans have been compiled by Vivo, 1973; Cardona, 1983; Herrera, 1979; Wasserman, 1983; Cordasco, 1972; and Pérez, 1987. A major bibliography on Cubans has been compiled by MacCorkle, 1984. Casal, 1975, has also contributed an important bibliography on Cubans.

Educational Sources

Education is one of the favorite topics for those writing about Latinos. Unfortunately, the literature is extremely uneven and there is no critical bibliography on this topic. Rangel and Alcalá (1972) wrote a major review of Chicano education. They pay particular attention to the legal aspects of education. San Miguel (1987) has recently contributed a survey of historical research on Chicano education. Hernández (1970) provided us with a devastating critique of Chicanos and the educational system. Benitez, Villarreal (1979) have compiled the most comprehensive bibliography in this area. Cordasco, 1979, and Thomas, 1982, have focused on bilingual education. Leggett, 1978, compiled a bibliography on Chicanos and higher education. Haro, spring 1983; Rincón, 1981, and Webster, summer 1981, have written reviews of the higher education literature. Parker, 1978, provides access to dissertations on Puerto Ricans and the educational system. Finally Durán, 1983; Orfield, November 1986; Arías, November 1986; and Schon, 1982, provide general reviews on Latino educational literature.

Fine and Performing Arts

The fine and performing arts are the least documented bibliographically. The exception to this general assessment is Chicano art which is wonderfully documented by Goldman, Ybarra Frausto, 1985. Quirarte 1973, 1983, 1984, has also provided us with two major works on Chicano art. González-Rich and Quirarte, 1982, developed a directory of Hispanic American art organizations. Bensusan, 1982, has provided a more limited review of Chicano art. Wall, 1982, has reviewed the work on Puerto Rican art. Latino art exhibits are becoming more common. Many of these exhibits are documented in catalogs, such as *Hispanic Art in the United States* (Beardsley, 1987).

The area of photography remains undocumented within the literature. Some examples of this medium are provided by the Chicano Communication Center, 1976; Fusco, 1970; Hall, 1988; and Martín, 1983. Film is another area which needs more bibliographic documentation. Cine Aztlan, 1974, provided a filmography of Latino works. The Chicano libraries at UCLA (Chicano Studies Research Center, 1989), Austin (Chavaría, 1983), and Los Angeles County, 1987, documented their film holdings. Durán, 1979, and Caballero, 1981, have provided additional material on this topic. Keller, 1985, has edited an excellent anthology on Chicano cinema which includes a filmography.

Given the dramatic influence of Latino music it is surprising that there is no major bibliography or discography in this area. Girard, 1982, has provided a review of this topic. Heisley, 1988, has provided an excellent review of Chicano music in California. Sources which are regularly cited in this literature include: Geijerstam, 1976; Paredes, 1976; Robb, 1980; and Roberts, 1979. The topic of Chicano theater has been documented in *Chicano Theatre,* which includes an extensive bibliography on this topic (Huerta, 1982).

Folklore Sources

There is a rich tradition of folklore studies in the Southwest. This literature is excellently documented in Heisley, 1977. Najer Ramírez, 1987, has updated this source. Weigle, 1983, has also contributed to documenting this literature. Recently Glazer, 1987, compiled a dictionary on Mexican-American proverbs.

Health and Mental Health Sources

The early literature on health discusses primarily folk beliefs. Policy issues which discuss the social context of health are rare in the literature.

This literature is reviewed by Roeder. The emerging literature, which is more epidemological, has been documented by Villaescusa, 1986. Cervantes, 1985, has reviewed the literature on Chicanos and stress. There has been substantial work carried out on Latino mental health. By far the most important work in this area is by Newton et al., 1982. Greenblatt, summer 1982, has also provided a review of mental health utilization.

Historical and Archival Sources

Chicano historical studies have constituted a major part of the literature. Early reviews and critiques are represented by Gómez-Quiñones, fall 1971; Arroyo, summer 1975; Gómez-Quiñones and Arroyo, April 1976; Corwin, summer 1973; Jones, January 1969; and Guzmán, 1972. More recent reviews include works by Acuña, spring, 1989; Almaguer, January 1981; Arroyo, 1983; Camarillo, spring 1986b; García and García, 1982; Saragoza, 1987; and Weber, autumn 1977. The most important historical bibliography was compiled by Meier, 1984. This work is complemented by Camarillo, 1986; Camarillo, 1986a, and Gómez-Quiñones, 1982.

Guides to archival sources are provided by Beers, 1979; Barnes, Naylor and Thomas, 1981; Cardoso, 1978; Griswold del Castillo and Martínez, 1984; and Güereña, 1988. Oral history efforts have been described by Martínez, 1978; the Mexican revolution by Raat, 1982; and the Mexican American War by Tutorow, 1981. Acuña, 1988, and Weber, 1982, have written two survey monographs on Chicano history, while Meier, 1981, has compiled a dictionary of Mexican-American history. Puerto Rican historical studies has been surveyed by Martínez de Carrera, 1982.

Language Sources and Dictionaries

Language has been recognized as a key constituent of the social life of Latinos. Topics such as language loyalty, language shifts, and dialects are common topics within the literature. Teschner, 1975, identifies key studies on Latinos. This work was partially updated in 1982 (Teschner, 1982). Macías, 1981, and Macías, 1981a, have reviewed language policy studies. Peñalosa, 1980, and Sánchez, 1983, have authored key sociolinguistic monographs. Blanco, 1971, has provided us with a classic study of language in California.

In the 1930s Julio G. Arce (Jorge Ulica) forecast the need for a regional language dictionary. Today numerous such dictionaries have been produced. The major Latino dictionaries were compiled by Fuentes, 1974; Galván, 1980; Polkinhorn, 1986; and Vásquez, 1977.

Literary Sources

The 1960s witnessed the *florecimiento* of Chicano literature. Rojas, December 1973, was perhaps the most ambitious effort to document this literature. This work is especially important because it includes creative works within books, periodicals and newspapers. Trujillo and Rodríguez, 1985, provide us with an important listing of separately published creative titles. Numerous review articles exists on Chicano literature. Some of the most significant are by Paredes, 1987, 1987a, 1988; Ramos, 1982; Rodríguez, 1982; and Shirley, 1984. Important anthologies and monographs which survey this literature are by Bruce Novoa, 1980; Leal, 1985; Leal et al., 1982; Sommers, Ybarra Frausto, 1979; and Tatum, 1982. *Chicano Literature* (Martínez and Lomelí, 1985) and *Chicano Writers* (Lomelí, 1989) are encyclopedic works which provide information on several authors and various genres. Eger's (1982) *A Bibliography of Criticism of Contemporary Chicano Literature* provides access to Chicano literary criticism, and, although published eight years ago at this writing, remains a key source. Chabram's forthcoming review of Chicano criticism surveys the major tendencies within this literature (Chabram, no date announced). Foster, 1982, and Hill and Schleifer, 1974, have compiled bibliographies on Puerto Rican literature. Acosta Belén, 1978, has provided a brief review of this literature. Finally, Lindstrom, 1982, has surveyed Cuban and Puerto Rican literature.

Social Science Sources

Cubans in the United States provides a listing of social science resources on Cubans (MacCorkle, 1984). There are no comparable works on Chicanos or Puerto Ricans. Instead there exists a multitude of more specialized bibliographies and literature reviews. General reviews of Chicano social science literature have been provided by Almaguer, 1981; Flores, 1986; Hennessy, May 1984; Mirandé, winter, 1989; and Ortiz, 1983. Critiques of traditional social science literature have been produced by Romano-V., 1973; Romano-V., 1973a; Romano-V., 1973b; Montiel, 1973; Rocco, 1970; and Vaca, 1970. The sociological literature on Chicanos has been reviewed by Alvarez, Sánchez and Solache, 1982; Tienda, 1983; Barrera, 1979; and Mirandé, 1985. The sociological literature on Cubans is surveyed by Cobas, 1982, while the literature on Puerto Ricans is surveyed by Duncan, 1982a. Chicano anthropological literature is reviewed by Rosaldo, 1985, and Zavaleta, 1982. Puerto Rican anthropological literature has been surveyed by Duncan, 1982. Barrera, spring 1974; Muñoz, spring 1974; and Muñoz, 1983, have surveyed the literature on Chicanos and political science. The labor literature has been reviewed and listed by Almaguer, Camarillo, 1983; Barrera, 1983; Delgado, 1984; Fodell, 1974;

Fogel, 1983; and Sable, 1987. Surveys of the literature on families are extensive and are here represented by Baca Zinn, 1979; Baca Zinn, 1983; Andrade, 1983; García, 1980; Griswold del Castillo, 1983; Ramírez and Arce, 1981; Saragoza, 1983; Valdéz, 1982; Ybarra, 1983; and Zapata, 1981. Becerra, 1984; Newton, 1981; and Bigelow, 1983, have reviewed the literature on the elderly. Border literature is surveyed by Bustamante, 1980; Valk, 1988; Carillo, 1981; Fernandez Kelly, 1981; Fischer de Figueroa, 1982–; Hall, 1985; Peña, 1981; and Villalobos, 1988. The immigration literature has been surveyed by Cornelius et al., 1982; Cornelius, 1983; Cornelius, Chávez, Castro, 1982a; and Spaulding, 1983. The childbearing literature is listed by Darabi, 1987. The media literature is detailed by Greenberg, 1983. Nelson and Tienda, 1985, and Munguía, 1984, have surveyed the literature on ethnicity. Finally, Trujillo, 1974, has reviewed the criminological writings.

Women's Sources

General bibliographic reviews of the literature on women have been developed by Loeb, 1980; D'Andrea, April 1986; and Chábran, 1986. General bibliographies on women have been compiled by Castillo Speed, forthcoming; Cabello et al., 1976; Candelaria, 1980; Chapa, 1976; Cotera, 1982; Knaster, 1977; Portillo, Ríos and Rodríguez, 1976; Stoner, 1989; and Timberlake, 1988. Historical reviews have been prepared by Apodaca, 1977; Driscoll, 1986; González, fall 1984; Sweeney, 1977; and Orozco, 1984. García, 1986; Baca Zinn, 1982; and Baezconde and Salgado, September 1987, have reviewed the sociological literature, while McKenna, 1988, has edited a bibliography on educational resources. Literary sources are covered in Ordoñez, 1980; and Sonntag, 1980. Soto, 1976, has reviewed the periodical press, while Waldman, 1980, has developed a statistical profile.

Conclusion

There is no one Latino bibliographic source which contains the entire universe of Latino resources. There are, however, a multitude of rich bibliographic reference and source materials which will lead users to appropriate materials. These reference materials reflect a growing sophistication and specialization. Over the next decade we will see an increase in the availability of many of these tools in an online environment. For the reader's benefit I have included below the bibliographic citations for sources included within the text.

REFERENCES

Acosta Belén, Edna. "The literature of the Puerto Rican national in the United States." *Bilingual Review* **5**, 1–2 (August 1978): 107–116.

Acuña, Rodolfo F. *Occupied America: A History of Chicanos.* New York: Harper & Row, 1988.

_____. "The struggle of class and gender: current research in Chicano studies." *Journal of American History* **2**, 8 (Spring 1989): 134–138.

Alarcon, Norma. "Chicana writers and critics in a social context: towards a contemporary bibliography." *Third Women* 4 (1989): 169–178.

Almaguer, Tomás. "Recent contributions to Chicano studies research." *Contemporary Sociology* **10**, 1 (January 1981): 27–30.

_____, and Alberto Camarillo. "Urban Chicano workers in historical perspective: a review of the literature." *The State of Chicano Research in Family, Labor and Migration Studies.* Alberto Camarillo, Tomás Almaguer and Armando Valdéz. 3–32. Stanford: Stanford Center for Chicano Research, 1983.

Alvarez, Rodolfo; Juan J. Sánchez and Saul Solache. "Mexican Americans — sociology." *Sourcebook of Hispanic Culture in the United States.* David William Foster. 57–85. Chicago: American Library Association, 1982.

Amaro, Hortensia. *Hispanic Women in Psychology: A Resource Directory.* Washington, D.C.: American Psychological Association, 1984.

Andrade, Sally, ed. "Bibliography on Latino families in the United States." *Latino Families in the United States.* Sally J. Andrade. 72–79. s.l.: Planned Parenthood Federation of America, 1983.

Anuario Hispano: Hispanic Yearbook. Mclean: 1987–.

Apodaca, María Linda. "The Chicana woman: an historical materialist perspective." *Latin American Perspectives* **4**, 1–2 (1977): 70–89.

Arías, M. Beatriz. "Content of education for Hispanic students: an overview." *American Journal of Education* (November, 1986): 27–57.

Arroyo, Luis. "Notes on the past, present, and future directions of Chicano labor studies." *Aztlan* **2**, 6 (Summer 1975): 137–149.

_____. "The state of Chicano labor history 1970–1980." *Chicanos in the Social Sciences: A Decade of Research and Development (1970–1980)* Isidro Ortiz. 1–8. Santa Barbara: Center for Chicano Studies, 1983.

Baca Zinn, Maxine. "Chicano family research: conceptual distortions and alternative directions." *Journal of Ethnic Studies* **7**, 3 (1979): 59–71.

_____. "Familism among Chicanos: a theoretical review." *Humbolt Journal of Social Relations* **10**, 1 (1983): 224–238.

_____. "Mexican American women in the social sciences." *Signs: Journal of Women in Culture and Society* **8**, 2 (Winter 1982): 259–272.

_____. "Mexican heritage women: a bibliographic essay." *Sage Race Relations Abstracts* 9 (August 1984): 1–12.

Baezconde Garbanati, Lourdes, and Nelly Salgado. "Mexican immigrant women: a selected bibliography." *Hispanic Journal of Behavioral Sciences* **9**, 3 (September 1987): 331–358.

Baker, Houston A., Jr., ed. *Three American Literatures: Essays in Chicano, Native American, and Asian American Literatures for Teachers of American Literature.* New York: Modern Language Association, 1982.

Barnes, Thomas C.; Thomas H. Naylor and Charles W. Polzer. *Northern New Spain: A Research Guide.* Tucson: University of Arizona Press, 1981.

Barrera, Mario. *Race and Class in the Southwest: A Theory of Racial Inequality.* Notre Dame, Ind.: University of Notre Dame Press, 1979.

_____. "The study of politics and the Chicano." *Aztlan* **5**, 1 (Spring 1974): 9–26.

_____. "Traditions of research on the Chicano worker." *The State of Chicano Research in Family, Labor, and Migration Studies*. Alberto Camarillo, Tomás Almaguer and Armando Valdéz. 51–74. Stanford: Stanford Center for Chicano Research, 1983.

Barrios, Ernie. *Bibliografía de Aztlan: An Annotated Chicano Bibliography*. San Diego: San Diego State Foundation, 1971.

Bean, Frank D.; Elizabeth H. Stephan and Wolfgang Optiz. "The Mexican origin population in the United States: a demographic overview." *The Mexican American Experience: An Interdisciplinary Anthology*. Rodolfo de la Garza et al. 57–75. Austin: University of Texas Press, 1985.

_____, and Martha Tienda. *Hispanic Population of the United States*. New York: Russell Sage Foundation, 1988.

Beardsley, John, and Jane Livingston. *Hispanic Art in the United States*. New York: Museum of Fine Art, 1987.

Becerra, Rosina, and David Shaw. *The Hispanic Elderly: A Research Reference Guide*. Lanham, Md.: University Press of America, 1984.

Beers, Henry P. *Spanish and Mexican Records of the American Southwest: A Bibliographical Guide to Archive and Manuscript Sources*. Tucson: University of Arizona Press, 1979.

Benítez, Mario A., and G. Villarreal, comps. *The Education of Mexican Americans: A Selected Bibliography*. Rosslyn, Va.: National Clearinghouse for Bilingual Education, 1979.

Bensusan, Guy. "Mexican Americans—art." *Sourcebook of Hispanic Culture in the United States*. David William Foster. 112–130. Chicago: American Library Association, 1982.

Bibliographic Guide to Latin American Studies. Boston: G.K. Hall, 1967–.

Bigelow, Abbie. "The aged in Hispanic groups: a review." *International Journal of Aging and Human Development* **17**, 3 (1983): 177–201.

Blanco S., Antonio. *La lengua española de California: Contribución a su estudio*. Madrid: Ediciónes Cultura Hispanica, 1971.

Bonilla, Frank; Ricardo Campos and Juan Flores. "Puerto Rican studies: promptings for the academy and the left." *The Left Academy: Marxist Scholarship on American Campuses*. Bertell Ollman and Edward Vernoff. 67–102. New York: Praeger, 1986.

Bruce Novoa, Juan. *Chicano Authors: Inquiry by Interview*. Austin: University of Texas Press, 1980.

Bustamante, Jorge. *Mexico–Estados Unidos: Bibliografía General sobre Estudios Fronterizos*. Mexico: Colegio de Mexico, 1980.

Caballero, César. *Chicano Organizations Directory*. New York: Neal-Schuman, 1985.

_____. "Non print materials and the Mexican American." *Library Resources on Latin America: New Perspectives for the 1980s*. Dan Hazen. 179–185. Madison, Wis.: SALALM, 1981.

Cabello Argandoña, Roberto; Juan Gómez-Quiñones and Patricia Herrera Durán. *La Chicana: A Bibliographic Study*. Los Angeles: Chicano Studies Center Publications, 1976.

Camarillo, Alberto. "The 'new' Chicano history: historiography of Chicanos of the 1970s." *Chicanos and the Social Sciences: A Decade of Research and Development (1970–1980)*. Isidro Ortiz. 9–17. Santa Barbara: Center for Chicano Studies, 1983.

_____. *Latinos in the United States: A Historical Bibliography*. Santa Barbara: ABC-CLIO, 1986.

_____. *Mexican Americans in Urban Society: A Selected Bibliography*. Berkeley: Floricanto Press, 1986a.

_____. "Perspectives on Mexican American urban life and culture." *Journal of American Ethnic History* **5**, 2 (Spring 1986b): 72–79.

Campos Carr, Irene. "A survey of selected literature on la Chicana." *NWSA Journal* **1**, 2 (1988–89): 253–273.

Candelaria, Cordelia. "Six reference works on Mexican American women: a review essay." *Frontiers* **5**, 2 (1980): 75–80.

Cardona, Luis A. *An Annotated Bibliography for Puerto Rican Materials and Other Sundry Matters*. Bethesda, Md.: Carreta Press, 1983.

Cardoso, Lawrence A. "Archival sources in Mexico for the study of Chicano history." *New Scholar* **7**, 1–2 (1978): 255–258.

Carrillo, Jorge V. *La Industria Maquiladora Mexico: Bibliografía, Directorio e Investigaciónes Reciéntes/Border Assembly Industry and Recent Research*. La Jolla, Calif.: Program in United States–Mexican Studies, 1981.

Casal, Lourdes, and Andres R. Hernández. "Cubans in the United States: a survey of the literature." *Cuban Studies* **5**, 2 (July 1975): 25–51.

Castillo-Speed, Lillian. "La Chicana: a selected list of materials from 1980 to the present." *Frontiers* (forthcoming).

_____; Richard Chabrán and Francisco García-Ayvens. *Chicano Periodical Index*. Berkeley: Chicano Studies Library, 1981–.

_____; Richard Chabrán and Francisco García Ayvens. *The Chicano Index: A Comprehensive Subject, Author, and Title Index to Chicano Materials*. Berkeley: Chicano Studies Library, 1989–.

Center for the Continuing Study of the California Economy. *Projections of Hispanic Population for California, 1985–2000: With Projections of Non-Hispanic White, Black and Asian & Other Population Groups*. Palo Alto: Center for the Continuing Study of the California Economy, 1982.

Centro de Estudios Puertorriqueños. *Index to Articles in the New York Times Relating to Puerto Rico and Puerto Ricans Between 1899 and 1930*. New York: Centro, 1981.

Centro de Estudios Puertorriqueños. *Preliminary Guide to Articles in Puerto Rican Newspapers Relating to Puerto Rican Migration Between 1900 and 1929*. New York: Centro, 1981a.

Centro de Estudios Puertorriqueños. *Preliminary Guide to Articles in La Prensa Relating to Puerto Ricans in New York City Between 1922–1929*. New York: Centro, 1981b.

Centro de Estudios Puertorriqueños. *Sources for the Study of Puerto Rican Migration, 1879–1930*. New York: Centro, 1982.

Cervantes, Richard. "Stress, coping, and Mexican American mental health: a systematic review." *Hispanic Journal of Behavioral Sciences* **7** (1985): 1–73.

Chabram, Angie. "Chicano critical discourse: an emerging cultural practice." *Aztlan* (forthcoming):

Chabrán, Rafael. "Spaniards." *The Immigrant Labor Press in North America, 1840s–1970s: An Annotated Bibliography*. Dirk Hoeder. 151–190. New York: Greenwood Press, 1987.

Chabran, Richard. "Chicana reference sources." *Chicana Voices: Intersections of Class, Race and Gender*. Teresa Córdova, et al. 146–156. Austin: Center for Mexican American Studies, 1986.

_____. *Hispanic Bibliographic Services in the United States*. Ann Arbor: National Chicano Research Network, 1980.

The Changing Profile of Mexican America: A Sourcebook for Planning. Claremont: The Tomás Rivera Center, 1985.

Chapa, Evey, and Sally Andrade, eds. *La Mujer Chicana: An Annotated Bibliography*. Austin: Chicana Research and Learning Center, 1976.

Chavaría, Elvira. *Chicano Film Guide*. Austin: Mexican American Library Program, The General Libraries, University of Texas, 1983.

Chicano Communication Center. *450 Años del Pueblo Chicano/450 Years of Chicano History in Pictures*. Albuquerque: Chicano Communication Center, 1976.

Chicano Studies Research Center. *Chicano Films: A Listing of Films Available in the Chicano Studies Research Library*. Los Angeles: Chicano Studies Research Center, 1989.

Cine Aztlan. *La Raza Film Bibliography*. Santa Barbara: Cine Aztlan, 1974.

Cobas, José A. "Cuban Americans — sociology." *Sourcebook of Hispanic Culture in the United States*. David William Foster. 203–218. Chicago: American Library Association, 1982.

Cole, Katherine W. *Minority Organizations: A National Directory*. Garrett Park, Md.: Garrett Park Press, 1987.

Comité de Mexico y Aztlan. *News Monitoring Service*. Oakland: COMEXAZ, 1972–1980.

Cordasco, Francesco. *Bilingual Education in American Schools: A Guide to Information Sources*. Detroit: Gale, 1979.

_____. "Bilingual education in American schools: a bibliographical essay." *Immigration History Newsletter* **14**, 1 (May 1982): 1–8.

_____, et al. *Puerto Ricans on the United States Mainland: A Bibliography of Reports, Texts, Critical Studies and Related Materials*. Totowa, N.J.: Rowman & Littlefield, 1972.

Cornelius, Wayne, et al. *Mexican Immigrants in the San Francisco Bay Area: A Summary of Current Knowledge*. San Diego: Center for United States-Mexican Studies. 1982.

_____. "The study of Mexican migration." *The State of Chicano Research in Family, Labor and Migration Studies*. Albert Camarillo, Tomas Almaguer, and Armando Valdéz. 187–200. Stanford: Stanford Center for Chicano Research, 1983.

_____; Leo Chávez and John Castro. *Mexican Immigrants and Southern California: A Summary of Current Knowledge*. San Diego: Center for United States-Mexican Studies, 1982a.

Cortés, Carlos, comp. *Mexican American Bibliographies*. New York: Arno Press, 1974.

_____. "Mexicans." *Harvard Encyclopedia of American Ethnic Groups*. Stephan Thernstrom. 697–719. Cambridge: Harvard University Press, 1980.

Corwin, Arthur. "Mexican immigration history, 1900–1970: literature and research." *Latin American Research Review* **2** (Summer 1973): 3–24.

Cotera, Martha. *Latina Sourcebook: Bibliography of Mexican-American, Puerto Ricans and Other Hispanic Women Materials in the U.S.* Austin: Information Systems Development, 1982.

D'Andrea, Vaneeta-Marie. "Ethnic women: a critique of the literature, 1971–1981." *Ethnic and Racial Studies* **9** (April 1986): 235–246.

Danky, James. *Hispanic Americans in the United States: A Union List of Periodicals and Newspapers Held by the State Historical Society of Wisconsin and the*

Libraries of the University of Wisconsin–Madison. Madison: State Historical Society of Wisconsin, 1978.

Darabi, Katherine F. *Childbearing Among Hispanics in the United States: An Annotated Bibliography.* New York: Greenwood Press, 1987.

de Platt, Lyman. "Hispanic-American records and research." *Ethnic Genealogy: A Research Guide.* Jessie Carney Smith. 365–401. New York: Greenwood Press, 1983.

Delgado, Melvin, and Denise Humm-Delgado. "Hispanics and group work: a review of the literature." *Social Work with Groups* 7, 3 (Fall 1984): 85–96.

Driscoll, Barbara. "Chicana historiography: a research note concerning Mexican archival sources." *Chicana Voices: Intersections of Class, Race, and Gender.* 136–145. Austin: Center for Mexican American Studies, 1986.

Duncan, Ronald J. "Puerto Ricans — anthropology." *Sourcebook of Hispanic Culture in the United States.* David William Foster. 151–169. Chicago: American Library Association, 1982.

————. "Puerto Ricans — sociology." *Sourcebook of Hispanic Culture in the United States.* David William Foster. 170–186. Chicago: American Library Association, 1982a.

Durán, Daniel Flores. *Latino Materials: A Multimedia Guide for Children and Young Adults.* New York: Schuman, 1979.

Durán, Richard P. *Hispanics: Education and Background.* New York: College Entrance Examination Board, 1983.

Eger, Ernestina. *A Bibliography of Criticism of Contemporary Chicano Literature.* Berkeley: Chicano Studies Library Publications, 1982.

Estrada, Leobardo, et al. "Chicanos in the United States: a history of exploitation and resistance." *Daedalus* 110, 2 (Spring, 1981): 103–131.

Falcón, Angelo. "Puerto Rican politics in urban America." *La Red/The Net* 70 (July 1983): 2–9.

Fernandez Kelly, María. "The U.S. Mexico border: recent publications and the state of current research." *Latin American Research Review* 16, 3 (1981): 250–267.

Fischer de Figueroa, Claire, ed. *Relaciónes Mexico–Estados Unidos: Bibliografía Anual.* Mexico: Colegio de Mexico, 1982–.

Fitzpatrick, Joseph P. "Puerto Ricans." *Harvard Encyclopedia of American Ethnic Groups.* Stephan Thermstrom. 858–867. Cambridge, Mass.: Harvard University Press, 1980.

Flores, Estevan. "Chicanos and sociological research, 1970–1980." *Chicanos and the Social Sciences: A Decade of Research and Development (1970–1980).* Isidro Ortiz. 19–45. Santa Barbara: Center for Chicano Studies, 1983.

Flores, Estevan T. "The Mexican-Origin People in the United States and Marxist Thought in Chicano Studies." *The Left Academy: Marxist Scholarship on American Campuses.* Bertell Ollman and Edward Vernoff. 103–138. New York: Praeger, 1986.

Flores, María. *Mexican American Archives at the Benson Collection: A Guide for Users.* Austin: Mexican American Library Program, The General Libraries, University of Texas, 1981.

Flori, Monica. "A selected and annotated filmography on Latin American Women." *Third Woman* 2, 2 (1984): 117–121.

Fodell, Beverly. *César Chávez and the United Farm Workers: A Selective Bibliography.* Detroit: Wayne State University Press, 1974.

Fogel, Walter. "Research on the Chicano Worker." *The State of Chicano Research in Family, Labor and Migration Studies.* Albert Camarillo, Tomás Almaguer and

Armando Valdéz. 33–50. Stanford: Stanford Center for Chicano Research, 1983.

Foster, David William. *Puerto Rican Literature: A Bibliography of Secondary Sources.* Westport, Conn.: Greenwood Press, 1982.

Fowlie-Flores, Fay. *Index to Puerto Rican Collective Biography.* New York: Greenwood Press, 1987.

Fuentes, Dagoberto, and José López. *Barrio Language Dictionary: First Dictionary of Caló.* La Puente: El Barrio Publications, 1974.

Fusco, Paul. *La Causa: The California Grape Boycott.* New York: Collier Books, 1970.

Gale. *The Latino Information Directory.* Detroit: Gale (forthcoming).

Galván, Roberto. *Bilingual Dictionary of Anglicismos, Barbarismos, Pachuquismos y Otras Locuciónes en el Barrio: Bilingual Dictionary of Anglicisms, Barbarisms, Pachuquisms, and Other Locutions in the Barrio.* Denver: Francisco García, 1980.

García, Alma. "Studying Chicanas: bringing women into the frame of Chicano studies." *Chicana Voices: Intersection of Race, Class and Gender.* 19–29. Austin: Center for Mexican American Studies, 1986.

García, Mario. "La familia: the Mexican immigrant family, 1900–1930." *Work, Family, Sex Roles, Language.* Alberto Camarillo, Francisco Hernández, and Mario Barrera. 117–139. Berkeley: Tonatiuh-Quinto Sol, 1980.

———— and Richard García. "Mexican Americans: history." *Sourcebook of Hispanic Culture in the United States.* David William Foster. 3–33. Chicano: American Library Association, 1982.

García, Richard. *Chicanos in America, 1540–1974: A Chronology and Fact Book.* Dobbs Ferry, New York: Ocean, 1977.

García-Ayvens, Francisco. *Chicanos in These Times: A Cumulative Subject Index to Articles About Chicanos in the Los Angeles Times.* Santa Fe Springs: ATM Information Services, 1985–.

————. *Chicano Anthology Index.* Berkeley: Chicano Studies Library (forthcoming).

————. *Ethnic Orange County: An Ethnic Resource Directory. 4th Edition.* Orange County: Santiago Library, 1989.

————, et al. *¿Quien Sabe?: A Preliminary List of Chicano Reference Materials.* Los Angeles: Chicano Studies Research Center, 1981.

————, and Richard Chabrán. *Biblio-Politica: Chicano Perspectives on Library Services in the United States.* Berkeley: Chicano Studies Library, 1984.

Geijerstam, Claes, af. *Popular Music in Mexico.* Albuquerque: University of New Mexico Press, 1976.

Girard, Sharon. "Music." *Sourcebook of Hispanic Culture in the United States.* David William Foster. 309–326. Chicago: American Library Association, 1982.

Glazer, Mark. *A Dictionary of Mexican American Proverbs.* New York: Greenwood Press, 1987.

Goldman, Shifra, and Tomás Ybarra Frausto. *Arte Chicano: A Comprehensive Annotated Bibliography of Chicano Art, 1965–1981.* Berkeley: Chicano Studies Library, 1985.

Gómez-Quiñones, Juan. "Pre-twentieth century Mexicans north of the Rios Bravo: selected social and economic sources." *Development of the Mexican Working Class North of the Rio Bravo: Work and Culture Among Laborers and Artisans, 1860–1900.* 55–118. Los Angeles: Chicano Studies Research Center Publications, 1982.

_____. "Towards a perspective on Chicano history." *Aztlan* **2**, (Fall 1971): 1–49.

_____, and Luis Arroyo. "On the state of Chicano history: observations on its development, interpretation, and theory, 1970–1974." *Western Historical Quarterly* 2 (April 1976): 155–185.

Gonzalez-Rich, Maria Elena, and Jacinto Quirarte. *Directory of Hispanic American Art Organizations*. San Antonio: Research Center for the Arts and Humanities, 1982.

Gonzalez, Rosalinda. "The Chicana in southwest labor history, 1900–1975 (a preliminary bibliographic analysis)." *Critical Perspectives* **2**, 1 (Fall 1984): 26–61.

Gonzales, Sylvia. *Hispanic American Voluntary Organizations*. Westport, Conn.: Greenwood, 1985.

Graham, Joe S. *Hispanic American Material Culture: An Annotated Directory of Collections, Sites, Archives and Festivals in the United States*. Westport, Conn.: Greenwood Press, 1988.

Greenberg, Bradley S., et al. *Mexican Americans & the Mass Media*. Norwood, N.J.: ABLEX, 1983.

Greenblatt, Milton, and Norman Margie. "Hispanic mental health and use of mental health services: a critical review of the literature." *American Journal of Social Psychiatry* **2**, 3 (Summer 1982): 25–31.

Griswold del Castillo, Richard and Julio Martínez. "Survey of Chicano manuscript collections." *Biblio-Politica: Chicano Perspectives on Library Service in the United States*. Francisco García and Richard Chabrán. 107–118. Berkeley: Chicano Studies Library Publications, 1984.

_____. "Chicano family history, methodology and theory: a survey of contemporary research direction." *History, Culture and Society: Chicano Studies in the 1980s*. 95–106. Ypsilanti: Bilingual Press, 1983.

Güereña, Salvador. "Archives and manuscripts: historical antecedents to contemporary Chicano collections." *Collection Building* **8**, 4 (1988): 3–11.

_____. "Latin America, Latino (U.S.), Spain and Portugal." *Magazines for Libraries*. Bill Katz and Linda Sternberg Katz. 600–623. New York: Bowker, 1989.

Gutierrez, Felix, and Jorge Reina Schement. "Chicanos and the media: a bibliography of selected materials." *Journalism History* 4, 2 (Summer 1977): 53–55.

Guzmán, Ralph. "Chicano control of Chicano history: a review of selected literature." *California Historical Quarterly* (1972): 170–175.

Haigh, Roger M. *Finding Aid to the Microfilmed Collection of the Genealogical Society to Utah: Preliminary Guide to the Mexican Collection*. 1978.

Hall, Douglas Kent. *The Border on the Line*. New York: Abbeville Press, 1988.

Hall, Linda B. "The United States–Mexican borders: historical, political, and cultural perspectives." *Latin American Research Review* **20**, 2 (1985): 223–229.

Haro, Carlos Manuel. "Chicanos and higher education: a review of selected literature." *Aztlan* **14**, 1 (Spring 1983): 35–77.

Haro, Roberto. *Developing Library and Information Services for Americans of Hispanic Origin*. Metchen, N.J.: Scarecrow, 1980.

Hayes-Bautista, David; Werner O. Schink and Jorge Chapa. *The Burden of Support: Young Latinos in an Aging Society*. Stanford, Calif.: Stanford University Press, 1988.

Heisley, Michael. *An Annotated Bibliography of Chicano Folklore from the Southwestern United States*. Los Angeles: Center for the Study of Comparative Folklore and Mythology, UCLA, 1977.

_____. "Sources for the study of Mexican music in California." California's

Musical Wealth: Sources for the Study of Music in California. Stephen Fry, Glendale, May 17–18, 1985. 1988.

Hendricks, Glenn. "Dominicans." *Harvard Encyclopedia of American Ethnic Groups.* Stephan Thermstrom. 282–284. Cambridge, Mass.: Harvard University Press, 1980.

Hennessy, Alistair. "The rise of the Hispanics: Chicanos." *Journal of Latin American Studies* **16** (May 1984): 171–194.

Hernández, Deluvina. *Mexican American Challenge to a Sacred Cow.* Los Angeles: Aztlan, 1970.

Herrera, Diane. *Puerto Ricans and Other Minority Groups in the Continental United States: An Annotated Bibliography.* Detroit: B. Ethridge, 1979.

Hill, Marnesba, and Harold B. Schleifer. *Puerto Rican Authors: A Biobibliographical Handbook/Autores Puertorriqueños: Una Guia Biobibliográfica.* Metuchen: Scarecrow, 1974.

Hispanic Division. Library of Congress. *Handbook of Latin American Studies.* Austin: University of Texas Press, 1935–.

Hispanic Policy Development Project. *The Hispanic Almanac.* New York: Hispanic Policy Development Project, 1984.

Hispanic Media and Markets. Wilmette: Standard Rate and Data Service, 1988–.

Hispanic Studies Update. Ann Arbor: University Microfilms, 1984–.

Huerta, Jorge. *Chicano Theater: Themes and Forms.* Ypsilanti, Mich.: Bilingual Press, 1982.

Indiana University. Libraries. *Pueblo Latino: The Puerto Ricans.* Bloomington: Indiana University, 1975.

International Guide to Research on Mexico/Guía Internacional de Investigaciónes sobre Mexico. San Diego and Tijuana: Center for U.S.-Mexican Studies and Colegio de la Frontera Norte, 1987.

Jaffe, Abram J.; M. Cullen and Thomas D. Boswell. *The Changing Demography of Spanish Americans.* New York: Academic Press, 1980.

Jones, Oakah L. "Borderlands: a selected reading list." *Journal of the West* 8 (January 1969): 137–142.

Keller, Gary. *Chicano Cinema: Research, Reviews and Resources.* Binghamton, N.Y.: Bilingual Press, 1985.

Knaster, Meri. *Women in Spanish America.* Boston: G.K. Hall, 1977.

Koldewyn, Phillip. *Latino Volunteer and Non-Profit Organizations: A Directory.* Claremont: The Rose Institute, 1988.

Kuhn Al-Bayti, Barbara, et al. *Ethnic Serials at Selected University of California Libraries: A Union List.* Los Angeles: Ethnic Studies Centers, 1977.

Larralde, Carlos. *Mexican Americans: Movements and Leaders.* 1976.

Leal, Luis. *Aztlan y Mexico: Perfiles Literarios e Historicos.* New York: Bilingual Press, 1985.

————, et al. *A Decade of Chicano Literature (1970–1979): Critical Essays and Bibliography.* Santa Barbara: Editorial La Causa, 1982.

Leggett, Delia C. *Chicanos in Higher Education: A Bibliography.* Ann Arbor: Survey Research Center, University of Michigan, 1978.

Lindstrom, Naomi E. "Cuban American and continental Puerto Rican literature." *Sourcebook of Hispanic Culture in the United States.* David William Foster. 221–245. Chicago: American Library Association, 1982.

Loeb, Catherine. "La Chicana: a bibliographic essay." *Frontiers* **5**, 2 (1980): 59–74.

Loh, Eudora, and Medford, Roberta. *Statistical Sources on California Hispanic Population, 1984: A Preliminary List.* Oakland: California Spanish Language Data Base, 1984.

Lomelí, Francisco and Carl Shirley. "Chicano writer's (first series)." *Dictionary of Literary Biography.* Detroit: Gale, 1989.

Los Angeles County Public Library. Chicano Resource Center. *Chicano Resource Center Film Guide.* Los Angeles: Los Angeles County Public Library, 1987.

MacCorkle, Lyn. *Cubans in the United States: A Bibliography for Research in the Social Sciences, 1960–1983.* Westport, Conn.: Greenwood Press, 1984.

Macías, Reynaldo F. "Language policy, planning, and politics in the United States concerned with language minority issues." *Annual Review of Applied Linguistics* (1981): 86–104.

_____. "U.S. Language-in-Education Policy: Issues in the Schooling of Language Minorities." *Annual Review of Applied Linguistics* (1981a): 144–160.

Maldonado, Adal Alberto. *Mango Mambo: Portraits by Adal.* San Juan: Marrozzini/ Illustres, 1988.

_____. *Portraits of the Puerto Rican Experience.* New York: IPRUS, 1984.

Márques, Pauline R. *Caminos National Hispanic Media Directory.* Caminos: 1985.

Martín, Patricia Preciado. *Images and Conversations: Mexican Americans Recall a Southwestern Past.* Tucson: University of Arizona Press, 1983.

Martínez, Al. *Rising Voices: Profiles of Hispanic American Lives.* 1974.

Martínez, Arthur D. *Who's Who, Chicano Officeholders.* Silver City, N. Mex.: Martínez, 1975–.

Martínez, Julio A. *Chicano Scholars and Writers: A Biobibliographical Directory.* Metuchen, N.J.: Scarecrow, 1979.

_____. *Mexican Americans: An Annotated Bibliography of Bibliographies.* Saratoga: R&E, 1984.

_____, and Francisco Lomeli. *Chicano Literature: A Reader's Guide.* Westport, Conn.: Greenwood Press, 1985.

Martínez, Oscar. "Chicano oral history: status and prospects." *Aztlan* 9, 1 (1978): 119–131.

Martínez de Carrera, Teresita. "Puerto Ricans — history." *Sourcebook of Hispanic Culture in the United States.* David William Foster. 133–150. Chicago: American Library Association, 1982.

Marting, Diane E. *Women Writers of Spanish America: An Annotated Bio-Bibliographical Guide.* New York: Greenwood Press, 1987.

McKenna, Teresa. "Select bibliography on Hispanic women and education." *The Broken Web.* Teresa McKenna and Flora Ida Ortiz. 221–254. Berkeley: Floricanto Press, 1988.

Medford, Roberta. *Online Information on Hispanics & Other Ethnic Groups.* Berkeley: Floricanto Press, 1986.

Meier, Matt S. *Bibliography of Mexican American History.* Westport, Conn.: Greenwood Press, 1984.

_____. *Mexican American Biographies: A Historical Dictionary, 1836–1987.* New York: Greenwood Press, 1988.

_____, and Rivera Feliciano. *Dictionary of Chicano History.* Westport, Conn.: Greenwood Press, 1981.

Metress, James F. *Mexican American Health: A Guide to the Literature.* Monticello, Ill.: Council of Planning Librarians, 1976.

Mirandé, Alfredo. *The Chicano Experience: An Alternative Perspective.* Notre Dame, Ind.: University of Notre Dame Press, 1985.

_____. "Latinos in the United States: new directions in research and theory." *Mexican Studies* 5, 1 (Winter 1989): 127–144.

Montiel, Miguel. "The social science myth of the Mexican-Americans." *Voices:*

Readings from El Grito: A Journal of Contemporary Mexican American Thought 1967–1973. Octavio I. Romano-V. 57–64. Berkeley: Quinto Sol, 1973.

Munguía, Edward, et al. *Ethnicity and Aging: A Bibliography.* San Antonio, Tex.: Trinity University, 1984.

Muñoz, Carlos. "Politics and the Chicano: on the status of the literature." *Aztlan* **5**, 1 (Spring 1974): 1–7.

Muñoz, Carlos, Jr. "The state of the art in the study of Chicano politics." *Chicanos and the Social Sciences: A Decade of Research and Development (1970–1980).* Isidro Ortiz. 47–58. Santa Barbara, Calif.: Center for Chicano Studies, 1983.

Nájera Ramirez, Olga. "Greater Mexican folklore in the United States: an annotated bibliography." *Ethnic Affairs* **1**, 1 (Fall 1987): 64–115.

National Association of Latino Elected and Appointed Officials. *National Roster of Hispanic Elected Officials.* Washington, D.C.: NALEO Education Fund, 1984–.

Nelson, Candace, and Marta Tienda. "The structuring of Hispanic ethnicity: historical and contemporary perspectives." *Ethnicity and Race in the U.S.A.: Toward the Twenty-First Century.* Richard D. Alba. 49–74. Boston: Routledge & Kegan Paul, 1985.

Newton, Frank. "The Hispanic elderly: a review of health, social, and psychological factors." *Explorations in Chicano Psychology.* Augustine Baron. 29–49. New York: Praeger, 1981.

_____; Esteban L. Olmedo and Amado M. Padilla. *Hispanic Mental Health: A Research Guide.* Berkeley: University of California Press, 1982.

Ordoñez, Elizabeth. "Chicana literature and related sources: a selected and annotated bibliography." *Bilingual Review* **7**, 2 (May/August 1980): 143–164.

Orfield, Gary. "Hispanic Education: Challenges, Research, and Policies." *American Journal of Education* (November 1986): 1–25.

Orlov, Ann, and Reed Ueda. "Central and South Americans." *Harvard Encyclopedia of American Ethnic Groups.* Stephan Thernstrom. 210–217. Cambridge: Harvard University Press, 1980.

Orozco, Cynthia. "Chicana labor history: a critique of male consciousness in historical writing." *La Red,* 77 (1984): 2–5.

Ortiz, Isidro, ed. *Chicanos and the Social Sciences: A Decade of Research and Development, 1970–1980.* Santa Barbara: Center for Chicano Studies, 1983.

Padilla, Raymond. "Apuntes para la documentación de la cultura chicana." *El Grito* **5**, 2 (Winter 1971–72): 1–43.

Paredes, Americo. *A Texas-Mexican Cancionero: Folksongs of the Lower Border.* Urbana: University of Illinois Press, 1976.

Paredes, Raymund. "Contemporary Mexican-American literature: 1960–present." *Literary History of the American West.* 1101–1118. Fort Worth: Texas Christian University Press, 1987.

_____. "Early Mexican-American literature." *A Literary History of the American West.* 1079–1100. Fort Worth, Tex.: Texas Christian University Press, 1987a.

_____. "Mexican-American literature." *Columbia Literary History of the United States.* Emory Elliot. 800–810. New York: Columbia University Press, 1988.

Parker, Franklin, and Betty June. *Education in Puerto Rico and of Puerto Ricans in the United States: Abstracts of American Doctoral Dissertations.* San Juan: Inter-American University Press, 1978.

Peña, Devon G. *Maquiladoras: A Select Annotated Bibliography and Critical Commentary on the United States-Mexico Border Industry Program.* Austin: Center for the Study of Human Resources, University of Texas, 1981.

Peñalosa, Fernando. *Chicano Sociolinguistics: An Introduction.* Rowley, Mass.: Newberry, 1980.

Pérez, Lisandro. "Cubans." *Harvard Encyclopedia of American Ethnic Groups.* Stephan Thermstrom. 256–261. Cambridge: Harvard University Press, 1980.

Pérez, Nélida, and Amilcar Tirado. *Boricuas in el Norte.* New York: Center for Puerto Rican Studies, 1987.

Pino, Frank. *Mexican Americans: A Research Bibliography.* East Lansing: Latin American Studies Center, Michigan State University, 1974.

Polkinhorn, Harry; Alfredo Velasco and Malcolm Lambert. *El Libro de Caló: Revised Edition.* Berkeley: Floricanto Press, 1986.

Portillo, Christina; Graciela Ríos and Martha Rodríguez. *Bibliography of Writing on La Mujer.* Berkeley: Chicano Studies Library Publications, 1976.

Puerto Rico. Migration Division. *Directory of Puerto Rican and Community Service Organizations Throughout the United States.* New York: Commonwealth of Puerto Rico, Department of Labor, Migration Division, 1976–.

Quirarte, Jacinto. *Chicano Art History: A Book of Selected Readings.* San Antonio: Research Center for the Arts and Humanities, University of Texas, San Antonio, 1984.

_____. *The Hispanic American Aesthetic: Origins, Manifestations, and Significance.* San Antonio: Research Center for the Arts and Humanities, 1983.

_____. *Mexican American Artists.* Austin: University of Texas Press, 1973.

Raat, W. Dirk. *The Mexican Revolution: An Annotated Guide to Recent Scholarship.* Boston: G.K. Hall, 1982.

Ramirez, Oscar, and Carlos H. Arce. "The contemporary Chicano family: an empirically based review." *Explorations in Chicano Psychology.* Augustine Baron. 3–28. New York: Praeger, 1981.

Ramos Foster, Virginia. "Mexican Americans—Literature." *Sourcebook for Hispanic Culture in the United States.* David William Foster. 86–111. Chicago: American Library Association, 1982.

Redfern, Bernice. *Women of Color in the United States: A Guide to the Literature.* New York: Garland, 1989.

Rincón, Edward. "Aptitude theory, higher education, and minority groups: a review of the issues and research." *Explorations in Chicano Psychology.* Agustine Baron. 85–108. New York: Praeger, 1981.

Ríos-C., Herminio. "Towards a true Chicano bibliography: part two." *El Grito* 5, 4 (Summer 1972): 40–47.

_____, and Lupe Castillo. "Towards a true Chicano bibliography: Mexican American newspapers, 1848–1942." *El Grito* 3, 4 (Summer 1970): 17–24.

Robb, John Donald. *Hispanic Folk Music of New Mexico and the Southwest: A Self-Portrait of a People.* Norman: University of Oklahoma Press, 1980.

Roberts, John Storm. *The Latin Tinge: The Impact of Latin American Music on the United States.* New York: Oxford University Press, 1979.

Robinson, Barbara, and J. Cordell Robinson. *The Mexican American: A Critical Guide to Research Aids.* Greenwich, Conn.: JAI Press, 1980.

Robinson, David J. *Research Inventory of the Mexican Collection of Colonial Parish Registers.* Salt Lake City: University of Utah Press, 1980.

Robinson, Roger M. *Research Inventory of the Mexican Collection of Colonial Parish Registers.* Salt Lake City: University of Utah Press, 1980.

Robledo, Tey Diana. "Bibliography (Chicana creativity and criticism special issue)." *The Americas Review* 15, 3–4 (1987): 182–188.

Rocco, Raymond A. "Chicanos in the social sciences: traditional concepts, myths and images." *Aztlan* 1, 2 (Fall 1970): 75–97.

Rodríguez, Juan. "El florecimiento de la literatura Chicana." *La Otra Cara de Mexico: Los Chicanos.* David Maciel. 348–369. Mexico: Ediciónes El Caballito, 1982.

Roeder, Beatrice A. "Health Care Beliefs and Practices Among Mexican Americans." *Aztlan* 13, 1–2 (1982): 223–256.

Rojas, Guillermo. "Towards a Chicano/Raza bibliography: drama, prose, poetry." *El Grito* 7, 2 (December 1973): 1–85.

Romano-V., Octavio I. "Anthropology and sociology of the Mexican-Americans." *Voices: Readings from El Grito: A Journal of Contemporary Mexican American Thought 1967–1973.* 43–56. Berkeley: Quinto Sol, 1973.

_____. "The historical and intellectual presence of Mexican-Americans." *Voices: Readings from El Grito: A Journal of Contemporary Mexican American Thought 1967–1973.* 164–178. Berkeley: Quinto Sol, 1973a.

_____. "Social science, objectivity and the Chicanos." *Voices: Readings from El Grito: A Journal of Contemporary Mexican American Thought 1967–1973.* 30–42. Berkeley: Quinto Sol, 1973b.

Rosaldo, Renato. "Chicano Studies, 1970–1984." *Annual Review of Anthropology* 14 (1985): 405–427.

Rose Institute. *The Demographics of California's Latinos: Maps and Statistics.* Claremont, Calif.: The Institute, 1988.

Ryskamp, George. *Tracing Your Hispanic Heritage.* Riverside, Calif.: Hispanic Family History Research, 1984.

Sable, Martin H. *Mexican and Mexican American Agricultural Labor in the United States: An International Bibliography.* New York: Haworth, 1987.

San Miguel, Guadalupe. "The status of historical research on Chicano education." *Review of Educational Research* 57, 4 (Winter 1987): 467–480.

Sánchez, Rosaura. *Chicano Discourse: Socio-Historic Perspectives.* Rowley: Newberry House Publications, 1983.

Santillian, Richard. *California's Latinos: A Research Bibliography.* Claremont, Calif.: The Rose Institute, 1988.

Saragoza, Alex. "The conceptualization of the history of the Chicano family." *The State of Chicano Research in Family, Labor and Migration Studies.* Alberto Camarillo, Tomás Almaguer, and Armando Valdéz. 111–138. Stanford, Calif.: Stanford Center for Chicano Research, 1983.

_____. "The significance of recent Chicano-related historical writings: an appraisal." *Ethnic Affairs* 1, 1 (Fall 1987): 24–62.

Schon, Isabel. "Education." *Sourcebook of Hispanic Culture in the United States.* David William Foster. 246–271. Chicago: American Library Association, 1982.

Schorr, Alan Edward. *Hispanic Resource Directory.* Juneau, Alaska: Denali Press, 1988.

Shirley, Carl R. "A contemporary fluorescence of Chicano literature." *Dictionary of Literary Biography Yearbook* (1984): 7–16.

Sommers, Joseph, and Tomás Ybarra Frausto. *Modern Chicano Writers: A Collection of Critical Essays.* New York: Prentice-Hall, 1979.

Sonntag, Eliana. "Hacia una bibliografía de poesia feminina Chicana." *La Palabra* 2, 2 (Spring 1980): 91–109.

Soto, Carolyn. "A directory of Chicano serials." *Chicano Periodical Index.* Berkeley: Chicano Studies Library, 1983–.

Soto, Shirlene Ann. "The emerging Chicana: a review of the journals." *Southwest Economy and Society* 2, 1 (November 1976): 39–45.

Spaulding, Rose. "Mexican immigration: a historical perspective." *Latin American Research Review* 18, 1 (1983): 201–209.

Stoddard, Ellwyn R., et al. *Borderlands Sourcebook: A Guide to the Literature on Northern Mexico and the American Southwest.* Norman: University of Oklahoma Press, 1983.

Stoner, K. Lynn. *Latinas of the Americas: A Source Book*. New York: Garland, 1989.
Sweeney, Judith. "Chicana history: a review of the literature." *Essays on La Mujer*. Rosaura and Martínez Cruz, and Rosa Sánchez. 99–123. Los Angeles: Chicano Studies Center Publications, 1977.
Tatum, Charles. *Chicano Literature*. Boston: Twayne, 1982.
Teller, Charles, et al. *Cuantos Somos: A Demographic Study of the Mexican American Population*. Austin: Center for Mexican American Studies, 1977.
Teschner, Richard V. "Sociolinguistics." *Sourcebook of Hispanic Culture in the United States*. David William Foster. 272–308. Chicago: American Library Association, 1982.
_____, et al. *Spanish and English of the United States Hispanos: A Critical Annotated Linguistics Bibliography*. Arlington: Center for Applied Linguistics, 1975.
Thermstrom, Stephan, et al. *Harvard Encyclopedia of American Ethnic Groups*. Cambridge, Mass.: Belknap Press of Harvard University, 1980.
Thomas, Carol H., and James L. Thomas. *Bilingual Special Education Resource Guide*. Phoenix: Oryx Press, 1982.
Tienda, Marta. "Residential distribution and internal migration patterns of Chicanos: a critical assessment." *The State of Chicano Research in Family, Labor and Migration Studies*. Alberto Camarillo, Tomás Almaguer, and Armando Valdéz. 149–185. Stanford: Stanford Center for Chicano Research, 1983.
Timberlake, Andrea, et al. *Women of Color and Southern Women: A Bibliography of Social Science Research, 1975–1988*. Memphis: Center for Research on Women, 1988.
Trejo, Arnulfo. *Bibliografía Chicana: A Guide to Information Sources*. Detroit: Gale, 1975.
Trujillo, Larry. "La evolución del 'bandido' al 'pachuco': a reexamination of the criminology literature on Chicanos." *Issues of Criminology* **9**, 2 (1974): 43–67.
Trujillo, Roberto. *The Chicano Public Catalog: A Collection Guide for Public Libraries*. Berkeley: Floricanto, 1987.
_____, and Andrés Rodríguez. *Literatura Chicana: Creative and Critical Writing Through 1984*. Oakland: Floricanto Press, 1985.
Tutorow, Norman E. *The Mexican American War: An Annotated Bibliography*. Westport, Conn.: Greenwood Press, 1981.
U.S. Bureau of the Census. *Persons of Spanish Origin*. Washington, D.C.: Government Printing Office, 1974–.
U.S. Hispanic Market. Miami: Strategy Research Corporation, 1987.
Vaca, Nick C. "The Mexican American in the Social Sciences." *El Grito* **4**, 1 (Fall 1970): 17–51.
Valdéz, Armando; Albert Camarillo and Tomás Almaguer. *The State of Chicano Research on Family, Labor, and Migration*. Stanford: Stanford Center for Chicano Research, 1983.
Valdéz, Diana. "Mexican American family research: a critical review and conceptual framework." *De Colores* **6**, 2 (1982): 48–63.
Valk, Barbara, ed. *Borderline: A Bibliography of the United States-Mexico Borderlands*. Los Angeles: Latin American Center, 1988.
_____. *Hispanic American Periodical Index (HAPI)*. Los Angeles: Latin American Studies Center, 1977–.
Vásquez, Librado Keno. *Regional Dictionary of Chicano Slang*. Silver Spring, Md.: Institute of Modern Languages, 1977.

Veciana-Suárez, Ana. *Hispanic Media, USA: A Narrative Guide to Print and Electronic News Media in the United States.* Washington, D.C.: The Media Institute, 1987.

Villaescusa, Henrietta, ed. "Selected Hispanic health issues of the eighties: an annotated bibliography." *Report of the Secretary's Task Force on Black and Minority Health.* Washington, D.C.: Department of Health and Human Services, 1986.

Villalobos, Rolando M. *Research Guide to the Literature on Northern Mexico's Maquiladora Assembly Industry.* Stanford: Zapata Underground Press, 1988.

Vivo, Paquita. *The Puerto Ricans: An Annotated Bibliography.* New York: Bowker, 1973.

Waldman, Elizabeth. "Profile of the Chicana: a statistical fact sheet." *Mexican Women in the United States.* Magdalena and Castillo, Adelaida del Mora. 195–204. Los Angeles: Chicano Studies Research Center Publications, 1980.

Wall, Catharine E. "Puerto Ricans — art." *Sourcebook of Hispanic Culture in the United States.* David William Foster. 187–200. Chicago: American Library Association, 1982.

Wasserman, Paul. *Ethnic Information Sources of the United States: A Guide to Organizations, Agencies. . . .* Detroit, Mich.: Gale Research, 1983.

Weber, David. *The Mexican Frontier, The American Southwest Under Mexico, 1821–1846.* Albuquerque: University of New Press, 1982.

Weber, David J. "Mexico's far northern frontier 1821–1845: A critical bibliography." *Arizona and the West* 19 (Autumn 1977): 225–266.

Webster, David S. "Chicano students in American higher education." *Campo Libre* 1, 2 (Summer 1981): 169–192.

Weigle, Marta. *Hispanic Arts and Ethnohistory in the Southwest.* Santa Fe, N. Mex.: Ancient City Press, 1983.

Woods, Richard Donovan. *Hispanic First Names: A Comprehensive Dictionary of 250 Years of Mexican–American Usage.* Westport, Conn.: Greenwood Press, 1984.

————. *Mexican Autobiography/La Autobiografía Mexicana.* New York: Greenwood Press, 1988.

————. *Spanish Surnames in the Southwestern United States: A Dictionary.* Boston: G.K. Hall, 1978.

Ybarra, Lea. "Empirical and theoretical developments in the study of Chicano families." *The State of Chicano Research in Family, Labor, and Migration Studies.* Alberto Camarillo, Tomás Almaguer, and Armando Valdéz. 91–110. Stanford, Calif.: Stanford Center for Chicano Research, 1983.

Zapata, Jessie T., and Pat T. Jaramillo. "Research on the Mexican American family." *Journal of Industrial Psychology* 77, 1 (1981): 72–85.

Zavaleta, Antonio Noe. "Mexican Americans — anthropology." *Sourcebook of Hispanic Culture in the United States.* David William Foster. 34–56. Chicago: American Library Association, 1982.

LATINO DATABASES

Ron Rodríguez

In 1981 a collection of papers on Chicanos and library service was presented at the National Symposium for Academic Library Services for Chicanos in conjunction with the 1981 American Library Association annual meeting in San Francisco. I was one of the presenters. I discussed what had been done to date concerning library automation, bibliographic databases and Chicano research. A decade later there are some changes that have occurred. There is one more information provider, one has become inactive and one is moving toward activity at the cutting edge. This is significant, as each provider defines and redefines their activity and evaluates funding to accomplish work. There is, to be sure, no waning of interest in information on Chicanos. In 1990, the interest and need for information on Chicanos is stronger than ever.

The so-called "Decade of the Hispanic" produced, if nothing else, a great need for marketing information. Suddenly businesses became aware of the tremendous spendable income of Hispanics and needed basic information about these potential customers. They wanted to know what their favorite colors were, what brand names of automobiles were favored and why some Hispanics would prefer not to buy a car called Nova (*no va* = "doesn't go") or Matador (= "killer"). The list of inquiries goes on and on. The ever continuing debate over bilingual education has kept librarians busy searching for articles pro and con. Every Cinco de Mayo, newspaper and television station are in search of historical data or archival photos of revolutionaries in old Mexico. The bottom line to all of this is that the need for information on Chicanos and Hispanics by researchers, educators, business people, politicians and public policy planners is stronger than ever.

Bibliographic Output and Control

The amount of literature published is immense but efforts at bibliographic control are coming closer to achieving reasonable success especially for serials. Bibliographic control is knowing what is produced and where it is located. Books are largely in the domain of public, academic and special libraries. Chicano libraries are the strongest resources for Chicano books, serials and periodicals. They are located within a few public and academic libraries. The Chicano libraries and resource centers often have their holdings in card catalogs or private database catalogs, which provide a strong element of bibliographic control.

One element of bibliographic control is physical access by network, consortia or cooperative efforts. It should be noted that some Chicano collections are centralized, in this case meaning the materials are housed in a separate area apart from the main collection, or are decentralized, which means the materials are integrated with the other materials in the main collection. From the access point of view it may be more effective to have all the materials on Chicanos in one area. Indeed browsing and otherwise exploring alternatives in research is easier with centralized collections. Some Chicano collections do not participate in interlibrary loan due to the rarity of their materials. For those researchers not able to visit collections in person or interlibrary loan items, arranging for selective photocopying within legal limits or telefaxing may be a solution to the problem of few Chicano resource centers and physical distance for many would-be users.

"Chicano" as a Subject Term

Before any research is attempted on Chicanos or Hispanics it is necessary to clarify who is the subject of the search. It is wrong to assume that Hispanics, Chicanos, Spanish, Spanish Americans, Latinos, Mexican-Americans and Latin Americans are all synonymous terms. There are differences and each term defines a political and cultural profile of identity. There is no consensus about which term is the most correct. Wishing to leave the debate to other scholars, the author chooses to present various terms and define them as popularly accepted.

"Hispanic" is generally a catch-all term for the people of Mexican, Spanish, Hispano, Puerto Rican, Cuban, Latin American or any other Spanish-speaking ethnic group. "Chicano" is a political statement as well as an identifier. It symbolizes those of Mexican descent in the United States who work to improve the quality of life in the barrios and for all Mexican heritage people in the United States. The identifier "Chicano" signifies pride in ethnic identity. Chicano as an identifier reached its peak use in the late 1960s and early 1970s but has not declined out of usage.

"Latino" broadly indicates people of Latin American descent. It is much like the identifier "Hispanic" and is often used as a substitute. "Mexican-American" is used to describe a person of Mexican descent who is a United States citizen by birth or naturalization. The term identifies people who are for the most part acculturated into the mainstream of United States society. In other parts of the country this distinction is noted in usage.

In Texas, the term "Latin American" is used by Anglo Texans and middle-class Mexican-Americans instead of Mexican or Mexican-Americans. The substitution is an attempt to deny the Mexican heritage of Texas. Another case of substitution is the term "Hispano" used in New Mexico. Again the term is used as a superior replacement in an attempt to nullify Indian or mestizo heritage. Not to be confused with the Texas use of "Latin American," the term "Latin American" is often used to refer to a person from Latin America but it is largely a term of convenience rather than one of accuracy. Latin America as a geographical entity includes all of the continent of South America, Central America, and Mexico, as well as Cuba, Haiti, Puerto Rico and other islands of the Caribbean.[1]

After reading about these terms you will understand that terms of self-identification are complex but you will have a more precise idea of what group or groups of people you are really interested in. The real confusion begins once research begins. Since there is no standardization of terms for Chicano, Hispanics, et al., the researcher must check the thesaurus, authority list or subject headings list for terms used. In some instances there are brief definitions to help. It is best to keep all the terms in mind when conducting research. No doubt using the terms Mexican-American, Hispanic and Latino will bring up relevant citations, but an important article may be listed under Hispano. One should not assume that all relevant information will be listed under only one or two terms.

Databases of Chicano/Latino Information

In 1981, there were five major database efforts related to Chicano/Latino information. They were Borderline, the Spanish Speaking Mental Health Research Center Database, the California Spanish Language Database, BEBA (now BAGI) at the National Clearinghouse for Bilingual Education, and the Chicano Database. In 1990 three remain solidly active and two additional providers have entered. They are the Stanford Center for Chicano Research databases and the Chicano Studies Research Library (CSRL) online file at the University of California at Los Angeles. Before discussing the four active efforts, it is important to review the other two. Following the efforts mentioned above is a basic review of mainstream databases that provide bibliographic information on Hispanics.

Spanish Speaking Mental Health
Research Center Database (SSMHRC)

This database was established in 1975 and was the first searchable Hispanic database. Its scope of coverage was United States Hispanics and mental health. In addition to mental health there was also material from the following disciplines: anthropology, education, psychology, psychiatry, sociology, social work, public health, medicine and nursing.[2] The SSMHRC file was searched by the index field and Boolean operators. At last count the database held 6,235 records dating from 1927. Database searches and pre-programmed searches were available. Of importance are three outstanding publications spawned by the SSMHRC. They are the *Hispanic Journal of Behavioral Sciences* (HJBS), *Hispanic Mental Health Research: A Reference Guide*, and the *Research Bulletin*. Of the three the HJBS is the only survivor since SSMHRC closed operations in early 1989.

The *Hispanic Journal of Behavioral Sciences* continues to be published quarterly by Sage Publications. It is a valuable source for in-depth articles and critical reviews in Hispanic mental health. The *Reference Guide* mentioned earlier was the paper equivalent of the Hispanic Health and Mental Health Database (formerly the Spanish Speaking Mental Health Research Center Database). It contains bibliographic citations to thousands of articles on the mental health of Hispanics and peripheral topics. The *Research Bulletin* was a quarterly update of the latest research trends, events and publications, and included annotated bibliographies on various topics.

The SSMHRC and its various products, especially the Hispanic Health and Mental Health Database (formerly known as the Spanish Speaking Mental Health Database), were all outstanding. With the exception of the journal, researchers are left with a bibliographical void. Of course there are mainstream databases like Medline or Family Resources which help fill the void but they have not equalled the comprehensiveness of the Hispanic Health and Mental Health Database. At this time the database and the Spanish Speaking Mental Health Research Center are defunct. There are no plans at the present time to reactivate.

California Spanish Language Database (CSLDB)

Another database effort was the California Spanish Language Database, which began in 1977. It was conceived as a database of Spanish book records. The books represented would range among a wide variety of topics much like a public library would. The difference was that the books were in Spanish. Subject access was accomplished by English and Spanish subject headings, equivalents of themselves. This bilingual subject access was considered to be a strength by some. Spanish subject headings were matched as close as possible to the Library of Congress Subject Headings. This plan provided a degree of standardization. The drawback to the plan was the inadequacy of the Library of Congress Subject Headings themselves. Critics pointed out that LCSH was inaccurate and biased in its treatment of minorities in the United States. The CSLDB, now known as HISPANEX (Hispanic Information Exchange), is currently most active in

Spanish language book vending and review. The English/Spanish subject headings have been published in a publication entitled *Bilindex*. HISPANEX has a select portion of its bibliographic records database available online through the Research Libraries Information Network (RLIN) and the Auto Graphics Interactive Library Exchangee (AGILE II). The main HISPANEX bibliographic file comprises 126,000 machine-readable records. The subject authority files include 16,000 English subject headings and 12,000 Spanish cross references.

Still fully active are Borderline, BAGI (fomerly BEBA) at the NCBE, the Chicano Data Base, and the Stanford Center for Chicano Research Files.

Borderline

Borderline is an online bibliographic database begun in 1981. Its scope encompasses data about all aspects of the border between the United States and Mexico. Topics include politics, history, economics and labor characteristics and much more. Currently the database holds approximately 9,000 records and is available through the ORION library system at the University of California at Los Angeles. The database is searchable by keyword from the author, title, series and added descriptive fields.[3]

National Clearinghouse for Bilingual Education Databases: BAGI and CMR and Other Efforts

A major resource for information on bilingual education was begun in 1977 with the establishment of the National Clearinghouse for Bilingual Education (NCBE), which is a national information center dealing with the education of students with limited English proficiency. In the beginning NCBE had three files within their database. They were the bibliographic file, Bilingual Education Bibliographic Abstracts (BEBA); the Directory File; and the Catalog File. Beginning in 1986, NCBE, now contractually operated by Corporation Information Systems Division (COMSIS), embarked on a new set of four searchable databases. They are Bibliographic Abstracts and General Information (BAGI); Curriculum Materials Review (CMR); the Reference and Referral Database; and the Searches-on-File Database. BAGI and CMR are bibliographic databases that provide citations to print/nonprint materials about bilingual/bicultural and English-as-a-second-language (ESL) education. The BAGI database specifically contains citations to reference materials, research reports, state-of-the-art reviews, conference papers, bibliographies, program descriptions, monographs and journal articles from ESL and bilingual education-related serials. The CMR database specifically contains citations to curricular documents, including instructional materials for use in the bilingual/ESL classroom and teacher training materials.[4]

The Reference and Referral Database holds a list of resource organizations. Included are State Education Agencies and the Educational Resources Information Center (ERIC) network of clearinghouses. Included are two newly created files. One is a directory of more than 500 publishers and distributors serving minority language education. The other is a directory of software programs that can be used in the education of limited English proficiency students.[5]

The fourth database is called the Searches-on-File Database. It contains the results of searches on frequently requested topics. Searches from NCBE and ERIC databases are included. Paper copies of these searches are obtainable for a nominal charge from NCBE. Completing this information system is an electronic bulletin board offering news from federal, state and local education agencies as well as upcoming conferences. All the services described and others not described here are free of charge. The NCBE is funded by the Department of Education. Clearly NCBE is a leader in bilingual education information provision.

Chicano Database

The Chicano Database was begun in 1976 at the Chicano Studies Library at the University of California at Berkeley. The first success came with a 3,000 item database. The founders, Richard Chabrán and Francisco García-Ayvens, approached this project with the intent of avoiding Library of Congress subject headings. They determined that the user should be free to use the language of the literature to access whatever was needed and that subject terms used should be culturally sensitive. Library of Congress subject headings were determined to be inaccurate and offered poor treatment of subjects of interest to minorities.

In 1977 work began on the creation of a *Chicano Thesaurus* which utilized a combination of English, Spanish and Caló (slang) words or descriptors. These words were chosen because they approximated natural language. For example, if information on *quinceañeras* (the debutante-like celebration for 15-year-old Latinas) was needed it would appear under that term. The best bet for an equivalent term utilizing LCSH would be "Mexican-Americans — Social life and customs." An example illustrating cultural sensitivity is the thesaurus term "undocumented workers." Compared to the LCSH term "Aliens, illegal" the thesaurus term presents these people in a positive light, as contributors to society. The LCSH term is unflattering and biased against undocumented workers. The *Chicano Thesaurus* is a unique and well-respected attempt to blend efficiency and fairness. The most recent printing of the *Chicano Thesaurus* was in 1986 but it is continually being updated.

With the *Chicano Thesaurus* well underway in 1978, that same year saw the founding of the Chicano Periodical Indexing Project. The two primary goals were to provide comprehensive access to Chicano Studies literature and to develop a model for constructing a future Chicano periodical index and database. The immediate objectives of the ChPI project were to develop a vocabulary for indexing Chicano material, index 18 Chicano periodicals retrospectively, and publish the results.[6] Since then, rapid development and progress has taken place. Five printed indexes ranging from 1967 to 1988 have been published. After the second *Chicano Periodical Index* was published, the original goals gave way to the goal of identifying all types of literature on Chicanos in one source; providing subject access to this literature in one source, and accomplishing it all in a timely fashion.

The success of the *Chicano Periodical Index,* or ChPI, as it is popularly known, lead the founders to work further with the ChPI database in terms of exploring its possibilities. They came to the conclusion that a new range of timely access could be had by placing the database on-line. Since 1986 the ChPI has been available on-line to users of the Chicano Studies Library and to member libraries of the Chicano Information Management Consortium of California. In the mid–1980s the ChPI was well-established and recognized by library professionals as the most comprehensive source of information on Chicanos. The ChPI continues to grow and has begun to meet its retrospective coverage objectives. As of 1990, imprints are being added to the Chicano Database. As of this writing, a project has begun to add the entire card catalog contents of the Chicano Library at the University of California at Berkeley to the Chicano Database. The newest development is converting the Chicano Database to CD-ROM format, thus allowing greater dissemination. The CD-ROM utilizes the same technology as a music compact disc and both look quite the same. Searching on a personal computer hooked up to a CD-ROM drive unit is very much like searching on-line. With a printer attached there is no need for frantic note-taking. This development is being directed by Lillian Castillo-Speed. Furthermore, the entire *Chicano Thesaurus* will be included on CD-ROM. The first compact disc is expected in the winter of 1990. It will contain the entire Chicano Database including a subset whose scope will be Latinos and AIDS. The Chicano Database on CD-ROM will use state-of-the-art information retrieval software. The user will be able to search by subject, author, title, subject combination, language, date and publication-type, as well as perform free-text searching.[7] There are currently over 35,000 citations in the Chicano Database. Included are journal articles, chapters from books, and books. This database was used to create several bibliographic products including the *Chicano Periodical Index, Arte Chicano* and the *Chicano Anthology Index.*

Chicano Studies Research Library (CSRL) Online File

Around 1984 this database was made available to the public by arranging an account with the Office of Academic Computing at UCLA. This file gives access to citations representing monographs, documents, and dissertations owned by the Chicano Studies Research Library at UCLA. The file is on UCLA's information system, called ORION.

Mainstream Databases Providing Chicano Information

Information on Chicanos can be accessed through a variety of commercial mainstream databases as well as compact discs. An important point worth noting is that one should inquire as to what the database's scope is and which periodicals are indexed. Some mainstream databases are very selective about what periodicals or journals they index. To rely solely on mainstream databases for Chicano information is to perform an incomplete search.

There are many mainstream databases available through large suppliers like BRS and Dialog. BRS has some 42 databases in the social sciences, humanities and education fields. Dialog has some 22 databases in the social sciences and humanities. Some of the databases containing Chicano information are Medline, Sociofile, Mental Measurements Yearbook, Family Resources, Social and Behavioral Sciences, ERIC, Ageline and Alcohol Use and Abuse. From Dialog, popular databases are Child Abuse and Neglect, and Linguistics and Language Behavior Abstracts.

As mentioned CD-ROMs, or compact discs, are creating the ability for wider dissemination of information. The primary reason is that on-line searching incurs communication charges, database on-line charges, and per-citation charges. Charges vary from database to database. By contrast, CD-ROMs can be searched as often as wished and of course one's ability to print citations is unlimited. The negative aspect of CD-ROMs is that they are not as current as on-line databases. The time lag is usually one to six months. The disadvantage of the CD-ROM is mostly in its high cost of initial production but the cost per disk declines as they are reproduced. Given the advantage of greater dissemination and lower overall cost to the consumer, the CD-ROM is expected to be increasingly popular among researchers.

Concluding Remarks

Each database dealing with Chicano information has played an integral role in providing comprehensive coverage on information about Chicanos, Latinos and Hispanics. The individuals responsible for these database efforts are pioneers and perennial optimists. They have worked countless hours to make bibliographic dreams come true. The main obstacle to those dreams is funding. Some have been fortunate to secure partial or complete governmental funding or institutional sponsors to defray labor and material costs.

In 1981 there was much discussion on the new marketability of Chicano, Latino and Hispanic information. Time has proved this to be a nonissue. There are people willing to pay for this information but not in sustaining numbers to keep a for-profit organization in black ink. Another potential issue then was that of information dominion. It is not that one or some databases may be more useful than another but that no single database effort can have a monopoly on collections or materials. Thus there is no "king of the hill" but "many kings of many small hills" to stretch an analogy. Most projects are now driven by sincere scholarly interest in providing Chicano information for the benefit of all people. This altruism helps projects like the *Chicano Periodical Index* whose workers are almost all volunteers.

If there is a trend to watch it is probably that of new products that result from manipulation of bibliographic data within databases. The first of this wave may well be the upcoming Latinos and AIDS subset from the Chicano Database CD-ROM. These products will not be simply paper equivalents of a database but unique products whose demand is driven by an interested populace. Evidence of this may be the kinds of database searches conducted during a period of time. For example, Lourdes Baez-Conde Garbanati, formerly of the Spanish Speaking Mental Health and Research Center, pointed out that topics searched reflected interests of the time, ranging from bilingual education to immigration to stress to statistics and now AIDS.[8]

The future is a bright one for Latino, Chicano and Hispanic researchers thanks to the constant work of librarians, students and researchers. Their giving of time and scholarly effort now will hopefully last forever.

NOTES

1. Matt S. Meier, *Dictionary of Mexican American History* (Westport, Conn.: Greenwood Press, 1981), p. 189.

2. Richard Chabrán and Maricela Ayala Ordaz, "Hispanic Mental Health Bibliography: A Review Essay"; a review of *Hispanic Mental Health Research: A Reference Guide. Aztlan* **15**, 1 (1984).

3. Amy Lucas and Annette Novallo, eds. *Encyclopedia of Information Systems and Services* (Detroit: Gale, 1988), v. 1, p. 894.

4. NCBE Databases (information sheet), (Silver Spring, Md.: NCBE, 1987).

5. The National Clearinghouse for Bilingual Education (brochure) (Silver Spring, Md.: NCBE, 1988?).

6. Richard Chabrán, "Foreword" in the *Chicano Periodical Index: A Cumulative*

Index to Selected Chicano Periodicals Between 1967 and 1978 (Boston, Mass.: G.K. Hall, 1981), p. ix.

7. Lillian Castillo-Speed and Carolyn Soto, "Chicano Database Reduced to 5-inch Disc," *Chicano Studies Library, University of California at Berkeley Newsletter* 4, 2 (1989): 2.

8. Lourdes Baez-Conde Garbanati, interview with author, Westwood, Calif., 9 June 1989.

COLLECTION DEVELOPMENT FOR THE SPANISH-SPEAKING

Linda Chávez

The purpose of this chapter is to provide guidance for building a public library collection to serve the special needs of the Spanish-speaking community. Though there are some recommendations on specific titles to collect, the emphasis of this article is on the methods for selecting, evaluating, and acquiring. These guidelines are applicable for any level of collection that a library may be establishing, whether it be for adults, children or young adults, and all media are covered, with a special emphasis placed on the selection, evaluation, and acquisition of books.

Tips for building the Spanish-language collection are separate from guidelines for developing a Chicano collection. A distinction has to be made between the two collections because each serves a different purpose. A Spanish-language collection will more likely serve those whose first language is Spanish; often these patrons are recent arrivals from Mexico. A Chicano collection will be geared towards the interests of the individual of Mexican descent who is living in the United States, and is usually English-language dominant. Such a collection will also serve those who are interested in learning about Chicano history and culture. Most Chicano literature and nonfiction is written in English. A library serving a Mexicano/Chicano community needs to have both collections to adequately serve these patrons.

In May, 1988, a "State of Change Conference" was held in San Diego, California. It was sponsored by the state library and brought together library directors and staff, government officials, educators, and others in the community to formulate a policy agenda of library services for the increasing ethnic population in California.

This conference was one of the more recent notable efforts to address the issue of library services for California's ethnic communities. Those participating in the conference were reminded, or made aware perhaps for the first time, that there are barriers that have existed for years and can no longer be allowed to prevail that prevent ethnic communities from realizing the benefits of library services. Among the major barriers mentioned was the lack of adequate library collections. The recommendations for improvements in this area that were made at the conference included the need to increase collections in non–English languages to best serve the needs of ethnic communities, the need to add resources in English about other cultures as well as materials in nontraditional formats, and also to acquire materials to help those who wish to learn English and to acquire survival and coping skills.[1]

Model collections from which new efforts can be patterned already exist to serve the ethnic patron. For example, from its inception, the Latin American Library in Oakland, California, which was dedicated in 1966, took an innovative approach to collection development. Practical materials in both English and Spanish were purchased, including English-as-a-second-language (ESL) materials, child care information, and vocational guidance materials. Translations of English-language novels were purchased, but an effort was also made to build a good collection of standard Latin American literature in both English and Spanish. In addition, the library built a strong multimedia Chicano collection in English.[2]

The Spanish-Language Collection

When setting out to evaluate and select Spanish-language books, it is necessary first to establish a collection policy. Materials in Spanish must not be considered resources of secondary value within the context of the library's overall collection. Specific standards should be set by which all items can be evaluated. Yolanda Cuesta and Patricia Tarín, and the American Library Association, have prepared guidelines which may be consulted when developing a collection policy.[3]

Building a good Spanish-language collection involves a knowledge of the community's needs. A bilingual staff makes it easier to communicate with the users and develop an awareness of their interests. In the absence of professional staff with the necessary language skill, bilingual, nonprofessional staff and volunteers can play an important role in assessing the patrons' needs.

The collection should be made as visually attractive as possible. Librarians will sometimes make the mistake of placing the Spanish-language collection in a corner of the building where it cannot easily be seen. This collection has to be prominently displayed with appropriate signs, especially if bilingual staff members are not readily available.

Because Spanish-language books are published in small quantities, it is necessary to consider the acquisition of ephemeral materials, such as brochures, pamphlets, and newsletters, to ensure that as much reading material as possible is made available. Regardless of format, the content of the materials should be adequately evaluated before adding any item to the collection.

A good basic collection includes classics of Spain and Latin America. Libraries sometimes neglect to purchase the classics in substantial numbers and concentrate too much on Spanish-language translations of English-language bestsellers.

Nonfiction subjects that are asked for repeatedly include English as a second language, citizenship, biographies, child care and pregnancy, math, and United States history and government. Subjects that are difficult to find are, unfortunately, also some of the most popular; these include United States history and government, math, comtemporary surveys of countries of the world, and information on Mexican holidays and customs. Large-print books are popular but difficult to find.

There are some available guides to collection building (see the Bibliography at the end of this chapter). These include Restrepo's *Spanish-Language Books for Public Libraries*, published by the American Library Association, and *Spanish-Language Reference Books: An Annotated Bibliography* and *Linking Latino Youth and Books*, both compiled by Bibliotecas para la Gente. However, because Spanish-language books tend to go out of print quickly, it can be difficult to obtain a book listed in a bibliography which may already be a couple of years old. Nevertheless, these bibliographies are excellent guides for reviewing what may already be on the shelf, for determining popular subject areas, classic fiction titles, and standard fiction and nonfiction authors.

For children's Spanish-language collection development, Isabel Schon provides expert guidance to the many excellent books and articles, and she periodically issues bibliographies with evaluative annotations. These appear in the professional literature.

When reviewing distributors' catalogs and Spanish-language books, librarians will find that some publishers make more of an effort to reach the United States market. Editorial Limusa is one of the large publishing houses that specializes in a very broad selection of books on technical subjects from botany to solar energy. Editorial Diana, Grupo Editorial Planeta, Plaza y Janes, and Javier Vergara Editor emphasize popular nonfiction and fiction. Art, social sciences, humanities, and Mexican history are covered by Fondo de Cultura Económica. Mexican legends, costume, history and biographies, are well-represented by Panorama Editorial.

Among the noteworthy Mexican publishers of children's books are Editorial Trillas, Secretaría de Educación Pública (SEP), and Sistemas Técnicos de Edición (Sitesa). Editorial Amaquemecan publishes excellent books of legends and folktales for children and young adults. Sitesa is experimenting with improved binding for children's books; they were exhibited at the most recent Feria Internacional del Libro in Guadalajara, Mexico. When purchasing children's books it is a good idea, because of weak bindings, to buy in multiples so as to have as many copies of a good title as possible to serve as reserves when the book becomes shabby.

Spanish-language periodicals and pamphlets are an essential part of any basic collection. *Magazines for Libraries* contains reviews and information on available titles. Hispanic Books Distributors is one of the vendors that handles magazine subscriptions for libraries, even offering fotonovela packages. Pamphlets in Spanish can sometimes be obtained from local community organizations and from various United States federal agencies, such as the Consumer Information Center and the Social Security Administration.

Audiovisual Spanish-language materials are in high demand, particularly video and audio cassettes. Films in 16mm format are slowly decreasing in popularity, but are still requested by teachers for classroom use. The *Chicano Resource Center Film Guide* lists about 60 titles for adults and children pertaining to Mexican history and culture.

Because of the increasing demand and popularity of videos, film distributors are making an effort to serve the needs of public libraries. Some display their materials at library conferences and will even make special packages available at discount prices. Feature films are most popular, but videos on English as a second language are in high demand as well. There are distributors of educational materials, such as Cole in Houston, Texas, that offer audio and video cassettes for language learning and send catalogs to libraries. For feature films, an annual with three quarterly updates, *Variety's Complete Home Video Directory*, lists videos from Spain and Latin America, and provides descriptions, cast information, prices and distributors.

Musical audio cassettes and recordings are available from local vendors. It is possible to determine the most popular artists by visiting a record or music store that serves Spanish-speaking clientele.

Book Evaluation and Selection

In selecting and evaluating Spanish-language books, there are conditions which must first be taken into consideration. First, Spanish-language books are often poorly bound and printed on low quality paper. However, this factor should not deter libraries from purchasing a book if the content is of good quality and it is appropriate for the collection. If this is the only condition in which certain materials can be found, then that has to be accepted. If the alternative is to buy books that are in good condition, then this is truly not a viable alternative. Second, it is difficult to obtain an adequate supply of books from Mexico and other Latin American countries, because titles are printed in small quantities. Over the years, librarians have discussed at great length issues regarding language differences in the books from Spain versus those from Mexico. Librarians question if they should continue to buy as much from Spain because the language is different from that which is typically spoken by Mexicans in the United States. In response to this, one must take into account the availability of materials needed to round out a collection. Because the books from Spain are easier to acquire in greater number, libraries will continue to purchase those books.

Alternately, every effort should be taken, whenever possible, to obtain materials published in Mexico, because these are more relevant to Mexicans in the United States. This is especially important for obtaining children's books because youngsters need to be able to identify with the culture in the books they read, to reach an enriched appreciation of themselves and their heritage.

The lack of adequate coverage of Spanish-language books in the review media makes it difficult to evaluate titles for purchase. Excellent selection tools have appeared in the past, such as the reviewing journal *Lector*. Unfortunately, these have either been issued irregularly or have been discontinued. Such is the case with the recently defunct *La Lista*, which was an excellent review periodical published by the El Paso Public Library. *La Lista* focused on Spanish-language books suitable for public libraries.

Sometimes Spanish-language periodicals contain book reviews. One current politically-oriented magazine which includes reviews of Latin American publications and occasionally lists bestsellers in the various countries is *Visión: La Revista Latinoamericana*. But searching for reviews in periodicals can be time-consuming and does not yield enough information to make the effort worthwhile. Currently there is a need for a selection tool that appears often and regularly. There is no handy tool, such as *Library Journal*, that is filled with reviews of current titles. *Booklist* occasionally contains reviews of Spanish-language titles, but by the time these reviews appear the books may or may not be available for purchase.

There are some ancillary selection tools. For example, *Libros de México* is a Mexican publication with articles similar to the type found in *Publishers Weekly*. Especially helpful are its advertisements for recently published books. Included in each issue is a lengthy "Boletín Bibliográfico" that lists recent publications from Mexico, with full bibliographic information, but without reviews or annotations. *Fichero Bibliográfico Hispanoamericano*, published in Puerto Rico, is another listing which contains complete bibliographic information of new titles coming out of Spain and Latin America but it does not contain any reviews or annotations. These tools are useful as they provide an awareness of what is being produced, and can serve as updates to *Libros en Venta*. Both of the above-mentioned sources list titles by subject areas, which can be useful to librarians seeking out books to fill specific needs. Admittedly there is a risk involved in ordering materials based solely on bibliographic information, however, it is a risk worth taking if it will help to fill a serious gap in the collection.

Delibros is a magazine that is currently available from Spain. Accordingly, it focuses on books published in Spain. Arranged by publisher, it includes lengthy descriptive annotations for each publication. Presently it is issued in Spanish; there are plans, however, to publish an English-language version.

Librarians depend on distributors' catalogs for information on recent publications. Several distributors produce excellent catalogs on a regular basis with good annotations. But these vendors are trying to create interest in the titles they are marketing, so librarians cannot expect such annotations to be written from a completely objective viewpoint. Another problem with these catalogs is that the publication dates will not always be provided. A title may appear to be exactly what is needed to fill a gap in the collection, but after placing a call to the vendor to obtain the correct year of publication, it may be found to be way out of date. Another drawback is that these catalogs will primarily emphasize popular titles and cannot be relied on to list books that will fill specific subject gaps. In spite of these shortcomings, it is possible for the librarian to at least become more aware of recent popular titles by relying on such catalogs. Moreover, distributors have been dealing with public libraries for many years and have a good idea as to the type of material that interests the general reader.

Selecting books after firsthand examination is the best method for evaluating the appropriateness of material for the collection. If there is a shortage of librarians with the language capability to evaluate the books, a pooling of resources can serve a purpose. Patricia Tarín in her article, "Books for the Spanish Speaking: Sí Se Puede," presents a "professional solution" which utilizes such a strategy. Relying on knowledgeable community members who are proficient in Spanish or requesting copies of order lists from a neighboring library with a strong collection are two solutions she suggests.[4] Workshops on collection development, conducted by specialists, can be extremely helpful to build and improve selection skills among staff members and should be offered on a regular basis, perhaps emphasizing a different aspect of the collection each time.

Several distributors offer approval plans which make it possible to examine the books before purchasing; other methods of firsthand examination involve visiting Spanish-language bookstores and attending conferences, such as those of the American Booksellers Association and the American Library Association, where vendors display their publications. The Feria Internacional del Libro (FIL), which has been held for the past two years in Guadalajara, Mexico, is a particularly useful conference to attend. Approximately 30 librarians from the United States attended in November of 1988 to purchase or place orders for materials. That year about 450 publishers displayed thousands of attractive children's and adult books from Mexican, Latin American, and Spanish publishers and distributors.[5]

Even if one is not able to purchase books at the conference it is still an excellent opportunity to review recent publications for future orders. Some librarians place orders through United States distributors who attend FIL, while others purchase directly from the publishers. One of the shortcomings in purchasing directly is that the publishers vary in their methods for invoicing materials, which can make the paperwork complicated. A distributor, on the other hand, will take care of the paperwork for the librarian, but this service will increase the price. The booths at the conference are sometimes staffed by individuals who have limited knowledge of the publications and can provide little guidance or assistance in recommending specific titles. Another difficulty is that very few of the publishers provide catalogs or flyers with sufficient information, other than titles and prices of the books. Despite these drawbacks, the FIL is well worth attending, even if it is for no other reason than to be made more aware of the publications from Mexico. It is also a good opportunity to see the newest titles without having to wait for distributors to advertise these in the United States.

Through firsthand examination of the books, it is possible to determine the original date and country of publication. Many Spanish-language books are translations. Though the Spanish version may have been published just the previous year, by checking the verso of the title page, one might find that the book was originally published several years earlier. In the case of a medical book, this could seriously undermine its value and make it an inappropriate addition to any library. For children's books, as mentioned earlier, the factor of the country of origin is important. It is also worth reviewing children's books to check for grammatical and typographical errors. In particular, many bilingual books translated into Spanish from the original English contain such errors.[6]

Acquisitions

Librarians need to be aware of the constraints involving Spanish-language book publishing that make the acquisition of these materials a true challenge for any public library attempting to build a strong collection. First, as mentioned earlier, these materials are printed in small runs and tend to go out of print quickly, making it important to obtain these materials as soon as possible. Another obstacle is that these materials are not widely marketed to the United States audience, which makes it difficult for library staff to be aware of what is available. The job becomes a search for sufficient materials that are appropriate for the collection. The acquisitions process is even more complicated for large public library systems that submit multiple orders. Small public libraries can submit purchase orders in a more timely manner, but the large public library system has to decide whether to utilize a centralized or a decentralized method of acquisitions.

In a talk delivered at the 1986 annual American Library Association conference, Marie Zielinska presented the advantages and disadvantages of centralized and decentralized acquisitions of multilingual materials.[7] Various models exist; with centralized purchasing, one or a few individuals are responsible for selecting and ordering for a number of libraries within a system. Using a decentralized method allows individual branches to select and buy materials suited specifically to their communities, and this is done either through buying trips to local vendors or by each library placing orders directly with vendors. Centralized purchasing is more economical because it saves staff time and money when discounts are allowed for large multiple copy orders. There is a disadvantage, however, in that the selections may not be as responsive to the reading interests of the clientele of each library. However, on the downside of decentralized purchasing, orders can be duplicated at various times within a system, making the method less cost-effective. Depending on the number of branches involved and the percentage of the community that is Spanish-speaking, each public library system has to select the method of acquisitions that best serves its needs.

Selecting a vendor is another important factor in the acquisitions process. Public libraries tend to deal with Spanish-language book distributors in the United States rather than purchasing directly from the publisher because it decreases the amount of paperwork and avoids currency exchange rate details. Also, distributors can take the time to seek out publications that the library needs. The vendor has to serve the specific needs of the public library. It may be that one vendor is not sufficient to serve all of the library's needs, so it may be necessary to utilize two or more vendors. A good vendor will keep the librarian abreast of popular titles and will respond to special requests for books on particular subjects by searching for these. Some vendors will make a point of attending library conferences to more effectively reach their market. It is best to avoid dealing with a vendor who is not aware of the recent titles that your patrons are requesting; the vendor that is not staying up-to-date, or is not willing even to search for a specific title when requested, should probably be avoided.

When evaluating a vendor's services, consider the following factors:

1. How quickly are orders filled?
2. From which countries does the vendor purchase books?
3. Are multiple copies of individual titles stocked? (This is especially important for large library systems.)
4. How much of a discount is offered, and what are the average prices?
5. Are annotated catalogs provided that include full bibliographic data?
6. Is an approval plan offered?
7. In which subject area does the vendor specialize?
8. Are mostly popular, recent publications, offered, or does the vendor carry a retrospective collection of works?

For other factors to consider when selecting a vendor and for background information, consult the listings in *Library Journal* compiled by Daniel Josslin and Patricia Tarín which describe the services of Spanish-language vendors located throughout the United States.[8]

If a good rapport is established with the vendor, more personalized service will be offered. It is also a good idea to talk with other librarians to discover which vendors they do business with and get their evaluations of the services offered.

Up until quite recently, most distributors dealt primarily with Spain, but are now realizing the need for more publications from Mexico and other Latin American countries. The previously mentioned Feria Internacional del Libro is one way in which the United States distributors and Latin American publishers are seeking to establish more effective lines of communication.

NOTES

1. Nora Jacob, ed., *A State of Change: California's Ethnic Future and Libraries: Conference and Awareness Forum Proceedings* (Stanford, Calif.: Planning Group for the "State of Change" Project, 1988), 301.

2. Barbara L. Wynn, "Oakland, California: La Biblioteca Latino Americana," *Wilson Library Bulletin* 44 (March 1970): 751, 753.

3. Yolanda Cuesta and Patricia Tarín, "Guidelines for Library Service to the Spanish Speaking," *Library Journal* 103 (July 1978): 1354–1355.

4. Patricia A. Tarín, "Books for the Spanish-Speaking: Sí Se Puede," *Library Journal* 112 (July 1987): 26.

5. Patricia Glass Schuman, "Promise and Problems at Guadalajara Book Fair," *Publishers Weekly* 235 (6 January 1989): 24.

6. Mary Frances Johnson, "A Guide to Spanish-Language Books for Children," *Wilson Library Bulletin* 53 (November 1978): 247; Jaqueline Shachter, "Materials for Young Black and Latino Children," *Drexel Library Quarterly* 12 (October 1976): 58.

7. Marie Zielinska, "Acquisition of Multilingual Materials; Through a Central Resource Agency or by Individual Libraries?" *Library Acquisitions: Practice and Theory* 10 (1986) 255–260.

8. Daniel Josslin, comp., "Spanish-Language Books: A Source List," *Library Journal* 113 (15 April 1988) 48–51; Daniel Josslin and Patricia A. Tarín, comps., "Sources of Spanish-Language Books," *Library Journal* 112 (July 1987) 28–31.

BIBLIOGRAPHY

Resources Consulted for This Article

Cuesta, Yolanda, and Tarín, Patrica. "Guidelines for Library Service to the Spanish-Speaking." *Library Journal* 103 (July 1978): 1350–1355.

Jacob, Nora, ed. *A State of Change: California's Ethnic Future and Libraries; Conference and Awareness Forum Proceedings.* Stanford, Calif.: Planning Group for the "State of Change" Project, 1988.

Johnson, Mary Frances. "A Guide to Spanish-Language Books for Children." *Wilson Library Bulletin* 53 (November 1978): 244–248.

Josslin, Daniel, comp. "Spanish-Language Books: A Source List." *Library Journal* 113 (15 April 1988): 48–51.

Josslin, Daniel, and Tarín, Patricia A., comps. "Sources of Spanish-Language Books." *Library Journal* 112 (July 1987): 28–31.

Schuman, Patricia Glass. "Promise and Problems at Guadalajara Book Fair." *Publishers Weekly* 235 (January 1989): 6.

Shachter, Jaqueline. "Materials for Young Blacks and Latino Children." *Drexel Library Quarterly* 12 (October 1976): 54–63.

Tarín, Patricia A. "Books for the Spanish-Speaking: Sí Se Puede." *Library Journal* 112 (July 1987): 25–28.

Wynn, Barbara L. "Oakland, California: La Biblioteca Latino Americana." *Wilson Library Bulletin* 44 (March 1970): 751–756.

Zielinska, Marie. "Acquisition of Multilingual Materials; Through a Central Resource Agency or by Individual Libraries?" *Library Acquisitions: Practice and Theory* 10 (1986): 255–260.

Collection Development Resources

Bibliotecas para la Gente. "Linking Latino Youth and Books." Printed copy distributed at the California Library Association Annual Conference November 15, 1987.

Bibliotecas para la Gente Reference Committee, comp. *Spanish-Language Reference Books: An Annotated Bibliography.* Berkeley: Chicano Studies Library Publications Unit, University of California, 1988.

Booklist [periodical]. Chicago: American Library Association.

Chicano Resource Center Film Guide. Rev. ed. Los Angeles County Public Library, 1987.

Delibros. Madrid: Delibros, S.A.

Fichero: Bibliográfico Hispanoamericano. San Juan, Puerto Rico: Melcher Ediciónes.

Katz, Bill, and Katz, Linda Sternberg. *Magazines for Libraries.* 6th ed. New York: R.R. Bowker Co., 1989.

Lector. Encino, Calif.: Floricanto Press.

Libros de México. Mexico City: Cepromex, Camara Nacional de la Industria Editorial Mexicana.

Libros en Venta en Hispanoamerica y España. 3 vols. San Juan, Puerto Rico: Melcher Ediciónes, 1988.

La Lista. El Paso, Texas: El Paso Public Library [ceased].

Restrepo, Fabio, ed. *Spanish-Language Books for Public Libraries.* Chicago: American Library Association, 1986.

Schon, Isabel. *Basic Collection of Children's Books in Spanish.* Metuchen, N.J.: Scarecrow Press, 1986.

_____. *Books in Spanish for Children and Young Adults: An Annotated Guide.* Metuchen, N.J.: Scarecrow Press, 1978.

_____. "Recent Notable Books in Spanish for the Very Young." *Journal of Youth Services in Libraries* 2 (Winter 1989): 162–164.

Variety's Complete Home Video Directory. New York: R.R. Bowker, 1988.

Visión: La Revista Latinoamericana. New York: Visión Inc., S.A.

COLLECTION DEVELOPMENT ON THE MEXICAN AMERICAN EXPERIENCE

Roberto G. Trujillo and Linda Chávez

Public libraries, perhaps more than any other public institution, are in a position of opportunity and obligation to reflect and foster cultural diversity. Any public library serving a Mexican American population should have a core collection of Mexican American materials. Because of the growing Mexican American population in the United States, nearly every public library in the country should carry at least a representative selection of titles that reflect the history and literature of Mexican Americans. Assume that both the Mexican American public and the public at large do have an interest in this particular history and creative expression as well as in the public issues affecting this population.

A Mexican American collection concentrates on material by and about people of Mexican descent in the United States. For this reason it does not contain much material on the Cubans, Puerto Ricans or other Hispanics, because each of these groups has a distinct history, culture, and identity.

There are some myths and misunderstandings about publishing and on library collection building on the Mexican American experience. For example, many librarians do not know the world production of writings on the Mexican American and many do not know of the special characteristics of publishing in this field. This is a challenge for the public library of any size because of the different kinds of publications that exist and their appropriateness for public library collections. Nonetheless, there is a body of literature pertaining to the historical and contemporary condition of Mexicans in the United States—Mexican Americans—that is appropriate for public library collections and there are tools and resources which public librarians may use to develop collections or otherwise keep current.

Over the past 20 years, from 1969 to 1989, perhaps some 10,000 book titles have been published in this field. Add to this figure the literally hundreds of serials, government documents, microform collections, film and video materials, audio recordings, machine-readable data files, and archival and manuscript collections and one is faced with a dire need to define a collection development policy. For example, which journals and periodicals need one subscribe to? Well over 40,000 journal and magazine articles exist on the Mexican American. Many are published in mainstream publications and perhaps an equal number are published in periodicals produced for the United States Hispanic market.

The Nature of Core Collections

Most public libraries do not seek to develop research collections — these essentially support college or university and postgraduate-level scholarship. However, most do seek to have the Mexican American experience represented to some degree in their libraries. It is important for public librarians to realize that most publications in this field are published in English and are printed in the United States. Many materials are also produced from an academic base and tend to be scholarly in nature — save for creative writing, however, these do not account for the majority of publications. Trade publishers, though few in number, do deal with Mexican American authors and topics, although many books are produced by small alternative presses. Most creative works — novels, poetry, short fiction, theater or drama, etc. — are published by small alternative publishers. This material is also typically produced in relatively small numbers — sometimes one or two thousand copies or fewer. What all this means is that collection development can be quite labor intensive.

Librarians must become familiar with publishers, distributors, and review sources to keep up with new publications. There are various tools for identifying these kinds of materials. Several academic libraries have developed research collections on the Mexican American and do print and distribute, free of charge, acquisition lists and specialized topical bibliographies. This really is one of the best ways for public libraries to keep up with publishing in the field of Mexican American studies. We will provide sources for some of these materials further into this chapter.

Another notion that clouds collections policy is the mistaken perception that Mexican American materials are primarily in the Spanish language. This is simply not the case. Spanish language collections are quite another area with quite different characteristics and problems. To be sure, some works about Mexican Americans are in Spanish. There are even a handful of titles in German and French published in those countries. Some materials have originated in Mexico and a few published in Spain. But by far the majority are in English and published in the United States.

For public libraries with little previous experience in this area the task of developing collections from scratch might appear daunting. It really is not so. A core collection for most public libraries might be something like 500 to 1,000 titles. The world production annually on the Mexican American experience rarely exceeds 500 titles per year. This historical base includes materials that are primarily intended for an academic or scholarly audience. However, the problem for public libraries should not be volume but rather selectivity and appropriateness for public library collections.

We hope that it has been clear thus far in this chapter that we are focusing on collection development efforts pertinent to the Mexican American experience exclusively. We have used the phrase Mexicans in the United States and the term Mexican Americans interchangeably. We are in fact speaking of American people of Mexican descent but even with that relatively simple definition the distinctions are not always clear because we include in this population first-generation Mexican Americans as well as people who trace their family to the Spanish period of the Southwestern United States (people from New Mexico and Colorado, for example). Often Mexican Americans are categorized as Hispanics or Latinos and these terms are fine in context. The point is, not all Hispanics or Latinos are Mexican Americans and developing library collections relevant to Puerto Ricans, Cubans, Central and South Americans and others are not the same. The scope of your collection development policy needs to be clearly articulated. We hope to provide in this chapter some practical guidelines and perspectives.

Core Collections: What Exists?

Earlier we mentioned that several academic libraries have Mexican American research collections. Those most noted for the breadth of their collections include three campuses from the University of California—the UCLA Chicano Studies Research Library, the Chicano Studies Library of UC Berkeley (UCB), and the Colección Tloque Nahuaque of the University of California at Santa Barbara (UCSB). Stanford University Libraries have a curatorial office for Mexican American research collections—its scope includes developing archives and manuscripts. The University of Texas at Austin has a Mexican American Library Program within its Latin American library collection. Arizona State University at Tempe has a Chicano collections program as does the Fullerton campus of the California State University system. Not many public libraries have organized special collections pertaining to the Mexican American. A notable exception is the Chicano Resource Center of the East Los Angeles (California) Library, a branch of the Los Angeles County Public Library. Though there may be other collections with significant representation of Mexican American materials, those listed above are by far the best known and have been developing their collections for some time. The University of California's Berkeley, Los Angeles and Santa Barbara programs, for example, started in 1969, while Stanford began its concerted program only in 1982. Each of the libraries listed above has collections that support scholarship. They are distinguished primarily by their unique, special, or primary source materials—manuscript and archival materials that are one-of-a-kind.

The Collection Building Process

Defining a core collection for a public library entails a process of reviewing and selecting materials that would be appropriate for a public library collection. There are a number of bibliographic tools that, as we have noted earlier, can assist public librarians in this work. First, however, let us present some basics for public library collections.

Most publications in this area have been produced in the past 20 years, so that one really is limited to this time period. Also, most works are published in English, though public libraries need also hold materials in Spanish. Most works are published in the United States, so that relationships with distributors will primarily be United States–based. A great many publishers *and* dealers are small businesses and many do not subcontract with large library jobbers. This means that you will need to invest in the labor-intensive nature of collecting in this area and establish and maintain business relationships with several, if not many, small publishers and community organizations that publish relevant material, and several small book dealers that carry Mexican American materials.

The formats for Mexican American materials are many. Public libraries most need to be concerned about books, magazines, journals, government publications, technical reports (e.g. materials published by nonprofit organizations that often pertain to human or social service concerns of the Mexican American community), films, and videos. One can also consider collecting primary source materials (e.g., oral histories) that pertain to the local community.

For research-level materials, public libraries are probably better off relying on local colleges and universities. To build such collections would require obtaining about 10,000-plus titles and providing physical access to literally thousands of journal and periodical articles. More typically, a public library will attempt to develop a core collection that is at once representative of the field and reflective of the culture, as is suggested in *The Chicano Public Catalog: A Collection Guide for Public Libraries* (Floricanto Press, 1987). The public library collection would not be comprehensive, but rather represent a solid basic collection. The collection should include acknowledged classics in the field and works that are representative of certain bodies of scholarship and interpretation. It should reflect the historical period from 1848 (the date the American Southwest was annexed from Mexico) to the present, though it may also include notable works whose subjects date back to the Spanish colonial period as well. The collection should include most recent publications and should reflect the work published in the humanities and social sciences as well as children's literature, nonprint format materials and periodical literature.

Bibliographic Aids

Gutierrez and Trujillo's *The Chicano Public Catalog* provides an annotated list of some 487 titles that the compilers suggest is a core collection for any public library. This work, however, does not include children's literature. For a comprehensive list of creative writing by Mexican American authors, readers are referred to *Literatura Chicana: Creative and Critical Writings Through 1984,* by Trujillo and Rodríguez (Floricanto Press, 1985).

These two latter works cited are not the only bibliographies to consider. They do, however, identify titles which are representative of the field of Mexican American studies. Again, periodical literature is important for public libraries. The principle source for identifying this literature is *The Chicano Periodical Index* (ChPI). Formerly published by G.K. Hall, ChPI is now issued by the program that essentially developed it, the Chicano Studies Library at the University of California at Berkeley. There are currently five volumes of this work in print and it has begun publishing a quarterly index. It will soon be available in CD-ROM format. An essential reference tool, it identifies the most important periodicals on Mexican Americans. Most, if not all, of the periodical titles are available on microfilm so that public libraries can, in fact, have both the index and source documents. Any public library that held the titles covered by the periodical index or by either of the two bibliographies cited above would be well on its way to having an important core collection on the Mexican American experience.

Reference guides are always vital to library collections, and this holds true for those on the Mexican American experience as well. In *The Chicano Public Catalog* the compilers list 38 important, some would argue essential, titles. Again, identifying bibliographies that can assist public librarians in collection development in this area is not a problem. What is a problem is acquiring in a timely manner materials that can go out of print very quickly. There is no equivalent for *Books in Print* for Mexican American materials — though some titles are themselves included in *BIP*. There is no single distributor for Mexican American materials and simply no easy way to guarantee that you will be informed of publications in this field without the investment of time as a bibliographer.

Experienced librarians in the field know that the subjects that are most difficult to locate are sometimes also those which are most often requested, including foods, customs and holidays, gangs, and children's literature that depicts realistic images of Mexican American children. The last is a very difficult request to fill. The lack of this type of literature has been a problem for librarians for years. Isabel Schon's (1978) bibliography, *A Bicultural Heritage: Themes for the Exploration of Mexican and Mexican American Culture in Books for Children and Adolescents,* is a helpful guide for selecting the appropriate and weeding out the inappropriate. Daniel Duran's

(1979) publication, *Latino Materials: A Multimedia Guide for Children and Young Adults,* is still useful for collection development guidelines. Though some of the titles listed in these tools may no longer be in print, these guides are important for reader's advisory and for guidance in weeding. Literature which depicts stereotypical images is harmful to children developing a sense of identity and self awareness; both Duran and Schon evaluate materials in terms of relevancy to the Latino child and in terms of the image of the culture that is portrayed.

Material on women is becoming easier to find. Fortunately there are publishers, such as Kitchen Table: Women of Color Press, which are addressing this area.

The 1980s were heralded as the decade of the Hispanic. A number of publications came out which dealt with Hispanics as a group; Cubans, Puerto Ricans, Mexicans, and other groups have been consolidated and studied. This type of publication should be evaluated for relevancy to the Mexican American collection, and purchased if the information included is substantial enough to warrant its inclusion.

For the reference collection, a number of good basic titles exist; *Mexican American Biographies: A Historical Dictionary 1836–1987* (Meier, 1988), and *Chicano Literature: A Reference Guide* (Martínez and Lomelí, 1985), both published by Greenwood Press, are essential reference books for any library. Mentioned earlier were the *Chicano Periodical Index, The Chicano Public Catalog,* and *Literatura Chicana.* Two very important reference works are *The Mexican American: A Critical Guide to Research Aids* (Robinson and Robinson, 1980), and *Mexican Americans: An Annotated Bibliography of Bibliographies* (Martínez, 1984). There is also an early work reflecting the Chicano reference collection at the UCLA Chicano Studies Research Library, *[¿]Quien Sabe?: A Preliminary List of Chicano Reference Materials* (Garcia et al., 1981). Thus there is much to work with in defining a core collection. There are numerous librarians, both in the public and academic library communities, with expertise and publications.

There is a tremendous body of literature pertaining to the Mexican American. There is probably in excess of 50,000 individual writings, government reports, films, videos, etc. For the work produced by Robinson cited above, our 2,000 individual bibliographies were considered for inclusion in this work—all were specific to the Mexican American experience. There are many subject-specialized bibliographies in this field. Particular works exist for education, health, mental health, literature, history, women, labor studies, immigration, bilingualism, children's literature, film, machine-readable data files, book reviews, United States–Mexico border studies, and more. There are specialized listings to unpublished doctoral dissertations and masters' theses on Mexican Americans of which there are several hundred. The volume of publishing and scholarship is substantial. The format is varied. Publishing has local, regional, and national characteristics.

Additional Resources

Again, the collection development policy statement can be a critical tool for defining the scope of a public library collection. Allow the policy to include materials that reflect local, regional, and national characteristics. Rely on academic libraries for more retrospective collections and antiquarian materials, microform research collections, and nonlocal primary source materials. Get on the mailing lists for publishers and distributors. Get on the mailing lists for those academic libraries noted above that regularly produce acquisition lists in this area of study. Subscribe to periodical titles that identify new publications—for example, the *Hispanic Link Weekly Report* (1420 N Street NW, Washington, DC 20005), and *La Red/The Net: The Hispanic Journal of Education, Commentary, and Reviews* (Floricanto Press, 16161 Ventura Blvd., Suite 830, Encino CA 91436). Both of these titles provide timely information about new publications including books and pamphlets. Neither is comprehensive; in fact, no single source does exist. Librarians and bibliographers must simply keep informed of the multiple sources available for current publications information. These will include online bibliographic utilities such as OCLC, RLIN (Research Libraries Information Network), and, of course, national trade journals such as the *Library Journal.* Networking with other librarians individually is often effective.

Latino periodicals tend to have short life spans and, perhaps due to poor marketing, librarians are not made aware of what is available. Even the more general Hispanic-oriented popular magazines have had difficulty staying in print, such as *Nuestro* and *Caminos. Hispanic* and *Hispanic Business* are two that have been successful for several years, but these deal with Hispanics in general and not exclusively with Mexican Americans. Because there is such a dearth of popular periodicals, libraries may want to subscribe to one or two of the more successful academic journals such as *Aztlan,* to have at least a representative selection. For the most important periodicals to subscribe to, it is helpful to consult the latest edition of Katz's *Magazines for Libraries* along with the *Chicano Periodical Index* mentioned earlier. The most recent edition of *Magazines for Libraries* includes the section "Latinos (U.S.)" which identifies titles that are appropriate for public libraries. Some local organizations and newspapers print publications that cover Hispanic topics. A good example is *Nuestro Tiempo,* which is issued by the *Los Angeles Times* and is intended for a general audience. This type of publication is a good resource for the public library because it appeals to the general reader.

Collection Development Variables

Mexican Americans are a subgroup of United States Hispanics although they are the largest component. Even within the Mexican American community, however, there is great diversity and this is reflected in the available materials: there are regional histories and literatures — New Mexico, Texas, California, Arizona, the Midwest; urban and rural; conservative and liberal. Public library collections should represent historical literature as well as creative writing reflecting local, regional and national scope. Major authors should be represented — libraries should have the most important novelists, poets, short story writers, women writers, and literary critics. The collections should reflect the Spanish period, the Mexican period, early political and civic participation, and creative writing during territorial periods, as well as the early struggles for civil and human rights. Collections should reflect the histories and writings of contemporary figures in the Mexican American communities.

A core collection, in the end, should be influenced by what the community expects of its library. To the degree that community members know of what exists they can expect a particular size and type of collection that is representative of Mexican American history and literature. When the community is unaware of what exists, and therefore what is possible, it is incumbent upon the library staff to convey this knowledge and so develop an acquisitions or collection development policy that is responsive and reflective of the community's particular needs and history.

Multimedia

We have only touched on the subject of audiovisual materials. A core Mexican American collection will include appropriate selections. In many cases, films can be found in both video and 16mm format. One of the best sources of information on new titles is the annual issue of *Tonantzín*, distributed by San Antonio's Guadalupe Cultural Arts Center, for its Cine Festival, an international Latino film and video exhibition held each year. Films and videos in this annual are annotated and the addresses and telephone numbers of the distributors are provided. Information on films and videos can also be obtained from some of the library review media, such as *Choice*, and occasionally from recent acquisition lists issued by university Chicano studies libraries. The Los Angeles County Public Library's *Chicano Resource Center Film Guide* (1987) is a list of available 16mm films. New films are also previewed at the annual conference of the National Association for Chicano Studies.

Educational audio cassettes on Chicano topics are offered by various distributors, such as Cole, that specialize in classroom resources for teaching language and culture, and by the Pacifica Radio Archive. A good recording collection should contain representative examples of traditional Mexican music, including boleros, norteños, and corridos. The music of popular Chicano artists, such as the rock group Santana, Los Lobos, and individual singers, such as Linda Ronstadt, should be acquired too.

Other audiovisual items worth considering fall under the category of ephemeral materials. These would include such items as posters and calendars that can be found on shopping trips to specialized book stores and gift shops in Chicano neighborhoods. This type of material can also occasionally be found advertised in Hispanic periodicals and newspapers and in the catalogs of distributors of educational resources. Ephemeral items are popular for displays, especially at school and community functions.

Book Selection and Evaluation

We have provided what we hope is a framework for understanding some basic elements of publishing within the field of Mexican American studies. Given all of the above as a context for developing a core Mexican American collection, what guidelines might be appropriate to help libraries become more responsive in this area? We have provided numbers, dates, and, we hope, a sense of world production in this area.

Though literature by and about the Mexican American has steadily appeared over the past 20 years, not enough of it reaches the shelves of the community library, partly due to the lack of adequate and timely selection aids.

Much like Spanish-language books that public libraries typically acquire, materials on the Mexican American experience can be difficult to select because of the lack of review sources. As stated earlier, most Mexican American titles are not published by mainstream United States publishers and therefore they sometimes have to be selected based on very little information save for author, title, and publisher. Special resources have to be utilized to pinpoint these materials and acquire them within as short a period as possible because, again, these publications are generally printed in small runs and tend to go out of print relatively quickly. Keeping informed of the available literature involves diligently going through special resources such as Mexican American magazines and journals, recent acquisitions lists of university Chicano libraries, publishers' and distributors' catalogs, and lists of available dissertations, as discussed earlier. Some scholarly journals, such as *Hispanic Review,* can serve as sources of information on recent publications, again, because academic publishers are producing much of the currently available Chicano material. A glance through *Forthcoming Books in Print* will provide leads to upcoming publications. *Choice* is one mainstream library journal that covers some of these materials, but more reviews can be found in the previously mentioned *La Red/The Net.* Once the material is available for acquisition it is especially important to evaluate its relevancy to the public library. Though many of the titles that one will come across are from academic presses, this does not mean that all of these items should be judged as being too scholarly for public libraries. Sometimes these publications are general historical surveys, *An Illustrated History of Mexican Los Angeles* (Rios-Bustamante and Castillo, 1986) is one example, which belong in public libraries.

Helpful guidelines do exist for the evaluation of Mexican American materials. For example, *The Interracial Books for Children Bulletin* published a "Checklist for Evaluating Chicano Material" (1975, 9), which is invaluable for use in reviewing materials. Evelyn Escatiola (1984) provided criteria for evaluating Chicano collections in her article, "Toward Acceptable Norms for Chicano Collections in Public Libraries."

Acquisitions

There are a number of small presses from which libraries can order materials, but sometimes, unfortunately, these have short life spans. Arte Público Press and the Bilingual Review Press are two of the well-established small publishing operations. To locate small publishers, refer to the *International Directory of Little Magazines and Small Presses* (Fulton; the 24th edition is dated 1988). In 1988, Path Press published the first issue of its *Pathways: A Minority Press Review*, which is quite helpful for locating recent and older publications. Path Press plans to issue an update. Relampago Press and Books, located in Texas, is an important source for literary materials — perhaps the single best source! The Mexican Book Service in Pennsylvania is also helpful.*

Through a visit to local, progressive bookstores one can see some of the recent titles. One way to identify such bookstores is by consulting college professors of ethnic studies in the area and asking where it is that they find their reading material. By attending the previously mentioned conferences of the National Association for Chicano Studies, one can view titles exhibited by vendors and publishers.

In his excellent editorial in *American Libraries*, Leonard Kniffel (1989, 100) writes about the dearth of classic black literature titles in print; these titles can be extremely difficult, if not impossible, to acquire because the publishers are saying that the books are "currently unavailable," which is a euphemism for "out of print." As a result, public libraries are finding it impossible to replace important works of literature. Kniffel also writes that a few small presses are trying to keep classics in print. Classic Mexican American titles can also be difficult to acquire. If one wishes to obtain a copy of a classic work of fiction or nonfiction that is no longer in print, the best method for doing so may be to pursue the out-of-print market, including secondhand book dealers. It is worth the effort expended in seeking out these sources to obtain valuable works.

*Addresses for these two sources: Mexican Book Service, St. Peters, PA 19470; Relampago Press, P.O. Box 43194, Austin, TX 78745; or 4601 Sojouner, Austin, TX 78725.

Information and Referral Files

Much information about Mexican American customs and traditions is communicated orally from generation to generation and is not documented in traditional reference sources. A local individual might be an expert in Mexican music; another might have some knowledge about curanderas and folk remedies. The library should build an information and referral file that lists resources and contact persons in the community to be relied on for referral purposes. An informal network should be established with nearby libraries to utilize other information and referral files whenever necessary.

Summary and Conclusion

The Mexican American community is a sizable one that will continue to grow in coming years. For too long, the special needs of this population have been inadequately served by existing public library collections.

Building a core collection of Mexican American materials takes long-term commitment, sensitivity, and hard work. Obviously, the materials in this field are not as easily obtainable as American best sellers. Approval plans generally do not work in this area. Ideally, every library should have a staff member specifically assigned to the acquisition of these materials. Library staff who work in this field must become competent in recognizing the literature, the publishers and distributors.

The volume of publications in this field over the years is strong evidence that this is an area of study with some stability. This means that we can expect to see at least a steady stream of scholarship and publications. The demographics of the United States are such that one can expect the level of learning about Mexican Americans to remain high — both within the Mexican American communities and the larger American society. We noted earlier that public libraries are unique public institutions with an opportunity and obligation to reflect and value cultural diversity. There is little doubt that libraries need to be a part of an increasingly multicultural society, and public library collections should be a testament to this.

We hope whatever myths or misunderstandings one may have had about collecting in this field have been clarified. Know your community, know what is being produced in the literature, and share in the value of reflecting a multicultural society through Mexican American library collections and services.

BIBLIOGRAPHY

Bibliotecas para la Gente. "Linking Latino Youth and Books." Printed copy distributed at the California Library Association Annual Conference, November 15, 1987.

Bibliotecas para la Gente Reference Committee, comp. *Spanish-Language Reference Books: An Annotated Bibliography.* Berkeley: Chicano Studies Library Publications Unit, University of California, 1988.
"Checklist for Evaluating Chicano Material." *Interracial Books for Children* **5**, 9 (1975).
Chicano Periodical Index. 2 vols. Boston: G.K. Hall, 1981, 1983.
Chicano Periodical Index. 3 vols. Berkeley: Chicano Studies Library Publications Unit, University of California, 1985, 1987, 1988.
Chicano Resource Center Film Guide. Rev. ed. Los Angeles County Public Library, 1987.
Cuesta, Yolanda, and Tarín, Patricia. "Guidelines for Library Service to the Spanish-Speaking." *Library Journal* **103** (July 1978): 1350–1355.
Duran, Daniel Flores. *Latino Materials: A Multimedia Guide for Children and Young Adults.* New York: Neal-Schuman, 1979.
Escatiola, Evelyn. "Toward Acceptable Norms for Chicano Collections in Public Libraries." In *Biblio-Politica: Chicano Perspectives on Library Service in the United States.* Edited by Francisco García-Ayvens and Richard Chabrán. Berkeley: Chicano Studies Library Publications Unit, University of California, 1984.
Forthcoming Books. New York: R.R. Bowker.
Fulton, Len, ed. *International Directory of Little Magazines and Small Presses.* 24th ed. Paradise, Calif.: Dustbooks, 1988.
García, Francisco. *[¿]Quien Sabe?: A Preliminary List of Chicano Reference Materials.* Los Angeles: Chicano Studies Research Center, University of California, Los Angeles, 1981.
Gutierrez, David G., and Trujillo, Roberto G. *The Chicano Public Catalog: A Collection Guide for Public Libraries.* Berkeley, Calif.: Floricanto Press, 1987.
Hispanic Business (periodical). Santa Barbara, Calif.: Hispanic Business, Inc.
Hispanic Link Weekly Report. Washington, D.C.: Hispanic Link News Service, Inc.
Hispanic Review. Philadelphia: University of Pennsylvania.
Jacob, Nora, ed. *A State of Change: California's Ethnic Future and Libraries: Conference and Awareness Forum Proceedings.* Stanford, Calif.: Planning Group for the "State of Change" Project, 1988.
Johnson, Mary Frances. "A Guide to Spanish-Language Books for Children." *Wilson Library Bulletin* **53** (November 1978): 244–248.
Josslin, Daniel, comp. "Spanish-Language Books: A Source List." *Library Journal* **113** (April 15, 1988): 48–51.
_____, and Tarín, Particia A., comps. "Sources of Spanish-Language Books." *Library Journal* **112** (July 1987): 28–31.
Katz, Bill, and Katz, Linda Sternberg. *Magazines for Libraries.* 6th ed. New York: R.R. Bowker, 1989.
Kniffel, Leonard. "Out of Print, Out of Mind." *American Libraries* **20** (February 1989): 100.
Lector (periodical). Encino, Calif.: Floricanto Press.
Library Journal. New York: R.R. Bowker.
Libros de México (periodical). Mexico City: Cepromex, Camara Nacional de la Industria Editorial Mexicana.
Libros en Venta en Hispanoamerica y España. 1988. 3 vols. San Juan, Puerto Rico: Melcher Ediciones.
La Lista. El Paso, Texas: El Paso Public Library.
Martínez, Julio A. *Mexican Americans: An Annotated Bibliography of Bibliographies.* Saratoga, Calif.: R. & E. Publishers.

_____, and Lomelí, Francisco A., eds. *Chicano Literature: A Reference Guide.* Westport, Conn.: Greenwood Press, 1985.

Meier, Matt S. *Dictionary of Mexican American History.* Westport, Conn.: Greenwood Press, 1982.

_____. *Mexican American Bibliographies: A Historical Dictionary 1836–1987.* Westport, Conn.: Greenwood Press, 1988.

Nuestro Tiempo (periodical). Los Angeles: Los Angeles Times.

Pathways: A Minority Press Review. Chicago: Path Press, 1988.

Publishers Weekly. New York: R.R. Bowker.

La Red/The Net: The Hispanic Journal of Education, Commentary and Reviews. Encino, Calif.: Floricanto Press.

Restrepo, Fabio, ed. *Spanish-Language Books for Public Libraries.* Chicago: American Library Association, 1986.

Rios-Bustamante, Antonio, and Castillo, Pedro. *An Illustrated History of Mexican Los Angeles.* Los Angeles: University of California Los Angeles, Chicano Studies Research Center, 1986.

Robinson, Barbara J., and Robinson, J. Cordell. *The Mexican American: A Critical Guide to Research Aids.* Greenwich, Conn.: JAI Press, 1980.

Schon, Isabel. *A Bicultural Heritage: Themes for the Exploration of Mexican and Mexican-American Culture in Books for Children and Adolescents.* Metuchen, N.J.: Scarecrow Press, 1978.

_____. *Basic Collection of Children's Books in Spanish.* Metuchen, N.J.: Scarecrow Press, 1986.

_____. *Books in Spanish for Children and Young Adults: An Annotated Guide.* Metuchen, N.J.: Scarecrow Press, 1978.

_____. "Recent Notable Books in Spanish for the Very Young." *Journal of Youth Services in Libraries* 2 (Winter 1989): 162–164.

Schuman, Patricia Glass. "Promise and Problems at Guadalajara Book Fair." *Publishers Weekly* 235 (January 6, 1989).

Shachter, Jaqueline. "Materials for Young Black and Latino Children." *Drexel Library Quarterly* 12 (October 1976): 54–63.

Tarín, Patricia A. "Books for the Spanish-Speaking: Sí Se Puede." *Library Journal* 112 (July 1987): 25–28.

Tonantzín (periodical). San Antonio, Texas: Guadalupe Cultural Arts Center.

Trujillo, Roberto G. "California Public Library Collections and Multicultural Literacy." *California State Library Foundation Bulletin* 27 (April 1989): 5–8.

_____, and Rodríguez, Andres. *Literatura Chicana: Creative and Critical Writings Through 1984.* Berkeley, Calif.: Floricanto Press, 1985.

Variety's Complete Home Video Directory. New York: R.R. Bowker, 1988.

Visión: La Revista Latinoamericana (periodical). New York: Visión, Inc., S.A.

Wynn, Barbara L. "Oakland, California: La Biblioteca Latino Americana." *Wilson Library Bulletin* 44 (March 1970): 751–756.

Zielinska, Marie. "Acquisition of Multilingual Materials; Through a Central Resource Agency or by Individual Libraries?" *Library Acquisitions: Practice and Theory* 10 (1986): 255–260.

CUBAN AMERICAN LITERATURE: AUTHORS AND RESOURCES

Danilo H. Figueredo

This article was prepared to give librarians a panoramic overview of the various genres of Cuban American literature and its major writers. Also provided are sources of information which will help librarians to identify the available literature as well as selected publishers and vendors which carry such works.

An annotated, basic collection of popular Cuban American writers is recommended in the bibliography at the end of this chapter. These are suggested titles which should be held by any medium-sized library serving Latinos. Most of these books are available only in Spanish, with exception of the major writers whose works have been translated into English.

Cuban American literature is a relatively recent phenomena. Unlike Chicano and Nuyorican literature, it is written primarily in Spanish and it does not yet document the migrant's experience in the adopted homeland. Its dominant feature is its anti–Castro testimonial mission. Cuban American literature might be divided into three groups: anti–Castro literature; the Mariel Generation; Cuban literature in exile.

Anti-Castro Literature

Anti-Castro literature is the direct result of Fidel Castro. It dates back to 1959, the year the rebel leader came to power. Originally, Castro had been welcomed by all sectors of Cuban society. However, as it became evident that the young leader's agenda was based on a Communist outline and his governmental style echoed Stalin's, dissatisfaction developed, especially within the middle class and among the intellectuals. Some of these dissenters started to conspire. Many were sent to jail. The majority went into exile.

The exiles felt betrayed by the Revolution. They had opposed strongman Fulgencio Batista, whom Castro overthrew, and they had believed Castro when he had stated that he was not a communist. Thus, their disillusionment when the rebel leader allied himself with the Soviet Union. The exiles concluded that it was their mission to witness this betrayal to the world.

As soon as they had settled in their new homes in the United States primarily in Miami and the New York–New Jersey area, they began to write their depictions of life in Cuba. The genres they chose were the novel and poetry, which afforded them flexibility, universality, and certain liberties.

The first anti–Castro novel was published in 1960. Its title was *Enterrado Vivo* (Buried Alive) by Andrés Rivera Collado. Other works soon followed, and by the end of the decade, nearly 30 anti–Castro novels had been published. Typical of these works were: *Los Dioses Ajenos* by Ricardo Luis Alonso, *Refugiados* by Angel A. Castro, *El Cielo Será Nuestro* by Manuel Colo Sausa, and *El Gallo Cantó* by Miguel F. Márquez y de la Cerra.[1]

The anti–Castro novels were all thematically linked. The themes may be summarized as (1) anti–Communist sentiments and condemnation of Castro; (2) criticism of the inefficiency of the communist economy in Cuba; (3) condemnations of the government's emphasis on loyalty to the state over loyalty to the family; (4) human rights abuses; (5) difficulties of life in exile; and (6) glorification of pre–1959 Cuba.[2]

These novels were not well written. The characters were drawn simplistically, with the Communists being all bad and the anti–Castro protagonists all good. Dialogue was stilted; action was often interrupted by the author's editorials.

The creators of these works, though, did not intend to make a lasting contribution to the world's literature. They were not professional writers. These were attorneys, physicians, and teachers, who, according to Cuban critic Alberto Gutierrez de la Solana, wanted to write a testimony.[3] A good example of this testimony is *Obrero Vanguardia* (Vanguard Worker), by Francesco Chao. It told the story of a fervent Castro supporter who founds a center for the rehabilitation of counter-revolutionaries, sends his children to school in the Soviet Union, and becomes a counterespionage agent. But the honeymoon ends when the protagonist, due to a misunderstanding, is accused of plotting against the Revolution, is arrested, and executed.[4] This novel was, according to scholar Seymour Menton, one of the better testimonial works.[5]

Testimony was also the objective of the poetry written by Cuban exiles. One of the most prolific is the poet Pablo Le Riverend, now in his eighties. Le Riverend laments in his poetry Castro's arrival. His poems, though, tend to examine his loneliness and nostalgia for Cuba, and, as such, the political theme becomes secondary.

This is also the case with another prolific writer, José Sánchez Boudy. His poems often describe the university where he works, a place that he finds cold and lonely, suggesting that for him, only life in Cuba could bring him happiness.

This is the prevalent mood in much of the poetry penned by Cuban exiles. Typical of these poets are Ernesto Carmenante, José Beamud, Oscar

Fernández de La Vega, and Orlando Saa. These poets, like the writers of the anti–Castro novels, are not professional writers and their tendency is to sacrifice art for the sake of presenting a particular point of view.

Most of the poems written by these poets were published in "periodi-quitos," weeklies and monthlies of limited circulation which are distributed unevenly. Some of the poems appeared in books and journals which were published by the writers themselves, thus making retrospective acquisition rather difficult. Samples of these poems, however, can be found in diverse anthologies; *17 Poetas Cubanos en el Exilio* (Barcelona: Azor, 1981); *Colectivo de Poetas Q-21* (Newark: Q-21, 1983); *Poetas Cubanos de New York* (Madrid: Betania, 1988).

Though the poets continue to produce volumes, the anti–Castro writers have ceased their activities. This might be the result of two factors: once they published their lamentations, their inspiration was gone; the ar-rival of new writers in the 1980s Freedom Flotilla shifted attention to the Mariel Generation.

The Mariel Generation

The term "The Mariel Generation" (la generación del Mariel) describes a group of young writers who arrived in the United States through the Freedom Flotilla. This was an event which took place in the summer of 1980 when Castro invited Cuban exiles to sail to the port of El Mariel, in northern Cuba, to pick up relatives who wished to migrate. The invitation resulted in the flight of 125,000 Cubans. Among these refugees there were scores of young writers.

These writers had never been published in Cuba. They did write, but their works were read by small circles of friends. The literature they pro-duced was anti-revolutionary. One novel, for example, *El Jardín del Tiempo* (Miami: Editorial Sibi, 1984), published four years after the flotilla, tells the story of a young author who is denied a prestigious award (and therefore the right to publish) because his book takes place in a South American coun-try and does not deal with socialist issues.[6]

Once they arrived in the United States, these writers grouped together and founded several short-lived little magazines. One journal in particular, *Mariel*, became their voice.

Mariel was conceived to promote the idea of a generation.[7] Most of the pieces published were written by writers who had left Cuba through the Mariel port. The contributors' intentions were to offer the world a testimony of the situation in Cuba as they saw it. Poems and short stories documented the oppression experienced by those who did not support Castro. Articles and essays criticized Castro's government.

Many of the *Mariel*'s contributors went on to publish novels. Most of the works were fictionalized autobiographies, detailing human rights violations in Cuba. But, unlike the anti–Castro novelists of an earlier generation, the *Mariel* writers did not only want to protest—they also wanted to create literature.

The Mariel Generation novels are influenced by contemporary Latin American literature. These writers do not create realist vehicles that serve as tools of propaganda. They use avant-garde and experimental techniques borrowed from the likes of Borges, Gabriel García Márquez, and Carlos Fuentes, among others. A typical book is *Al Norte del Infierno* (North of Hell; Editorial Sibi, 1987). Though the author, Miguel Correa, called it a novel, it is a collection of short stories. Divided into two parts, the first part takes place in Cuba, the second in the United States. There are no protagonists. The stories are told by different narrators with the objective of creating a scrapbook of different voices. Part I consists of sketches depicting a political rally in Havana, a man's attempt to leave Cuba on the claws of a vulture, a would-be-refugee listing the reasons for his departure. Part II describes the arrival to the United States and getting adjusted to the new country.[8]

A characteristic of those stories is the sense of anger and defiance felt by the authors, a trait shared by the Mariel Generation. The defiance emerges from the fact that once the Mariel writers arrived in the United States, they did not feel welcomed by either the Cuban community or the Americans. This has led some of the writers to color their works with a certain sadness and nostalgia.

These sentiments are evident in the poetry of the Mariel writiers:

> Grandmother sleeps in my wallet,
> her smile floats in memory
> The absence of a beloved friend
> And the knowledge of long walks
> in old streets
> accompany my steps[9]

This poem is by Roberto Valera, a young man whose work has been praised by the classic writer Eugenio Florit and who exemplifies the Mariel Generation. Valera is more interested in the creation of poetry than in making a political statement. In his poetry he uses imagery from Greek mythology and classical literature in an attempt to grasp a universal reality. His subject is not Castro and the Revolution, but Valera's wife, his childhood and his memories of Cuba. And when he does write against oppression, the subject is not the oppressor but the oppressed:

> To Key West an unknown has arrived
> We know he was barefooted
> and shirtless
> his skin was covered with blisters
> They say he was crying.[10]

This emphasis on writing is what separates Valera and the other Mariel writers from the authors of the anti–Castro novels. The former are interested in the creation of a body of creative literature. The latter wanted to make a political statement.

Cuban Literature in Exile

The interest in the creation of literature is the driving force behind the writers responsible for the output which falls under the umbrella term of Cuban literature in exile. The term applies to major writers who were already famous when they left Cuba and who continued to write from abroad. These writers have settled in Europe and South America and among them we find: Guillermo Cabrera Infante, Carlos Alberto Montaner, Juan Archocha, Severo Sarduy, César Leante. These are writers whose works are published by major houses and are often translated into several languages, including English. Their published works are reviewed in major journals like *World Literature Today*, and their writings are often textbooks used in Latin American programs in the United States. They belong to the mainstream of Latin American literature.

Several of these writers have chosen the United States as their home. Among them, Reinaldo Arenas is the best known and most productive. Reinaldo Arenas had been silenced in the 1960s for espousing nonsocialist ideas in his fiction. Unable to publish, he sought an opportunity to escape from Cuba. The Freedom Flotilla provided him with the means to migrate.

In the United States, he supports himself with the novels he writes and often is a visiting professor at major universities. Though he has published several books which are clearly anti–Castro, his emphasis has been on the act of writing. His novel, *Otra Vez, el Mar* (Farewell to the Sea), published in Barcelona by Seix Barral in 1985, is the account of a man, who, tired of life in Cuba, commits suicide. The novel consists of interior monologues, imaginary conversations with characters who are not present, and a long poem. Arenas' depiction of a concentration camp for homosexuals in *Arturo, la Estrella Mas Brillante*, (Arturo, the Brightest Star), published in Barcelona by Montesinos, 1984, was dubbed by critic Roberto Echavarren as one of the best novels written in Spanish.[11]

Arenas' writings appeal to other readers besides Cubans, a statement that might not be true of the anti–Castro writers and possibly the Mariel Generation. Arenas' works, like the other established Cuban writers, do not demand familiarity with Cuba and the Cuban Revolution. His works stand alone.

Other established writers working in the United States include Hilda Perara, whose novel *Plantado* (Barcelona: Planeta, 1986), tells the story of a political prisoner, and Heberto Padilla, whose *En Mi Jardín Pastan los*

Heroes (Heroes Are Grazing in My Garden; Barcelona: Argos Vergaras, 1981), recount his arrest in Cuba for writing antirevolutionary poetry.

New Writers

Cuban American literature has emphasized the turmoils of the Cuban Revolution and the nostalgia felt for the old country. The literature produced by the established writers continues to be part of the mainstream of Latin American writings. Authors like Guillermo Cabrera Infante and Reinaldo Arenas show little interest in documenting the exile's life in the United States. This task might fall on the shoulders of young Cuban Americans who have no direct contact with the island and the experiences of the Cuban Revolution.

But this is a new and developing area. A recently published work, *Cuban American Writers: Los Atrevidos,* by Carolina Hospital (Princeton: Line Lane Press, 1988), collects short stories written by Cuban-American writers who are more interested in what is happening in Dade County and the struggles of the Cuban community in exile, than in the Cuban Revolution. One promising writer is Elías Miguel Muñoz, author of *Crazy Love* (Houston: Arte Público, 1989). Muñoz writes in Spanish, but his fiction examines the linguistic relations between Spanish, the language of the migrant, and English, the language of the dominant culture. For Muñoz, English is the barrier that prevents the Cuban community from truly entering into American society. At the moment, very little has been written on Muñoz and the Cuban American writers who were raised in this country. In all likelihood, though, the next few years will see a new development in Cuban American literature: writers who will follow the trajectory taken by their Chicano counterparts.

Sources of Information

For a study of the anti–Castro novel, Seymour Menton's *Prose Fiction of the Cuban Revolution* (Austin: University of Texas, 1975) is still the best introduction to the subject. The author studies works written between 1960 and 1972, the period when most of the anti–Castro novels penned by amateurs were published. For information on anti–Castro writers, the Mariel Generation, and the major authors, Daniel C. Maratos's *Escritores de la Diaspora Cubana/Cuban Exile Writers: Manual Bibliográfico, A Bibliographic Handbook* (Metuchen, N.J.: Scarecrow, 1986) is an excellent source. For biographical details, bibliographies, and listings of lesser known writers and poets, Pablo Le Riverend's *Diccionario Biográfico de Poetas Cubanos en el Exilio (Contemporaneos)* (Newark: Ediciónes Q-21, 1988), which contains 180 entries, will prove very useful.

To identify new writers and trends, the following periodicals should prove fruitful: *Cuban Studies/Estudios Cubanos* (Pittsburgh, 1970–); *Mariel* (Miami, 1986–); *Noticias del Arte* (New York, 1976); and *Circulo de Cultura* (Verona, N.J., 1975).

Acquisitions

The early works of the anti–Castro writers were self-published, sometimes even xeroxed, and distributed to friends. Therefore, the acquisition of these novels is practically impossible. However, as more Cubans came to the United States, publishing houses and book stores managed by Cubans began to collect and even stock these works. This makes the acquisition of the latter writers, and those of the Mariel Generation in particular, an easier task. The major writers are published by important houses such as Planeta, Seix Barral, etc. Their works are often reprinted and are easily available through bookstores and dealers.

The following vendors, though, are known for their collections of Cuban American materials and their ability to obtain titles: Bilingual Publications Co., 1966 Broadway, New York NY 10023; Lectorum Publications, Inc., 137 West 14th St., New York NY 10011; Ediciones Universal, P.O. Box 450353, Miami FL 33245-0353. All the vendors publish informative catalogs identifying new writers.

The following libraries are known for their collections on Cuban American literatures. These can be consulted when conducting research in this field and for the use of the Cuban American books no longer in print: New York Public Libraries, the Research Libraries; the Library of Congress, Washington D.C.; Princeton University Library, Princeton, N.J.; and the Miami (Florida) Public Library.

NOTES

1. Naomi E. Lindstrom, "Cuban American and Continental Puerto Rican Literature," in David William Foster's *Sourcebook of Hispanic Culture*, (Chicago: American Library Association, 1982).

2. Seymour Menton, *Prose Fiction of the Cuban Revolution*, (Austin: University of Texas, 1975).

3. Alberto Gutierrez de la Solana, "La novela cubana escrita fuera de Cuba," *Anales de Literatura Hispanoamericana* 2–3, (1973–74): 767–89.

4. Francesco Chao, *Un Obrero de Vanguardia* (Miami: Universal, 1972).

5. Seymour Menton.

6. Carlos Díaz, *El Jardín del Tiempo* (Miami: Sibi, 1984), **61**.

7. *Mariel*, Primavera 1983, 1.

8. Miguel Correa, *Al Norte del Infierno* (Miami: Sibi, 1983).

9. Roberto Valera, *El fin, la Noche* (Miami: Solar, 1984) 7.

10. Valero, *Dharma* (Miami: Universal, 1985), **66**.

11. Roberto Echavarren. Interview with author, New York University, fall 1986.

SELECTED, ANNOTATED BIBLIOGRAPHY*

This collection of titles in Spanish focuses on literature written by and for Cubans in exile.

Acosta, Ivan. El super. 1982. 71p. Miami. Universal. $8. The humorous adventures of a Cuban building superintendent in Manhattan. The film version of this play won numerous European awards.

Aguilar, Luis E. De como se me murieron las palabras. 1984. 205p. Madrid, Playor, $9.95. Short stories by a respected historian and essayist.

Almendros, Néstor and Jiménez Leal, Orlando. Conducta impropia. 1984. 189p. Madrid, Playor, $5.75. Controversial documentary about Castro's treatment of dissidents.

Alonso, Luis Ricardo. El supremísimo. 1981. 265p. Barcelona, Destino, $9.95. A study of a dictator in Latin America. Fiction.

Aparicio Laurencio, Angel. La Cuba de ayer. 1984. 119p. Tlaquepaque (Mexico), Tlaquepaque Editorial, $5.50. A hard look at prerevolutionary Cuba, dismissing the popular myth that the island was a paradise and everything was perfect before Castro's rise.

Arenas, Reinaldo. Arturo: la estrella más brillante. 1984. 94p. Barcelona, Montesinos, $7.65. A powerful tale of a Cuban homosexual sent to a camp for the rehabilitation of antisocials.

Baquedano, Sarah. Rombo y otros momentos. 1984. 309p. Miami, Universal, $9.95. Poems, short stories, and a novel about a young girl growing up during the nineteenth century.

Cabrera Infante, Guillermo. La habana para un infante difunto. 1981. 711p. Barcelona, Seix Barral, $25. A witty autobiographical novel of growing up in pre–Castro Havana.

Cabrera, Lydia. Cuentos para adultos, niños y restrasados mentales. 1983. 231p. Miami, Universal, $7.50. Political satire and humorous stories.

Calatayud, Antonio. El testamento de los desheredados. 1981. 68p. Miami, Ponce, $4.95. Short narrative about the Cuban revolution.

Calleiro, Mary. Distancia de un espacio prometido. 1985. 80p. Miami, Universal, $6.95. Book of poetry by the mother of ballet star Fernando Bujones.

Castillo, Amelia del. Cauce de tiempo. 1981. 81p. Miami, Hispanova de Ediciones, $7. Contemplative poems about the search for God and the need for faith.

Catsroverde, Waldo de. El circulo de la muerte. 1985. 153p. Miami, Universal, $8.95. In this suspense novel, the Sandinistas plot the assassination of the president of the United States, while Cuban exiles plan an attempt on the life of Fidel Castro.

Consuegra Ortal, Diosdado. Cicerona. 1984. 63p. Miami, Universal, $5.95. A dialogue between two Cubans who have not seen each other for nearly 20 years. Fiction.

Conte Agüero, Luis. Cuando la muerte canta: María. 1981. 127p. Miami, Universal, $5.95. Reflective poems about the tragic death of the author's daughter.

*This bibliography originally appeared in Booklist **82**, 18 (May 15, 1986), 1363–64, and is reprinted here by permission of the American Library Association.

Cuesta, Tony. Plomo y fantasia. 1984. 187p. Miami, Sibi, $9.95. Autobiographical account of a commando raid into Cuba.

Cuza Malé, Belkis. El clavel y la rosa. 1984. 238p. Madrid, Cultura Hispánica, $7.65. Biography of Juana Borrero, a nineteenth-century Cuban artist and poet.

Díaz Rivera, Tulio. ¿Hácia donde vamos? 1984. 144p. Miami, Universal, $5. Memoirs about the political scene in Cuba before the revolution.

Fernández, Roberto G. La vida es un special. 1981. 93p. Miami, Universal, $6.95. A look at the frustrations, dreams, and hopes of the Cuban community in Miami.

Ferrer Luque, Rafael. El vuelo de la golondrina. 1983. 344p. West New York, N.J., Liberty Printing, $12.95. There is a Dostoyevskian touch to these adventures of a door-to-door book salesman.

González Argüelles, Eloy. Un golondrino no comopone primavera. 1985. 221p. Miami, Universal, $9.95. An account of the cultural shock and discrimination a group of Cubans experience upon reaching the United States.

Guigou, Alberto. Bruno. 1985. 71p. New York, Senda Nueva Ediciónes, $7. Two short plays: the dramatic story of young terrorists in flight, and a psychological study of a prostitute attracted to a young boy.

Gutiérrez Menoyo, Eloy. El radarista. 1985. 117p. Madrid, Playor, $9.95. An ex-leader of the Cuban revolution, now in prison, tells his daughter why he opposes Castro.

Hiriart, Rosario. Tu ojo, cocodrilo verde. 1984. 147p. Madrid, Biblioteca Nueva, $9.95. These vignettes and reflections about life in Cuba, Miami, and New York capture the sense of loss exiles often experience.

Le Riverend, Pablo. Hijo de Cuba soy, me llaman Pablo. 1980. 171p. Barcelona, Rondas, $7. A collection of poems about Cuba, life in exile, immortality, and the creative process.

León, Emilio J. Los hijos de las tinieblas. 1983. 231p. Miami, Sibi, $9.95. Life in Cuba's prisons. Nonfiction.

Lorenzo, Ismael. La hostería del tesoro. 1982. 88p. New York, Las Américas, $5.95. Allegorical fiction about a man who seeks escape through sexual activities.

Montes Huidobro, Matías. Segar a los muertos. 1980. 82p. Miami, Universal, $5.95. Picturesque characters with names to match (e.g., "Simplicity Duplicated") people this novel of the Cuban revolution.

Muñoz, Elías Miguel. Los viajes de Orlando Cachumbambé. 1984. 142p. Miami, Universal, $5.95. Short stories exploring the duality experienced by Cuban Americans caught between two cultures.

Olmedo, Raquel. Sé que spy. 1984. 87p. Miami, Sibi, $11.50. Poems of self-discovery.

Padilla, Heberto. En mi jardín pastan los heroes. 1981. 272p. Barcelona, Argos Vergara, $9.95. Padilla was imprisoned for writing antirevolutionary poetry. This is his fictional account of his literary struggles.

Palacios Hoyos, Esteban J. Memorias de un pueblito cubano. 1985. 110p. Miami, Universal, $6.95. Everyday life in a small town during the 1920s and 1930s. Nonfiction.

Penabaz, Manuel. La trampa. 1983. 461p. Miami, Zoom, $15. The author tells of his participation in the Bay of Pigs invasion, his involvement with drugs, and his years in an American prison.

Perera, Hilda. Plantado. 1981. 192p. Barcelona, Planeta, $9.95. The story of a *plantado*, a Cuban political prisoner who refuses to participate in a rehabilitation program. Fiction.

Quirós, Beltran de. La otra cara de la moneda. 1984. 62p. Miami, Universal, $5.95. A collection of stories depicting life in Cuba during the 1970s.

Rosas, Eugenio. De Cayo Hueso a Mariel. 1982. 132p. Hato Rey, Ramallo Brothers, $7.50. An account of the author's odyssey across the Florida Straits and into the port of Mariel on a mission to rescue his brother.

Sánchez-Boudy, José. Cuentos blancos y negros. 1983. 106p. Miami, Universal, $6. Short stories about war, love, and friendship.

Sardiño, Ricardo R. Cuando el verde olivo se torna rojo. 1982. 360p. Miami, Universal, $12.95. An idealistic young man forsakes his studies at an American university to join the Cuban revolution. Fiction.

Sarduy, Severo. La simulación. 1982. 134p. Caracas, Monte Avila, $7.50. Collection of essays about modern art.

Sarduy, Severo. Un testigo fugaz y disfrazado: sonetos, décimas. 1985. 54p. Barcelona, Ediciones de Mall, $7. This avant-garde author abandons experimental literature to take up *décimas*, a popular device used by Cuban peasants in their songs.

Valero, Roberto. Desde un oscuro ángulo. 1984. 109p. Madrid, Playor, $7.50. Poems originally written in Cuba by a young poet whose style and lyricism remind the reader of García Lorca.

Valladares, Armando. Contra toda esperanza. 1985. 447p. Barcelona, Plaza y Janes, $12. Controversial denunciation of Castro's prisons.

Valls Arango, Jorge. Donde estoy no hay luz y está enrejado. 1981. 125p. Madrid, Playor, $9.95. Mystical poems written behind bars.

DEVELOPING HISPANIC ARCHIVAL COLLECTIONS

Cesar Caballero

In this chapter I will first define some terms that cause problems with the conceptualization of projects and the writing of collection development policies. I will then relate historical periods to the problems of archival collections development and, finally, discuss some of the issues of importance to the efforts of developing Hispanic archives.

Defining the Term Hispanic

The name Hispania was used by the Romans to refer to that area of the Iberian peninsula now known as Spain. Thus, people whose origins can be traced to that part of the world are usually referred to as Hispanics. The Hispanic presence in the world today is a direct result of over 300 years of Spanish exploration and colonization that began in the 1400s and ended in the 1700s. Spanish incursions and outposts reached vast areas of today's Southwestern United States, Mexico and South America. The result of three centuries of expansionist activity left a strong Hispanic influence that is still felt and seen today in the culture, language and physical features of large numbers of people in the Western Hemisphere.

The term Hispanic is used currently in the United States to refer to a heterogeneous set of population groups identified by their national origin: Mexicans, Puerto Ricans, Cubans, and immigrants from Central and South America, Spain and the Canary Islands.

The Mexican, the largest and fastest growing group, is expected to represent 68.8 percent of the total Hispanic population in the United States by 1990. The Puerto Ricans will be approximately 11.6 percent, the Cuban Americans 4.5 percent and other Hispanics 14.8 percent of the total. The significant trend to notice here, in order to underline the importance of Hispanic materials, is that Hispanics are expected to surpass blacks as the nation's largest minority group by the year 2000. That means that the Hispanic population is expected to grow to a level of at least 12 percent of the total population, a very significant level indeed, considering that Hispanics were only 6.4 percent of the total population in 1980.[1]

The following are four major periods of history that should be taken into consideration in developing a Hispanic collection: The pre–Hispanic, exploration and colonization, nation building and the modern period.

The Pre-Hispanic Period, Up to 1492

Most Hispanic groups on this continent went through a process of *mestizaje* (mixing of the Spanish and Indian bloods) through the intermarriage of Spanish explorers, colonizers and conquistadors with Indian mothers. It is primarily for this reason that Hispanics tend to trace their ancestry to native peoples throughout the continent. It is also for this reason that *hispanistas* (those academicians concerned with Hispanic studies) find codexes (native records, written in a pictographic style, much like that of ancient Egypt) extremely important as a record type which should be preserved and studied. It makes me sad to think of the thousands of codexes that were once kept by the priests and scholars of ancient Mexico and Latin America that were burned up by zealous conquerors and Catholic priests in huge bonfires dedicated to the glory of God. Such ignorance and cruelty is difficult to imagine. What pain must have been felt by the priests and scholars at Cholula, the ancient Mecca of the Aztec Empire, when their entire libraries were set ablaze. It is a miracle that so many of these records survived. Many of those that did are housed in libraries and museums throughout the world, but many are still in the hands of private collectors and in hiding places. The question is: How many of us could recognize one, if one were brought to us? We should acquaint ourselves with this type of documentation as well as some of the more modern European types.

Exploration and Colonization, 1400s to 1500s

Much of the history of the so-called discovery and colonization, as well as development of a large portion of the American Continent in its broadest sense, is contained in Spanish archives. It is a good thing that Spaniards were such meticulous record keepers. El Archivo General de Indias, in Sevilla, Spain, as well as archives from the different *provincias* (provinces) and *municipios* (municipalities) in Mexico, contain much of this history. Many of these archives have been microfilmed and made available to scholars, but there are still vast numbers of archives covering thousands of linear feet of material barely surviving the harsh conditions in which they are stored, mainly due to the lack of resources, equipment and training in the proper conservation methods by the authorities charged with their care.

Attempts should be made to rescue and properly store, catalog, index and possibly microfilm the vast quantity of records that are in danger of being lost and which are extremely important to future generations. These efforts will require large amounts of money, international cooperation and commitment on the part of several academic institutions with programs to carry out such projects.

The Special Collections Department of the University of Texas at El Paso Library, where I work, has endeavored to do some of this work through its Mexican Microfilm Project, now in its 22nd year. During these years, we have been able to produce microfilm copies of Spanish and Mexican archives from Ciudad Juarez, Janos, Parral, and other important locations. These archives are being used by scholars throughout the United States, Mexico and other countries to study the development of a region of the "global village" known as the Borderlands. For a listing of these archives consult *Mexico and the Southwest*, a pamphlet published by the University of Texas at El Paso Library.[2]

More extraordinary is the recent project completed by the cooperative efforts of three academic institutions (the University of Minnesota, the University of California–Los Angeles and the University of Texas at El Paso) and coordinated by Robert McCaa of the University of Minnesota. That project found heretofore unidentified 16th century Spanish archives in Parral, Mexico, and had them cleaned, organized, microfilmed and indexed.

Our experience with all these activities has brought up several important issues: the need to continue developing trust and working relationships with officials from the countries where the archives are located, the need to continue funding projects that may take years to complete, and the need for resources to purchase archival collections currently in private collections, perhaps through cooperative acquisitions efforts.

A recent undertaking which merits a mention is the Documentary Relations of the Southwest (DRSW) project of the Arizona State Museum, under the direction of Charles W. Polzer. This project set out to provide a computerized data base of primary Hispanic documents. It has produced a master index, plus biographical and geographical indexes, called Biofile and Geofile respectively, which access information on Indian ethnohistory, Spanish colonial expansion, Spanish and Mexican social history and general Indo-Hispanic culture. The DRSW plans to locate, select, annotate and publish a series of volumes about the culture of Indian, Spanish and Mexican peoples in the Southwest. For an excellent description of this meritorious project you may want to consult the guide titled *Northern New Spain*, by Thomas C. Barnes and others, and published by the University of Arizona Press.[3]

By browsing the list of repositories which house significant holdings of Spanish and Mexican records, one can better understand the concept of a global village in documenting the Hispanic presence in the United States. The more obvious locations for repositories are in the states of the Southwest: Arizona, California, Colorado, and New Mexico. Other locations are not so obvious, such as Connecticut, New York, and the District of

Columbia. Some repositories in Mexico and Spain can be obvious locations as well, but who could guess that the Ignatiushaus Bibliotek in Bonn, Germany, or five major archival centers, including the Vatican Library, in Rome, hold collections important to Hispanics in the United States? Anyone wishing a description and specific locations of these repositories should consult *Spanish and Mexican Records of the American Southwest* by Henry Putney Beers, and published by the University of Arizona Press.[4]

Nation Building

There are many collections that contain documentation on the nation-building period of Hispanic nations, such as Mexico, but the point that I want to emphasize here is the fact that there are many archives relating to the founding and growth of many Hispanic nations that have not had any preservation work done to them. It has become imperative, for the sake of future generations of scholars, for archivists to start talking about cooperative efforts between the developed and developing nations to work on preservation projects. Future scholars in our country and other countries will want to have access to archives that relate the process of nation building in order to understand events that shaped the history and culture of entire regions. It is probably more imperative today, during times of world recession, for developed countries of the world to join developing countries in their struggle to preserve historical documentation.

The many barriers that exist that would impede cooperative efforts to take place cannot be ignored. Many international issues and politics have to be taken into consideration. World scholars must, however, work to retain a high level of objectivity in the preservation work that lies ahead. Much of this work will be in educating officials and in making them more sensitive to the anticipated needs of future scholars, especially in the realm of area studies.

The Importance of Hispanic Studies

One thing is becoming apparent. It is the growing influence that the Hispanic presence in this country is having in shaping the future culture and social fabric of American society. Social scientists and historians of the future will be searching for clues of the original seeds that developed into the new social fabric. It is the duty of librarians and archivists to document the germination stage of these social/cultural seeds. Many future Americans will demand to know about their roots. Thus, documentation of the cultural and social development of so-called minority groups is important.

Because of the pressures to assimilate, it is imperative that cultural aspects of Hispanic life be documented right now, when much of Hispanic culture is still alive and vibrant, not years later when social scientists might be trying to put the pieces together in order to get a glimpse of cultural history. Why not employ modern technology to do documentation? I am amazed that videotape is not employed more in a methodical manner to document our living American cultures.

Perhaps the upcoming Columbus Quincentennial of 1992 will provide some of the impetus necessary to implement some of the suggestions made in this chapter. This reminds me of the efforts being made by the emerging Center for Southwest Research, based on the University of New Mexico campus, which was recently awarded $5 million to "act as a clearinghouse and on-line information center for materials, programs, and research-in-progress on historical and comtemporary Southwest issues. The Center will serve as "the first library research instructional facility designed to serve resident and visiting scholars, faculty and students working on the 500 years of Hispanic history and influence in the Southwest."[5]

Documenting a Government Designation

The turn of the century ushered great historical events in the history of Hispanics. Most events speak of struggle, political or social, as well as great accomplishments. The struggles could be in faraway Latin American countries or at home. These struggles include revolutions against oppressive military dictators and demands for social and economic justice in a country that aspires to be the model of democracy for the world, the United States of America.

Immigration waves, labor strikes, political movements, as well as literary, philosophical and scholarly contributions merit documenting. Historians and other scholars in the future will be searching for answers to many questions about these and other major events.

Many recent events in the history of Hispanics in this country relate to labor history, mainly because Hispanics have had, for the most part, a working-class status in this country. Thus, labor organizations and activities in the Hispanic community should be well documented. It was with considerable foresight that over 20 years ago Wayne State University's Walter Reuther Library of Labor and Union Affairs acquired the papers of César Chávez's United Farm Worker's union. We need to ask: who is attempting to document the history of other groups, such as the Texas Farm Workers Union or other smaller but important groups? I am certain that social scientists are going to be wanting to research the papers of these organizations in the very near future.

In documenting the Hispanics' struggle in the areas of civil and human rights, legal proceedings dealing with school desegregation, voting rights, employment discrimination and abuse by Border Patrol and the police should also be collected. Court exhibits are part of these archival collections which historians will find very interesting and useful. The individuals, organizations and lawyers involved in such cases should be asked to donate their papers after these cases have been settled. It is only recently that major university archival centers have begun to collect the papers of important national Hispanic organizations such as LULAC (The League of United Latin American Citizens). Their papers are being actively collected by the University of Texas at Austin.

There are literally hundreds of Hispanic organizations that deal with a myriad of social and political issues. A directory that I compiled several years ago, titled *Directory of Chicano Organizations,* identified over 300 of these organizations.[6] A more recent publication, *Hispanic Resource Directory,* lists 951 Hispanic organizations nationwide.[7] How many archival centers have approached any of these organizations for their papers? It's probably only a handful. Is anyone else interested?

In terms of existing collections, the *Guide to Hispanic Bibliographic Services in the United States,* published by the National Chicano Research Network in 1982, lists 98 collections that are extremely important to Hispanic studies.[8] Although this listing is somewhat out of date, it is still very useful. A future edition will probably be more extensive, since my guess is that there are at least 300 collections which could be included in such a listing.

There are several university-based archival centers that have made great strides in documenting the Chicano in the Southwest. For example, Stanford University's curatorial office for Mexican American collections was instrumental in acquiring the archives of the Mexican American Legal Defense and Education Fund and the archives of Teatros Nacionales de Aztlán (TENAZ). Beginning in 1984, the Colección Tloque Nahuaque, of the University of California at Santa Barbara, initiated a systematic program of archival acquisitions that has attracted various collections of major interest to Chicano theater, art, and literature.

The Chicano Studies Research Library at the University of California at Los Angeles contains the papers of several Chicano activists, such as Grace Montañez Davis and Joe Ortis. Raymond Paredes and Richard Chabrán, both from the University of California, Los Angeles, have set out to conduct the first comprehensive survey of Mexican-American literary documents held in United States and Mexican libraries.

The Special Collections Department at the General Library of the University of New Mexico has acquired strong area studies collections that include important Hispanic Studies materials and has instituted specific guidelines to guarantee the inclusion of materials from culturally diverse communities. The library has been aggressive about collecting materials on Governor Tony Anaya. Important materials are also held by archival centers at Arizona State University and the University of Texas at Austin. The last one houses papers important to organizational and literary history. The papers of many notable Chicano leaders and writers are housed there.

When documenting the existence of Hispanics in the United States, with all their color and flare, it is the expression of the culture that we are concerned with. It is through language, music, literature, art and cultural events that culture finds expression. Archivists should, therefore, seek to document the expression of Hispanic culture in all its forms, keeping in mind its heterogeneity. A set of cultural traits common to one subgroup may not be common to the others.

Many of the problems or factors involved in documenting the Hispanic are the same as the factors involved in the low use of library resources by Hispanics. Lack of knowledge about the usefulness of libraries and lack of skills in accessing this resource, including language skills, are the main factors involved.

Scholars, writers, artists and leaders in the Hispanic community need to be educated about the usefulness of archival collections. Once they perceive the usefulness and benefit that can be derived from this source of information and knowledge, the more likely they are to become donors and users of personal papers and archival collections. The few writers that I have approached have been surprised, but glad, that I showed interest in collecting typescript copies of their works.

Once the Hispanic population has been identified in a particular region, efforts must be made to make contact with Hispanic leaders in order to inform them of collection development efforts and plans, and to educate them on archival practices. Many social, cultural and political groups do not know that archival centers are interested in collecting their papers, photos and other types of documentation. They may also not have a good way of keeping these documents for purposes of preservation. I suspect much material has already been lost or is scattered far and wide among past officers or leaders. Efforts must be made to recuperate these. Archival centers could hold workshops on how to preserve documents and how to approach repositories to accept documents. Publicity and education will be key elements in the success of all documentation efforts.

Then, there is the problem of trust. Many Hispanic leaders do not see universities, libraries or archival centers as places that they can trust with their historical records, perhaps because the recent history of Hispanic relations with educational institutions has been one of struggle, and some times, conflict. Therefore, archivists will need to develop trusting relationships with the Hispanic community if they are going to be effective in being all-inclusive with their collection development efforts. This implies starting with small steps and not expecting to leap forward into a period of great trust and long lasting working relationships overnight.

Different types of media are involved in documenting current culture and events. Do not overlook Spanish or bilingual newspapers, radio and television — these are excellent sources. In fact, since the Spanish language media has become a multimillion dollar industry, it is even more important. Also remember that some Hispanic groups have a strong oral history tradition. Thus, sound and video tape recordings are especially valuable. Archivists can ask area radio and television stations managers for copies of interviews and documentaries. Some stations are willing to provide copies for the cost of blank sound or video tapes.

The Need for Trained Personnel

The ideal person to work on developing Hispanic archival collections is one that has at least an undergraduate degree in Hispanic studies. In areas of the country where Mexican Americans make up the largest segment of the Hispanic population, the ideal person would be one with a Chicano studies degree. It should be pointed out that there are a good number of universities that offer such a degree plan. The person should be bilingual and knowledgeable, as well as sensitive to the cultural traits of the Hispanic population being documented. What is needed is a person that has a thorough knowledge of the history, literature and culture of the subject population. If such a person cannot be found or afforded, the person in charge of collection development should take survey courses in Hispanic studies.

It is my opinion that we will not start to develop the type of documentation that is needed for the Hispanic population until we inject this kind of expertise, no matter how well-intentioned administrators may be about developing collections. There are enough nuances with the culture, language, social structures, customs, etc., among the different Hispanic groups and subgroups, for a generalist to do justice to a serious undertaking.

Is the cost of additional personnel with the expertise required justifiable? You be the judge. Keep in mind, though, that in many parts of the country Hispanics are no longer a minority group. In El Paso, Texas, for example, Mexican Americans account for almost 70 percent of the city's total population.

Politics and Social Barriers

Another major problem is the fact that many organizations or individuals may be considered to be unacceptable by "establishment" individuals, especially if these persons or organizations have been involved in political or controversial activities. Let's face it, archival centers are usually part of institutions with very conservative policies. Perhaps we need to allow enough time to pass so that the passions, fears and antagonisms simmer down enough to approach organizations for their records. Archivists should be cautious not to let too much time pass or many important records will be lost forever.

The Chicano movement, an effort dedicated to social change aimed at improving the lot for Mexican Americans, has produced a number of very important personalities: Rodolfo Corky Gonzáles, Reyes López Tijerina, Jose Angel Gutiérrez and many others. The reference work, *Chicano Scholars and Writers,* lists many prominent Chicano scholars, and the recently published *Mexican American Biographies* lists well-known Chicanos from the 1800s to the present.[10] I wonder, though, if the political passions and social barriers have softened enough to allow for the preservation of papers that document the activities and contributions of these men to the shaping of American society. I certainly hope so.

At the local level, there are important individuals and organizations whose papers should be collected and preserved. A problem, here, is in defining standards or guidelines. For example, we may decide to acquire the papers of individuals who have held important positions. Therefore, we probably would acquire the papers of a Kika de La Garza, member of Congress, but would we acquire the papers of Carmen Félix, barrio activist and tenement grassroots organizer? Collecting the papers of both types of individuals is important to our understanding of history and social dynamics. In general terms, collection development policies should be broad and inclusive, and should allow for the acquisition of Hispanic political and social activists.

I am confident that future scholars will be happy for any improvements that are made in documenting the presence of Hispanics in this country, especially since Hispanics will surely continue to play an important role in the shaping of the American social tapestry.

NOTES

1. *The Hispanic Almanac.* Hispanic Policy Development Project, The Project, 1984.

2. *Mexico and the Southwest: Microfilm Holdings of Historical Documents and Rare Books at the University of Texas at El Paso Library.* Compiled by Cesar Caballero, Susana Delgado, Bud Newman. El Paso: University of Texas, Special Collections Department, 1984.

3. Thomas C. Barnes. *Northern New Spain: A Research Guide.* Tucson: University of Arizona Press, 1981.

4. Henry Putney Beers. *Spanish and Mexican Records of the American Southwest.* Tucson: University of Arizona Press, 1979.

5. This quote is from a brochure distributed by the Center for Southwestern Research.

6. Cesar Caballero. *Directory of Chicano Organizations.* New York: Neal-Schuman, 1985.

7. Alan Edward Schorr. *Hispanic Resource Directory.* Juneau, Alaska: Denali Press, 1988.

8. *Guide to Hispanic Bibliographic Services in the United States.* By the staff of the Hispanic Information Management Project and the National Chicano Research Network. Ann Arbor: The University of Michigan, 1980.

9. Julio A. Martínez. *Chicano Scholars and Writers: A Biobibliographical Directory.* Metuchen, N.J.: Scarecrow Press, 1979.

10. Matt S. Meier. *Mexican American Biographies: A Historical Dictionary, 1836–1987.* New York: Greenwood Press, 1988.

THE CENTRO DE ESTUDIOS PUERTORRIQUENOS LIBRARY AND ARCHIVES

Nélida Pérez and *Amilcar Tirado Aviles*

> *The struggle of man against power*
> *is the struggle of memory against forgetting.*
> —Milan Kundera,
> *The Book of Laughter*
> *and Forgetting (1981).*

Doña Genoveva de Arteaga is 90 wheelchair-bound, and hard of hearing. As we carefully sort through the scrapbooks full of clippings documenting her many concert tours, the letters and photographs she has collected throughout her long life, she repeatedly requests to see this or that item before it is packed away. Then, in a strong, clear, expressive voice which belies her age, she makes whatever she is viewing meaningful for us, providing names, dates, and circumstances, unveiling little pieces of her life in New York and Puerto Rico.

We know that it is hard for her to part with these papers that evoke so much memory. But gradually she releases them and the boxes fill up. When the packing is done, we take out the prepared deed of gift which we had carefully reviewed with her earlier. She asks us to read it out loud for her and then painstakingly begins to sign her name making extra efforts to steady her hand because she says she wants her signature to look good. It takes her a few minutes. When she finishes she looks around the room taking everyone in—her brother, a close friend, the woman who cares for her and the two of us from the Centro library. "Ahora me puedo morir en paz" she says. After drinking a toast with Spanish cidra and promising to keep in touch, we leave with her most precious possessions, deeply moved by her trust in us and greatly enriched.

Meeting Doña Genoveva was one of the high points of an archives survey project which we are now completing. A widely traveled concert pianist and organist, she was a promoter of Puerto Rican classical artists. She was also a devoted music teacher to young people both in New York and Puerto Rico. In 1929 she founded the Academia de Piano, precursor of the prestigious Conservatorio de Música de Puerto Rico. More than any

111

other person or organization we visited in these six months, she brought home to us the nature of our responsibility as archivists. This remarkable woman had such great confidence that we would take care of her things, that we would value them and teach others their value. It was not the first collection of this kind that we were accepting from an extraordinary, yet little recognized person.

Some years ago an elderly photographer—Don Justo A. Martí—entrusted the Centro library with his life's work proclaiming us his "heirs" and family. He worked for many years as a staff photographer for *La Prensa de Nueva York* (1952–1961) and other Spanish language publications covering events in the Latino community. He also worked as a freelance photographer out of his own studio. His photographs, dating from the start of the massive Puerto Rican migration in the late 1940s, document the entire range of Puerto Rican activities, from intimate family rituals to political and cultural affairs through the 1960s.

The Martí collection was preceded in our library by the Papers of Jesús Colón. Colón arrived in New York in 1917, and became a tireless organizer, journalist and writer, who left in his papers a history of the first Puerto Rican community organizations in New York City and of the role of politics in that early settlement. In processing these papers and the Martí photographs, we could only imagine what other riches lay untapped and endangered. Yet formally taking on the current archives project meant opening up the floodgates.

The project's objective was to identify records of permanent value in the New York City Puerto Rican community and to develop a long-range strategy for collecting them. Because we expected the survey to uncover a wealth of documents, we questioned our readiness to initiate a project which would inevitably grow into a full-fledged historical records program. Where were the resources? Where was the space to house materials properly? Who would organize them?

The responses to the survey reinforced our belief that regardless of our state of readiness, the time was ripe. The following comment from someone with a long history of service to the community is typical of the reactions to our first queries: "I will be most happy to cooperate in any way I can with your program.... I am most happy to hear that such a program is in progress for it is much needed and long overdue."[1]

In spite of the encouragement we received at the start, we were well aware of the complex and burdensome task it was going to be. The euphoric moments when something extraordinary is discovered and those emotional moments with our elders are energizing, but they are not, by far, the whole story in building archival holdings. Archives present enormous problems because of their volume and the cost of housing them in special materials and environments. They are also not organized like published materials and require a different mode of physical and intellectual control. This implies a need to hire trained archivists or to train personnel in archival methods.

Why then does a relatively small Puerto Rican studies library with limited resources take on this task? Certainly there is enough work to keep us occupied in the day-to-day operation of the library and its continued development. To some degree, we got into collecting original documents without making a conscious decision to do so. We were unexpectedly offered materials we could not refuse, although years back when this happened we knew nothing about archival management nor completely understood the value or use of these records. We did know that contained in these dusty, crumbling papers, and bulging boxes of photographs was a part of our history. Without actually planning for it, we had assumed the burden of their care and had entered the world of archives.

It is clear to us now that the dearth of published sources on the early development of the community here in the United States, the absence of documentation regarding the role of Puerto Ricans in United States history in mainstream repositories, and recent trends in historical research provide the most important rationale for developing Puerto Rican archives. This historical records component is a logical extension to our library, enhancing its research capacity and helping to fulfill original Centro goals.

The initial proposal to establish the Centro de Estudios Puertor-riqueños included the creation of a resource library to support the Centro's research agenda and the curriculum needs of the emergent departments of Puerto Rican studies. In 1969, the City University of New York (CUNY) adopted a policy to develop black and Puerto Rican studies and instituted open admissions. This led to a dramatic leap in the numbers of Puerto Ricans entering the University system, climbing from 5,425 in 1969 to 18,570 by 1975. Puerto Rican faculty also increased and by 1973 (the year the Centro was established) there were Puerto Rican studies departments in 17 of the 19 campuses, offering 155 courses.[2]

Needless to say, the college libraries were not prepared to meet the information needs of these newcomers. In a better but less than ideal position was the New York Public Library, with varying quantities of materials, primarily books, relating to Puerto Ricans dispersed in several branches. Notable holdings also existed in private institutions such as Columbia University, but these were practically inaccessible because of restrictive policies. An alternative resource was needed and the idea for the Centro library was born. There was no blueprint for such a library and no policies were elaborated in the Centro's founding document. Contrary to all the advice in library literature for building ethnic collections, this library did not begin with a coherent written policy defining the scope, content, and purpose of the collection.[3]

We were not guided as much by some future vision as by the pressing demands that grew out of the student movement of the late 1960s and by the Centro agenda which students, faculty and community leaders had forged. High on this agenda was the need to explain our presence in this country and the affirmation of Puerto Rican culture. Culture and history became central themes in Puerto Rican studies. Militant groups, among them the Young Lords, understood quite clearly why this was so:

> Many of our people see that our culture has been destroyed by this country, and they react in an extreme way and become cultural nationalists . . . we know that just going back to our culture is not gonna make it in and of itself. We have to use our culture as a revolutionary weapon to make ourselves stronger, to understand who we are, to understand where we come from, and therefore to be able to analyze correctly what we have to do in order to survive in this country.[4]

The library was founded primarily to serve this revolutionary mission: to give back to the community control over its cultural and intellectual heritage. Possessing the sources for the study of our history was not merely a goal, but a necessity to counter the negative, distorted visions of Puerto Ricans commonly circulated and in vogue at the time among social scientists.

The very first step taken in fulfilling this mandate was to assemble a core collection representing the basic works in the main areas of Puerto Rican studies instruction. While it might sound like a simple task, there were many obstacles to overcome, among them the lack of models for such a library both within and outside the university, and the problems of acquiring Puerto Rican materials. In contrast to black studies collections such as the Schomburg in New York and the Moorland-Spingarn at Howard University, for example, we did not start out with a rich source of materials collected carefully through the decades by bibliophiles.[5] We were also lacking specialized bibliographical tools to use in acquisitions. Trade publications such as *Books in Print* were only minimally useful. We learned to use all resources at hand, such as newspapers and journals, networks with vendors and scholars, alternative press catalogs, and friendly collectors of Puerto Rican materials willing to share their sources and their knowledge.

Those of us hired to carry out this work were fresh out of library school and were developing self confidence and expertise along the way. We received advice and encouragement from Lillian López, Daniel Chávez, and others who pioneered services to Latino communities in the New York Public Library, but we were basically on our own. The autonomy which we so prized and which has been so necessary to our survival was at times also a drawback since we were forced to learn every aspect of library work, carry out all library tasks, and take care of a growing public as well.

The library, currently housed within the Hunter College Library, operates autonomously as an integral part of the Centro de Estudios Puertorriqueños. In keeping with the Centro commitment to integrate the island and mainland–United States realities in its research, the present scope of the collection is the totality of the Puerto Rican experience. That is, the collection represents as completely as possible both communities in an attempt to maintain continuity and to provide adequate support for the complex issues facing Puerto Rican researchers and scholars today. Because the library is located in New York, still the center of Puerto Rican migration, we have a special interest in developing strong holdings on Puerto Ricans in the United States without neglecting Puerto Rico. Again, in keeping with the Centro practice of maintaining close links with the community it was created to serve, the library is open to the general public, not just academics. The majority of its users, nevertheless, are CUNY students and other students from the metropolitan area. The collection is noncirculating, with the exception of films and videocassettes.

Difficulties notwithstanding, the library's holdings have progressed over the years from a core collection to a comprehensive research collection and the library has been transformed from a local resource to a recognized national resource. As the only collection of its kind in the United States, it is filling a significant gap in information services to Puerto Ricans and to others studying the Puerto Rican experience.

Besides the general book collection of approximately 8,000 volumes, the library regularly acquires doctoral dissertations on Puerto Rican topics, which now number 1,200, subscribes to more than 200 periodicals, has developed wide-ranging retrospective periodical holdings which include both mainland United States and island publications, has gathered on microfilm documents focused on labor, migration, and economic policies from various archives in the United States and Puerto Rico, and maintains a vertical file of articles, clippings, and other materials. There is also a growing collection of films, video and audio tape, and a selection of art work.

The library uses the OCLC system for cataloging and will be participating in NOTIS, the integrated computerized library system coming into use throughout CUNY. It is expected that in the near future the library will have an online public access catalog. While participation in these shared systems makes our holdings more broadly accessible and makes library operations more efficient, we have to resist pressures to standardize completely, particularly in subject description of materials so that we continue to provide culturally relevant and nonalienating library access to Latinos who are our main user group.

Close work with undergraduate students has always been a reference priority, considering the fact that most of them enter the university with many academic needs and are poorly prepared to use libraries. Orientations to college classes and to younger groups are a regular part of our work. The orientations serve both to instruct and to break down barriers in library use and to help in formulating research strategies. We conduct the orientations in Spanish or English as is required and will either focus them on a particular assignment or make them more general. Our experience indicates that once college students feel at ease in the library, they will also make use of it for self-enrichment and not just for completing assignments.

Usage by a diverse clientele outside of CUNY undergraduates has increased significantly in recent years. Numerous advance graduate students use the collection to develop dissertations; some practically reside in the library since they can find most of the materials they need under our roof. A long-time "resident" is now winding up a thesis about the urbanization of 19th century Puerto Rico, for example.

The library also attracts international students and scholars from Europe and Latin America. Many come here looking for information on the cultural expression of Puerto Ricans in the United States, on language, and migration given the Centro's strength in those areas. Other main areas of research for those from abroad include ethnicity, urban politics, and other issues of urban life as they relate to Latinos.

Researchers from Puerto Rico, often frustrated by the lack of information on U.S. Puerto Ricans in the island libraries, pay us regular and lengthy visits. They make in-depth use of the dissertations and the many documents we have collected on microfilm from different repositories.

Joining the graduate students and other serious researchers are journalists requiring quick answers relating to breaking news or assistance in researching special reports. Equally important to us are the many users from the general public who come to borrow films and cassettes, to read the newspapers, to browse in the collection, or to develop ideas for community programs.

One of our responsibilities to our users is to facilitate their searches through the provision of adequate access tools. To this end, we produce a bibliographic series based on our holdings, a process which will now be made more efficient through the use of PROCITE, a bibliographic software. In addition to the bibliographies, we produce lists of recent acquisitions and maintain an updated list of microfilm holdings. These publications allow for better access to specific holdings in our collection, but do not solve the problem of those needing more comprehensive searches.

Lack of access to periodical articles on Puerto Ricans, for example, remains a great obstacle to researchers. A tool such as *The Chicano Index* which is a major achievement for Chicano scholarship, is needed for Puerto Ricans. Chicano librarians and scholars have been quite active as well in producing bibliographies that go beyond specific collections. Despite the usefulness of our in-house guides, we also need to move in the direction of creating more comprehensive tools. Our sister Chicano studies libraries provide a model and have substantial experience that we can draw on for this work.

The Centro is celebrating in 1990 its seventeenth anniversary. Anniversaries provide opportunities for reflection about accomplishments and shortfalls, and about future directions. Reflecting on 16 years of existence, we in the library ask ourselves how it is that we were able to grow and flourish in a sometimes hostile and always indifferent university system? What allowed us to progress in spite of the fumblings of an inexperienced library director and despite the limitations of restricted budgets and inadequate space? We may also ask what unique contribution we have made to Puerto Rican scholarship and librarianship and whether the library remains relevant in light of the present situation of Puerto Ricans here and in Puerto Rico?

The key element in our ability to flourish has been the consistent support of the Centro as an institution. The library is a product of collective efforts. Not only have Centro research staff made important contributions in the area of collection development, but it is primarily through them that we keep on top of research needs and trends. The administrative support that the library staff receives as a part of the Centro, such as in handling budgets or dealing with the College bureaucracy, saves valuable time. Of course, being fully integrated into a busy research center where collective work practices are the rule can at times cause conflicts about work priorities. At the same time that we participate fully in Centro governance and activities, frequently involved in assignments not directly related to the library, we have to run the library and keep up with other professional duties. For us the advantages of this situation by far outweigh the problems. The Centro's nourishing environment provides us with a context for the library work and helps us to carry it out purposefully.

The autonomy which we have been able to maintain has played an important role in shaping policies and is essential to protecting the integrity of the collection. It has permitted us to establish our own priorities in terms of services and collection building and in interacting with the community outside the university. While it is advantageous for us to participate to some extent in the larger library system, as in the union catalog, we reject all efforts to dismantle the collection or to integrate it into a general library. Each time that we outgrow our space, as has happened twice before and is once again the case at Hunter College, the solution offered is not more space to maintain our growth, but dispersal of the collection. After all these years we are still viewed as interlopers, occupying space that was only reluctantly surrendered to us.

The fight for legitimacy for Puerto Rican studies which started in 1969 is still being fought. It is a fact that in a system with a high Latino enrollment rate, there has been no sustained effort on the part of the college libraries to meet specific needs through the acquisition of pertinent Latino materials or the hiring of Latino personnel.[6] Despite this serious gap in services, neither the richness and uniqueness of our holdings nor the service we perform for students CUNY-wide are recognized as assets. Our most recent experience regarding a request for an increase in space confirms this attitude. Instead of reinforcing the value of our special collection by seeking to strengthen it, particularly in the absence of other significant Latino resources, our efforts are dismissed with a callous admonition to curtail growth so that we fit into presently allotted space.

At this juncture, just as at the time of our inception, linkages to the community are vital. Without the involvement of the broader community in the struggles that culminated in the creation of Puerto Rican Studies departments, the university might not have been pressured enough to comply with demands. By the same token, we continue to need a strong base in the community if we are to survive the present crisis within CUNY. Three years ago, a Friends of the Centro Library group was founded to promote library use and to support library development. The Friends are individuals representing different community spheres who are active in fundraising activities to help sustain growth, in sponsoring programs that focus on the library's services, and in pushing for more adequate facilities to accommodate our growing collections and increasing numbers of users. Appropriately, the very first activity sponsored by the Friends was the dedication of the library to Evelina López Antonetty, a prominent activist who fought throughout her life to better conditions for Puerto Ricans and other minorities in New York City. She was especially committed to children and education.

The Centro is a product of an era of protest over civil rights and of the struggles of the Puerto Rican community for recognition of its cultural identity. The 1980s ironically labeled "the decade of the Hispanic," turned out to be devastating for Latinos in the United States. The situation of Puerto Ricans is particularly grim:

> Our standard of living and quality of life have changed little in comparison to that of previous generations. Indeed, in some socio-economic categories our situation has worsened. Almost 38% of Puerto Rican families live in poverty. Forty-four percent of Puerto Rican families are headed by single women, who in turn experience a poverty level of 65%. The median income for Puerto Ricans is less than half that for non–Latinos. It is also the lowest among Latino groups.[7]

What possible bearing could collecting old papers, developing comprehensive bibliographies, and acquiring dissertations have on this somber reality in the United States? For one thing, the work of Puerto Rican and other Latino researchers trying to influence policy makers will intensify as they grapple with increasingly complex and intractable issues in employment, health, education, and housing. The use of historical records as well as the latest data, and service by knowledgeable librarians will have a role to play in bringing about a change in our present circumstances.

Secondly, the relative decline in the economic conditions of Puerto Ricans is only part of the story of what is happening with Latinos nationwide. The population of Puerto Ricans and other Latinos in the United States has grown substantially. In some cities and a few states Latinos will soon be a plurality or the "majority" minority. They constitute a significant market and a political as well as cultural force not just in the areas where their numbers are concentrated, but nationally.[8] They will need more than ever to have sustained knowledge about their past and the current situation in their own localities and beyond, especially in their countries of origin. On the road to empowerment, it will be the job of those of us entrusted with special collections or special responsibility for service to Latinos to keep information accessible and to fight trends to make information an expensive commodity.

When the Centro library started it had a clear mandate, but no clear plan of action. We started out perhaps naively addressing the needs of the moment. Gradually, as we have grasped the importance of what we were doing, we have also understood the need to plan with a wider vision of the centrality of information as a community resource.

NOTES

1. Letter from José Monserrat to Nélida Pérez, January 30, 1989. Monserrat was director of the Migration Division of the Office of the Commonwealth of Puerto Rico in New York.

2. Frank Bonilla, Ricardo Campos, and Juan Flores, "Puerto Rican Studies: Promptings for the Academy and the Left," in *The Left Academy: Marxist Scholarship on American Campuses,* eds. Bertell Ollman and Edward Vernoff (New York: Praeger, 1986), p. 69.

3. Examples are Ann Knight Randall, "Dreams, Reality, and Tailor-Made Service," in *What Black Librarians Are Saying,* ed. by E.J. Josey (Metuchen, N.J.: Scarecrow Press, 1972); also Bruni Vergés, "Developing Collections on Puerto Rican Heritage," in *Ethnic Collections in Libraries,* eds. E.J. Josey and Marva L. DeLoach (New York: Neal-Schuman, 1983).

4. Michael Abramson, *Palante: The Young Lords Party* (New York: McGraw Hill, 1971), p. 68.

5. Dorothy B. Porter, "Bibliography and Research in Afro-American Scholarship," *The Journal of Academic Librarianship,* 2 (1976): 77–81.

6. Carlos Rodríguez-Fraticelli, "Puerto Ricans and CUNY: Twenty Years After Open Admissions," *Centro Bulletin* 2 (Summer 1989): 22–31.

7. National Congress for Puerto Rican Rights, *The Status of Puerto Ricans in the United States 1989* (New York: NCPR, 1989), p. 1. See also, Joan Moore, *An Assessment of Hispanic Poverty: Is There an Hispanic Underclass?* (San Antonio, Texas: The Tomás Rivera Center, 1988); Robert Greenstein, et al., *Shortchanged: Recent Developments in Hispanic Poverty, Income and Employment* (Washington, D.C.: Center on Budget and Priorities, 1988).

8. See Latino Commission of Tri-State, *Outlook: The Growing Latino Presence in the Tri-State Region* (New York: Regional Plan Association, 1988). Also, Hispanic Policy Development Project, *The Hispanic Almanac* (New York: Project, 1984); "Hispanic Americans: An Emerging Group," *Statistical Bulletin* (Oct.–Dec. 1988).

SELECTED BIBLIOGRAPHY

Abramson, Michael. *Palante: The Young Lords Party.* New York: McGraw-Hill, 1971.
Bonilla, Frank; Campos, Ricardo; and Flores, Juan. "Puerto Rican Studies: Promptings for the Academy and the Left." In *The Left Academy: Marxist Scholarship*

on American Campuses, pp. 67–102. Edited by Bertell Ollman and Edward Vernoff. New York: Praeger, 1986.

Chabrán, Richard. "Mapping Emergent Discourses: Latino Bibliographic Services in Academia." In *Alternative Library Literature, 1986–1987*, pp. 11–15. Edited by Sanford Berman and James P. Danky. Jefferson, N.C.: McFarland, 1988.

Flores Durán, Daniel. *Latino Materials: A Multimedia Guide for Children and Young Adults.* New York: Neal-Schuman, 1979.

García-Ayvens, Francisco, and Chabrán, Richard F., eds. *Biblio-Política: Chicano Perspectives on Library Service in the United States.* Berkeley: University of California, 1984.

Greenstein, Robert, et al. *Shortchanged: Recent Developments in Hispanic Poverty, Income and Employment.* Washington, D.C.: Center on Budget and Policy Priorities, 1988.

Güereña, Salvador. "Archives and Manuscripts: Historical Antecedents to Contemporary Chicano Collections." *Collection Building* 8, 4 (1988): pp. 3–11.

Hispanic Policy Development Project. *The Hispanic Almanac.* New York: The Project, 1984.

Latino Commission of Tri-State. *Outlook: The Growing Latino Presence in the Tri-State Region.* New York: Regional Plan Association, 1988.

Josey, E.J., ed. *What Black Librarians Are Saying.* Metuchen, N.J.: Scarecrow Press, 1972.

_____, and Deloach, Marva L., eds. *Ethnic Collections in Libraries.* New York: Neal-Schuman, 1983.

National Congress for Puerto Rican Rights. *The Status of Puerto Ricans in the United States, 1989.* New York: The Congress, 1989.

Payne, Judith. *Public Libraries Face California's Ethnic and Racial Diversity.* Santa Monica, Calif.: Rand Corporation, 1988.

Porter, Dorothy B. "Bibliography and Research in Afro-American Scholarship." *The Journal of Academic Librarianship* 2 (1976): 77–81.

Rodríguez Fratecelli, Carlos. "Puerto Ricans and CUNY: Twenty Years After Open Admissions." *Centro Bulletin* 2 (Summer 1989): 22–31.

Sánchez, Maria E., and Stevens-Arroyo, Antonio M., eds. *Toward a Renaissance of Puerto Rican Studies.* Highland Lakes, N.J.: Atlantic Research Publications, 1987.

Tarín, Patricia A. "Rand Misses the Point: A Minority Report." *Library Journal* (Nov. 1, 1989): pp. 31–34.

Vázquez, Jesse M. "Puerto Rican Studies in the 1990s: Taking the Next Turn in the Road." *Centro Bulletin* 2 (Summer 1989): 8–19.

THE HISTORY AND ROLE OF REFORMA

Patrick José Dawson

Now, more than ever, the ability to retrieve information can determine one's success in work and society. In the United States, because of the predominance of the English language, information sources have traditionally been available to those who read English but not necessarily those who read other languages. The prevailing attitude was that in order to succeed, in order to have access to information, people needed to locate it themselves, and sometimes in a language with which they may not be familiar. There was not a great deal of outreach on the part of libraries because the needs of non–English readers had not yet been assessed. Fortunately, with the increasing number of Spanish-speaking people in the United States, a few saw the need for outreach to this community and this foresightedness led to the creation of REFORMA, the National Association to Promote Library Services to the Spanish Speaking. This chapter will examine REFORMA, its history, its structure, its concerns and its future.

It is too seldom that one can write of an organization that started as the dream of a single person and prospered to include eight national chapters, an affiliate and close to 700 personal and institutional members. However, this can be written of REFORMA. What started as a dream grew to be a national association as well as an affiliate of the American Library Association, actively pursuing its mission "to promote library services to the Spanish-speaking."

Even though REFORMA was not established until 1971, there were earlier attempts to impart library services to the Latino community. The most notable of these was the Seminar for the Acquisition of Latin American Library Materials, SALALM, which was founded in 1956. This is an international association of librarians, scholars and book dealers who work to provide information on Latin American publications so that libraries and librarians can have at their disposal a forum for information on the development of collections from and about Latin America. However, although SALALM concentrates on the Spanish (and Portuguese) speaking, it focuses more on Latin America rather than the United States and on academic and research libraries more than public libraries.

One factor accelerating the need for outreach to the Spanish-speaking community was the increasing publication of Chicano authors. The year 1959 is viewed by many as the genesis of the Chicano literary movement with the appearance of *Pocho* by José Antonio Villarreal. Although REFORMA works toward extending library services to all Spanish-speaking, it was the activity of Chicano authors and activists which ignited the idea behind the creation of an outreach to the Spanish-speaking population in the United States. Arnulfo Trejo is the man who took the idea for REFORMA, laid the groundwork for the organization, named it and even carried the organization forward in its early years. It can be said that Trejo and REFORMA were one and the same for the first four years.

The American Library Association's annual convention at Dallas in 1971 led to the creation of REFORMA. At one of the programs of the convention, Trejo and Elizabeth Martínez Smith showed the film *I Am Joaquín* based upon the poem of the same title by the Chicano poet Rodolfo "Corky" González. The film was enthusiastically received and this interest on the part of the audience made Trejo aware of the need for an organization which would serve as an outreach to the Latino population of the United States and as a forum for information and resource sharing. Arnulfo Trejo met with William Ramírez, Esperanza Acosta, Emma Morales González, Modene Martín, Alicia Iglesias, María Mata and others to resolve the problems inherent in creating a new organization. As is the case with most who plan a new group, development falls upon whoever raises the issue. Thus, Trejo became REFORMA's first president, a post he would hold from 1971 through 1974.*

The group was not yet known as REFORMA but referred to as the "National Association of Spanish-Speaking Librarians." After the Dallas meeting it was necessary to work on membership recruitment as well as goals and objectives for the organization. Under the name of the "National Association of Spanish-Speaking Librarians in the United States," Trejo applied for and received HEW funds to present a special institute in Fort Worth, Texas, in 1971, where the foundation was laid for what would become REFORMA. A second institute was held in Las Vegas later that year to work on association visibility and membership recruitment. From the Las Vegas meeting the George I. Sánchez award was created. The award is a special recognition to be given annually to one who has worked on behalf of the Latino population in educational or library innovation. The award was named in honor of George I. Sánchez, an educator who worked on behalf of the Spanish-speaking in the United States, fighting in the courts

---

The roster of REFORMA presidents: 1971–74 Arnulfo Trejo, 1974–75 Alberto Irabien, 1975–77 John Ayala, 1978 Roberto Cabello Argandoña, 1978–80 Daniel Flores Durán, 1980–82 Cesar Caballero, 1982–83 Luis Herrera, 1983–84 Albert A. Milo, 1984–85 Salvador Güereña, 1985–86 Susan Luévano, 1986–87 Elena Tscherny, 1987–88 Elizabeth Rodríguez-Miller, 1988–89 Ingrid Betancourt, 1989–90 Rhoda Ríos-Kravitz, 1990–91 Ron Rodríguez.

against the educational segregation of Spanish-speaking students and for the development of bilingual and bicultural education programs. The presentation of this award to Sánchez's widow in Las Vegas in 1972 also allowed for the press to nationally report on the activities and existence of the association.

Toward the end of 1972, REFORMA completed two major internal projects. The first was to develop its name, the second was to adopt its constitution.* The origin of the name is of notable interest. Trejo had in mind what the organization was — an association of Spanish-speaking librarians dedicated to outreach to the Spanish-speaking/Latino community. What was lacking was a name. After the Las Vegas institute, while visiting UCLA and browsing through some old newsletters, Trejo encountered an article about some "Californistas" and their newspaper called *Reforma*. The name had appeal as it reflected the goal of the nascent organization: to reform the lack of outreach to Spanish-speaking people. Therefore, REFORMA is not an acronym, but rather, the verbalization of a concept. Thus, REFORMA, the National Association of Spanish-Speaking Librarians in the United States, was named and developed.

As noted, there was much to do. The first was to recruit members who shared the same goal. The following brief notice appeared in *Library Journal* in 1972 under the heading, "REFORMA Urges Library Service for Spanish-Americans."

> REFORMA, organized last year in Dallas, is seeking members, those of Ibero-American extract and librarians interested in working with the Spanish-speaking people of the U.S. REFORMA will have a general meeting in Chicago at ALA to map out policies and present position papers. Contact Arnulfo Trejo at the University of Arizona [*LJ* **97**, 5 (March 1972)].

Still, despite the dedicated work of Arnulfo Trejo and others, the early years of REFORMA were rather unstable. There was not a large membership nor chapter affiliates and a viable financial base was lacking.

Nevertheless, November of 1973 marked another accomplishment for the association, with the publication of the first newsletter. This was a significant event as up to that time it was incumbent upon the president to inform the membership of news and events. The newsletter established an alternative vehicle to impart information to Reformistas who were unable to maintain communication with the association where there was no local representation.

Finances continued to be a problem for REFORMA. Not only was there a small membership base, but the organization had not yet acquired tax exempt status. Therefore, in 1974, REFORMA was officially incorporated as a nonprofit organization. However, income was still minimal. The treasurer's

See Annex A at the end of this chapter.

report of 1974 related in the newsletter states that only 36 members had paid their dues.

From the beginning, Trejo had been aware that one means for effective outreach to the Latino population was increasing the number of Latino librarians. This issue was first raised by REFORMA at the time of its founding and continues to be a project with which REFORMA actively deals: recruitment of Latinos into the library profession. As a faculty member of the Graduate Library School at the University of Arizona, Trejo saw the opportunity for action. At the time, there existed at California State University, Fullerton, the Graduate Institute for Mexican-Americans, School of Library Science, directed by Patrick S. Sánchez. Although this program served to recruit and educate Latinos in librarianship it was not accredited by the American Library Association.

Trejo decided to develop an accredited program and in 1975 the Graduate Library Institute for Spanish-Speaking Americans, GLISA, applied for and received HEW funding, opening its doors at the University of Arizona. This program would be successful in its mission to increase the number of Latinos in the library profession. Among its graduates were three future REFORMA presidents. With the termination of the library program at Fullerton and the demise of the Graduate Institute for Mexican-Americans in 1978, GLISA would be the only program of this type. Despite the continued need to educate Latinos to become librarians, GLISA would lose its funding during the Reagan-era cuts in federal programs and close in 1980. These programs were very successful, graduating 104 Latino librarians.

Because of a commitment to his GLISA, Trejo did not run for re-election as president of REFORMA and Alberto Irabien became the association's second president, elected during the 1974 ALA conference. Because of reorganization and the absence of Trejo, the remainder of 1974 was quiet for the association. In April of 1975 Alberto Irabien resigned as president and was succeeded by John L. Ayala. It became apparent that the structure of the association was becoming difficult to manage.

REFORMA is a national association; nevertheless, there was no national headquarters nor support staff, a problem which still exists, and as a result the burden of organization falls upon the president. To alleviate this organizational deficiency, four regional chapters were created which would coordinate the efforts of their local members and assist the president by taking over some administrative and planning duties. Committees were also created to handle specific charges. These chapters were to be the Pacific-Southwest; Central; Northeast and Southeast. With reorganization, 1975 marked the year that REFORMA won recognition by the American Library Association as an affiliated organization, afforded excellent exposure and publicity among the library community and would facilitate program sponsorship at future ALA conventions. Membership increased to 129 through this period and into the next year while activities were being planned at the national level to coincide with the annual ALA convention.

By 1977 leadership had changed again, with José Taylor as the new president. REFORMA, besides meeting at the midwinter and annual ALA conferences, was beginning to sponsor or cosponsor workshops and presentations at those conferences. An organizational accomplishment for the association that year was the fact that the newsletter, previously an irregular publication, became a regular quarterly publication. This small event is significant in that the membership could now look forward to being apprised of events, news and issues on a regular basis, which would benefit the association's activities and causes by keeping the members well informed. Also, for the first time, there would exist a regular written record to chronicle the evolution of REFORMA. The membership strength which had been evolving through 1977 was beneficial to the association, as 1978 would mark a year when REFORMA could call upon its members to make public two causes affecting the Spanish-speaking population.

Two events in 1978 created an impact upon libraries and the Latino community. One was the so called "tax revolt" of Proposition 13 in California where voters elected to lower their taxes and, as a result, many tax-funded services provided by the state and local governments had to be curtailed. REFORMA, nationally and at the state level in California, lobbied against cutbacks in services for Latinos as budget slashing was terminating many library services. A second issue was the Supreme Court decision handed down in June of 1978 in the case of the Regents of the University of California vs. Bakke. The University of California, Davis, was ordered by the high court to end the "reverse racial discrimination" of reserving 16 percent of their places in medical school for minority candidates. Although this case was of doubtful value as a precedent, it did threaten the concept of programs for affirmative action such as GLISA. REFORMA took a stand in opposition to this decision.

The association was again reorganized in 1978. In the continued absence of a national headquarters, REFORMA allowed for the local chapters to develop their own by-laws and structure as well as take a share of the national REFORMA dues, or develop their own dues schedules. State councils were organized to facilitate communication between the local state chapters. This is especially important in California where there are four chapters and an affiliate. Regional councils were also established which served to coordinate activists between the various state councils and the REFORMA president. The concept behind this move was to allow the local chapters autonomy to work on programs for the Spanish-speaking at the grassroots level. This was successful where there were strong local chapters. The president and executive board of REFORMA were then supposed to concentrate on the national level and work closely with ALA.

The problem with this structure, however, is that it can lead to a lack of cohesion, a nonstandardized dues structure, and failure of communication and cooperation on the national level. Manifestations of these problems have continued to plague REFORMA, and it seems that the best remedy would be the establishment of a national headquarters and support staff to administer the daily activities from the top down rather than from the bottom up.

Nevertheless, REFORMA continued to exist and succeed in its mission, causing then president Daniel Flores Durán to give an optimistic account of the association in a 1978 interview in *Wilson Library Bulletin:*

> At this point REFORMA is entering a period of revitalization and growth. Emphasis has shifted from that of a primary public library/Chicano/Southwest-oriented organization to a truly national association that not only represents the needs of Chicano librarians, but also of Puerto Ricans, Cubans, and other Latino groups ["Library Services and the Spanish-Speaking," *WLB* 53, 3 (Nov. 1978)].

By 1980, the newsletter began to be used as a means to disseminate information on resources for developing Spanish-language collections in libraries, and to recommend and review new publications for use by Spanish-speaking patrons. The year 1981 marked the tenth anniversary of REFORMA. The location of the ALA annual conference was San Francisco, allowing the California chapters to work together on program presentations. A national colloquium entitled "Chicano Academic Library and Information Services" was cosponsored by REFORMA and the Chicano Library collections of the University of California compuses at Berkeley, Los Angeles and Santa Barbara. The colloquium was a success and afforded great recognition for REFORMA, allowing the sponsorship of a joint program on minority concerns with the Black Caucus the following year at the annual ALA conference in Philadelphia.

One of the early ideals of REFORMA was recruitment of Latinos into the library profession. In 1982 the REFORMA National Scholarship Program was instituted to be awarded annually to Latinos who are candidates for library school. This scholarship program has continued to the present time and has assisted many Latinos in completing their education to become librarians. The same year, REFORMA was included in the 17th edition of the *Encyclopedia of Associations.*

The San Francisco annual conference in 1981 had been a boon to REFORMA's membership and exposure. The annual conference for 1983 was held in Los Angeles, which presented another opportunity to REFORMA. Not only was there a strong local chapter, but also a large Latino population where outreach programs and the results of REFORMA activities could be displayed. One of the activities which REFORMA sponsored and undertook at the Los Angeles conference was an exchange meeting with the Ethnic Materials Information Exchange Round Table, EMIERT, which forged an understanding for future cooperation between these two ALA groups.

REFORMA also began to actively advance a slate of candidates for election to ALA Council, and has continued to do so with some success to the present. REFORMA gained broader recognition as an association by sponsoring a bus tour of selected libraries with Latino outreach programs, starting a tradition which would be repeated at the ALA conferences in Chicago and New York. During that year's REFORMA Executive Board meeting, the association undertook an action which would serve to codify its mission. From the beginning, REFORMA had been known as the "National Association of Spanish-Speaking Librarians in the United States." At the ALA Conference in Los Angeles the group's executive board felt that this did not reflect the association's purpose. They proposed to the membership to shift the emphasis beyond the composition of the organization itself, to identify more with the goals of the association. Therefore, that year the name was changed to REFORMA, the "National Association to Promote Library Services to the Spanish Speaking."

In 1984 the Executive Board also believed that the best way to increase visibility in ALA and to advance the concerns of serving the Spanish-speaking was to forge coalitions with other library and nonlibrary groups concerned with providing services to minorities. REFORMA continues to pursue this avenue by encouraging the local chapters to affiliate with local library and nonlibrary groups and for the executive board to solicit affiliations with like associations at the national level. Some of the beneficial results of this enterprise have been in 1988 at the ALA conference meeting in New Orleans, where the executive board voted to affiliate with EPIC, and in 1989 in Dallas, where the executive board voted to affiliate with NCLR. REFORMA will continue to actively reach out to other groups.

A final note on 1984 is that Dr. Arnulfo Trejo retired from his teaching post at the Graduate Library School of the University of Arizona. REFORMA took this opportunity to cosponsor a "despedida" in his honor, awarding him a plaque to thank him for and to acknowledge the work he had done, not only in creating REFORMA, but for his instrumental role in GLISA and in promoting library services to the Spanish-speaking.

In 1985 REFORMA elected its first woman president, Susan Luévano. The idea of creating coalitions was continued and ties were developed with EMIERT, the ALA Council Committee on Minority Concerns and the Reference and Adult Services Division, RASD. Through work with RASD, REFORMA was able to contribute to the development of ALA/RASD *Guidelines for Library Services to the Spanish-speaking*, which were eventually adopted by ALA in 1989. Also in 1985 REFORMA chose a site, the Colección Tloque Nahuaque at the University of California, Santa Barbara, to locate its archives, which will preserve the records of the association and assist future research on REFORMA and the evolution of library services to the Spanish-speaking. A REFORMA job line was also established that year.

Beginning in 1984 and building momentum into 1985 was the emerging "English-only" movement, which strives to amend the United States Constitution to make English the official language of the United States. In keeping with its goal to promote access to information, regardless of language, REFORMA developed a policy proposal opposing legislation that would designate English as the official language of the United States. This was presented to ALA Council via the Committee on Minority Concerns. It was adopted and passed by Council at the 1985 ALA Midwinter meeting. The ALA Washington Office now monitors and testifies against any such legislation at public hearings. Similarly in California, where the "English-only" bill did pass, REFORMA introduced a resolution to the California Library Association, CLA, which stated CLA's commitment to supporting multilingual library materials and services. ALA and CLA stand united in their commitment to provide information in a format the individual can utilize, regardless of language.

REFORMA has continued the campaign against a constitutional amendment making English the official language of the United States through the release of a position paper in April of 1989. Through REFORMA's association with ALA's Washington Office and its Washington, D.C., chapter, REFORMA has been able to become involved in influencing Congress on other legislative issues. REFORMA and ALA have been able to work to ensure continued funding for LSCA and Title II-B. Without the actions of REFORMA, ALA and other national associations, these programs might have been cut.

Not only has REFORMA committed itself to recruiting potential library school students, it has recognized the need to retain these students to complete their education. Toward this end and to encourage the education of Latinos to becoming librarians, the REFORMA/UCLA Mentor Program was initiated in 1986. This program pairs a prospective library school student with a practicing librarian to assist the student in matters of curriculum and the profession, and provides continuing workshops to reinforce this assistance. The two also continue their association during the student's tenure in library school. Now in its fourth year, this program has received national attention as a model program for recruitment and retention of minority students into professional training programs, and is being considered by other library schools.

Through 1987 and 1988 REFORMA has continued to grow and prosper, establishing new chapters and professional associations with other organizations that share the same commitment. New members have been recruited, scholarships have continued to be awarded and the Mentor Program proven its merit. At the local and national levels REFORMA continued to work for library services on behalf of the Spanish-speaking. Major work done on internal issues was carried out by the Task Force on Long Range Planning which produced the REFORMA Five Year Plan, adopted at the 1989 ALA Midwinter meeting.*

What can be said about REFORMA? It is laudable that the association

*See Annex B at the end of this chapter.

started spontaneously and flourished as it has. This is a tribute to the dedication of those who have invested their time and energy in a cause to which they are dedicated. REFORMA has spearheaded genuine accomplishments in outreach to the Spanish-speaking community. First and foremost REFORMA is an advocacy organization, a "watchdog" whose basic goal must be accomplished by libraries and librarians themselves. REFORMA has actively monitored library activities and developments at national, statewide and local levels. Its members have worked with libraries to initiate and institute new library programs and to strengthen existing ones. Specific REFORMA accomplishments include the adoption of the position paper by ALA in opposition to "English-only" legislation, the REFORMA scholarship and the REFORMA/UCLA Mentor Program. There are also publications by REFORMA or "Reformistas" which deal with outreach programs to the Spanish-speaking or bibliographies to assist librarians in developing a collection to serve the Spanish-speaking.

Nevertheless, there are critiques as well. The greatest problem continued to be the lack of a national office or headquarters. Depending heavily upon the local chapters is acceptable for local exposure and work; with the lack of a national office and support staff, however, the headquarters has to travel every year to the location of the incoming president. This can be detrimental to REFORMA's communication and cohesion. Nevertheless, as with any organization, REFORMA is only as good as its members. In this there is no criticism. The future of REFORMA will depend upon its members, so hopefully the zeal of the past will continue beyond REFORMA's 20th anniversary to the future. REFORMA does not have the luxury to repose and reflect on its accomplishments, as there will always be more to do.

In the last 20 years, the percentage of library school graduates who are Latino has remained a constant 1.9 percent, while the percentage of Latinos in the population of the United States has dramatically increased. This problem has to be solved. A disturbing trend is the decrease in federal and state funding for library services for the underserved. This trend has to be stopped as well as the constant attacks on existing legislation which does promote library services to the underserved. Finally the question of how to serve the information needs of the growing Latino population has to be addresssed as well as informing the general public on the need to provide these services to the Spanish-speaking. Therefore, it can be seen that REFORMA will have a full agenda for the future.

Bibliographical Note

Most of the materials for this essay were gathered by examining the REFORMA archives, which include correspondence and newsletters located in the Special Collections Department of the University of California,

Santa Barbara. Many thanks to Salvador Güereña, former GLISA student, past REFORMA president (1984–1985), curator of the REFORMA archive and head of the Colección Tloque Nahuaque at UCSB for his assistance and willingness to answer questions. The archive is a treasure trove of information, however, to strengthen its viability, it is suggested that the outstanding papers from all past REFORMA officers be collected for the archive and that the archive be catalogued for future use.

Other sources consulted

American Library Association Yearbook of Library and Information Services. Vol. 1, 1975–   . Chicago: American Library Association.

Bruce-Novoa, Juan D. *Chicano Authors: Inquiry by Interview.* Austin: University of Texas Press, 1980.

REFORMA Newsletter. Vol. 1, no. 1 (1973–   ) Place of publication varies.

Specific articles

Durán, Daniel Flores. "Library Services and the Spanish-Speaking." *Wilson Library Bulletin* 53, 3 (Nov. 1978) (Special issue on library services to the Spanish-speaking).

Güereña, Salvador. "REFORMA: The National Association of Spanish Speaking Librarians." Paper presented to LS 304 Class, Graduate Library School, University of Arizona, November 1978.

Navarro Vielma, Zulema. "The History of REFORMA: Twelve Years of Work on Behalf of the Hispanics." MLS thesis, Texas Woman's University School of Library Science, 1984.

Russell, Joel. "New Stars of the Information Age." *Hispanic Business.* Vol. 11, no. 2 (Feb. 1989).

Annex A: The REFORMA Constitution, adopted 1972

Objectives

1) To unite librarians in the United States of Ibero-American extraction and all other librarians who are interested in working with the Spanish-speaking/ Spanish surnamed people in this country in activity of common interest.
2) Create and work toward implementation of policies which will fulfill in an adequate manner the needs of the Spanish-speaking/Spanish surnamed people in matters concerning librarianship in the broadest sense.
3) Study the findings of surveys, research and other available data which can be used to understand the Spanish-speaking ethnic groups so that libraries and library service can be made more useful and meaningful to these people.

4) Promote studies and research on current and potential problems concerned with the production, distribution and use of library materials, as well as compilation of general and subject bibliographies.
5) Develop a clearing house for the purpose of collecting and disseminating information about the Spanish-speaking.
6) Identify and evaluate those library programs which have been designed especially to provide adequate library service for the Spanish-speaking.
7) Identify the needs and establish priorities for librarians working with this ethnic group.
8) Formulate guidelines for libraries at all levels of library service for the Spanish-speaking.
9) Explore the application of computer technology in resolving problems relative to library services offered to the Spanish-speaking.
10) Make recommendations on how ALA, NEA and other national as well as state and regional associations can play a more active role in promoting services to the Spanish-speaking.
11) Help recruit prospective librarians from the various Spanish-speaking groups in the country for training in librarianship.
12) Conduct at least one annual meeting with the purpose of carrying forth the objectives of REFORMA.

Activities of REFORMA in Pursuance of Objectives

1) Foster understanding of Spanish-speaking peoples and their need for better library services.
2) Encourage cooperation among professors, librarians and specialists in Spanish language and culture studies to aid the development of library collections to support study and research.
3) Sponsor, support and/or participate in the publication and dissemination of information related to the purposes stated in this article.
4) Exchange reports, publications and information with organizations and institutions with similar objectives as those of REFORMA.
5) Serve as an information agency on book and non-book materials, programs, and people in matters related to library services to the Spanish-speaking people in the United States.
6) Sponsor, support, conduct or participate in periodic meetings including scientific, library and bibliographic conferences, seminars or round tables on topics related to the objectives of REFORMA.
7) Raise funds and accept contributions of money, materials, property, services and train personnel for the activities stated in this article.
8) Buy, own, receive, accept, sell, convey, assign, mortgage or otherwise exercise all privileges of ownership over any real estate and any personnel property necessary or incident to the scientific and educational non-profit purposes of the organization.
9) Engage in activities and perform and carry out contracts and agreements necessary to, or incidental to the accomplishment of any of one or more of the purposes of the organization.

Annex B: The REFORMA Five Year Plan, adopted January 1989

Goal 1. Recruitment of Bilingual/Bicultural Librarians.

Objective A: To establish a REFORMA Recruitment Committee to work on specific recruitment tasks, to coordinate the efforts of other REFORMA units and to communicate with ALA groups and committees.

Responsibility: President appoints committee chair who in turn selects committee members.

Objective B: To establish at least one new Mentor Program in the next five years targeting an area of the United States with a large Hispanic population.

Responsibility: Local chapters with the assistance of the Education and Recruitment Committees.

Goal 2. Marketing the Association.

Objective A: To submit a minimum of three articles a year promoting the association.

Responsibility: President writes or assigns task.

Objective B: To send press releases on REFORMA activities, programs and members' achievements to library and other publications. Minimum of 6 per year.

Responsibility: Public Relations Officer when appropriate.

Objective C: To lobby ALA Vice President/President-Elect every year to appoint at least one REFORMA member to the following committees: Minority Concerns, Office for Library Outreach Services (OLOS) Advisory, Accreditation and other appropriate committees.

Responsibility: President and Vice President.

Goal 3. Channeling growth and stability.

Objective A: To develop a Policies and Procedures Manual for REFORMA which will include specific policy statements regarding chapter responsibilities and duties of the Executive Board Members.

Responsibility: Current Treasurer with input from present Executive Board members and membership at large.

Objective B: To establish at least one new REFORMA chapter in the next five years.

Responsibility: Organizational Development Officer.

Objective C: To establish a uniform dues structure for all REFORMA Chapters.

Responsibility: Executive Board.

Objective D: To recruit at least 200 new members by 1995.

Responsibility: Chapter presidents and Membership Coordinator.

Objective E: To establish a permanent address for the Association.

Responsibility: Executive Board.

Goal 4: Developing greater political effectiveness and representation.

Objective A: To encourage the candidacy of at least one member of REFORMA for ALA Council every election.

Strategies: (1) Provide a designated amount of money for campaign funding per candidate. (2) Provide publicity via REFORMA newsletter and mailings to membership. (3) Provide publicity in other professional associations.

Responsibility: Executive Board designates amount. Public Relations Officer in charge of publicity.

Objective B: To endorse candidates for ALA offices and Council.
Strategies: (1) Establish small committee to evaluate candidates and present to Executive Board for vote on endorsement. (2) Announce endorsements in the REFORMA newsletter and other professional publications.
Responsibility: President appoints committee. Public Relations Officer in charge of publicity.
Objective C: To create an annual national REFORMA award for recognition of achievement in the area of library services to Latinos.
Strategies: (1) Expand Scholarship Committee to "Awards and Scholarships."
(2) Questionnaires can be sent to members requesting nominations for the award.
Responsibility: Executive Board establishes criteria for the selection of the recipient of the award, and decides what will be awarded, and when it will be presented. The Awards and Scholarship Committee will be responsible for drafting the questionnaire, requesting nominations and selecting the winner.
Objective D: REFORMA chapters affiliate with local, state and regional library associations and present programs at their annual conferences.
Strategies: (1) Chapters contact state library associations for information. Vote on affiliation. (2) If approved, chapter plans a program every year at the state library association conference.
Responsibility: Chapter presidents.
Objective E: To establish institutional memberships in at least one Latino educational, political or other professional organization during the next five years.
Strategies: Members recommend organizations. Executive Board votes on each year's selection(s) at ALA midwinter meetings.
Responsibility: President solicits recommendations. Executive Board makes selection.
Objective F: To write a minimum of one position paper statement per year on an issue that is not directly library related as needed.
Strategies: President solicits input from members. Executive Board votes on selection at midwinter meeting.
Responsibility: President writes or assigns task.
Objective H: To sponsor one annual program and a minimum of three programs and/or activities with other ALA divisions and round tables at each ALA summer conference.
Strategies: (1) To invite related groups to cosponsor REFORMA programs.
(2) To contact groups and offer to cosponsor and publicize their programs.
Responsibility: Vice President/President-Elect.

Goal 5: Nurturing communication and participation.
Objective A: To adopt an annual national theme and communicate it to chapters, requesting input and support.
Strategies: (1) Led by the Vice President/President-Elect, the Executive Board begins to work on next year's (July-June) agenda at midwinter and brings it to a vote at each ALA summer conference. (2) Agenda is sent to chapter presidents and published in REFORMA newsletter.
Responsibility: Executive Board.
Objective B: To obtain semiannual reports from all members of the Executive Board at the ALA midwinter conference and annual reports at the summer con-

Responsibility: President and Executive Board.

Objective C: To adopt a constant and recognizable format for the REFORMA newsletter and maintain high standards of professionalism in content and appearance.

Strategies: (1) Find a permanent home for the REFORMA newsletter. (2) Extend editorial term to three years. (3) Design and maintain a standard format for the cover and establish permanent sections/columns. (4) Require that chapter presidents and committee chairs submit articles for each issue. (5) Encourage membership at large to contribute by sending articles, letters, information for the various columns, etc. (6) Invite non–Reformistas to write about issues of interest to members. (7) Try to make the newsletter self-supporting through advertising revenue.

Responsibility: Executive Board and newsletter editor.

THE ENGLISH-ONLY MOVEMENT: A SELECTED BIBLIOGRAPHY

Salvador Güereña

The issue of English as the official language has been one of increasing controversy. Will it help immigrants advance and unify all Americans? Or is it a threat to the constitutional rights of the non–English speaking and a mask for racism and bigotry? Seventeen states have enacted legislation which have either declared English as the official language or which in varying degrees limit the use of non–English languages. There have been efforts to enact similar legislation in at least 20 other states. An active movement to amend the Constitution to make English the official language of the United States has been led by several national organizations which include U.S. English, based in Washington, D.C., and English First, located in Falls Church, Virginia.

The English-only movement has been motivated by a number of factors including concern over immigration and the increasing Latino presence in this country. The public policy implications of such legislation are many, affecting the provision of bilingual education programs, bilingual ballots, and government services in languages other than English.

Major national organizations such as the Mexican American Legal Defense and Education Fund and the National Council of La Raza and research centers such as the Tomás Rivera Center's National Institute for Policy Studies have produced analyses on this important topic and have sought to identify principles which would produce a language policy based on equity.

It is noteworthy that the American Library Association has adopted a policy stand against such federal legislation. A resolution was also adopted by the California Library Association, which declared the provision of library services, programs, and materials in languages other than English to be a valid and essential community service.

The following bibliography, while annotated, lists information on this topic published in various formats, including news items, journal articles . and selected position papers. The bibliographic entries are as complete as possible. Unpublished sources or testimony of congressional hearings were kept to a minimum.

Alfonso, Mirna. "English-Only Sign Proposal Sidetracked." *Los Angeles Times,* November 24, 1985, part X, p. 4.

_____. "South Gate Planners to Study Idea: English-Only Sign Bill Sidetracked." *Los Angeles Times,* November 17, 1985, part IX, p. 4.

Alter, J. "English Spoken Here, Please." *Newsweek,* January 9, 1984, pp. 24–25.

Anderson, Kurt. "Final Destination." *Time,* July 8, 1985, p. 46.

Anshen, Frank. "Tongues and Myths." *New York Times,* October 19, 1980, p. E21.

"Anti-Nativist Pact Declared." *Hispanic Link Weekly Report,* August 25, 1986, p. 1.

Arax, Mark. "Judge Upholds Foes of 'Official English' Vote." *Los Angeles Times,* December 25, 1985, part II, p. 4.

Are English Language Amendments in the National Interest? An Analysis of Proposals to Establish English As the Official Language. Claremont, Calif.: Tomás Rivera Center, 1986.

Armstrong, Scott. "English Classes Bulging with Immigrants." *Christian Science Monitor,* March 23, 1987, p. 1.

_____. "Should English Have Official-language Stamp?" *Christian Science Monitor,* July 31, 1986, p. 1.

Baker, Russell. "Dealing with California." *New York Times Magazine,* December 7, 1986, p. 36.

Ballin, Heinz Adolf. "English Only: Is It Necessary? Speaking a Common Language Is Vital to Keep Americans United." *Los Angeles Times,* November 2, 1986, part II, p. 16.

Barbaro, Kay. "The Cuckoo Nest." *Hispanic Link Weekly Report,* Nov. 24, 1986, p. 3.

"Battle Over Bilingualism: Opposition Intensifies to Ads Using Spanish." *Los Angeles Times,* September 8, 1986, part I, p. 21.

Baugh, J. "Linguistic Diversity and Justice in America: Growing Complexity in a Traditional National Paradox." *Urban Resources,* 3, 1985, pp. 31–35.

Beck, Joan. "America Needs a Common Voice." *Chicago Tribune,* July 7, 1986, p. 18.

Beers, David. "'Us' and 'Them': Push to Make English Official Goes Beyond the Issue of Language." *Los Angeles Daily Journal,* July 25, 1986, p. 4.

Bergholz, Richard, and Ellen Hume. "Mailing by Hayakawa Sent Postage-Free." *Los Angeles Times,* January 25, 1983, part I, p. 16.

"Big Vote Against Non-English Ballots." Editorial. *San Francisco Chronicle,* November 9, 1984, p. 70.

Bikales, Gerda. "From the Editor's Desk: What Can One Person Do?" *Up-date,* September-October 1985, p. 7.

"Bilingual Education." *Los Angeles Times,* September 8, 1986, part II, p. 4.

"Bilingualism Leads to Superior Cognitive Abilities." *National Council of La Raza Education Network News,* September/October 1985, pp. 8–9.

"Bill Pushes an Official State Prejudice." Editorial. *Atlanta Constitution,* February 18, 1986, p. 22.

Billiter, Bill. "Alternatives Offered for Teaching English to Immigrant Child." *Los Angeles Times,* March 13, 1986, part II, p. 3.

_____. "Bilingualism: Is Immersion Method Best?" *Los Angeles Times,* April 17, 1986, part II, p. 1.

_____. "Public Forum Slated on 'English Only' Measure." *Los Angeles Times,* October 14, 1986, part II, p. 2.

_____. "Torres Blasts English-Only Initiative." *Los Angeles Times,* November 7, 1986, part II, p. 5.

"Bradley Assails 'English Only' Idea as 'Evil'." *Los Angeles Times,* July 15, 1986, part II, pp. 1, 2.

Brownstorm, Ronald, Richard E. Cohen and Rene T. Riley. "Great Debates: English As the Official Language." *National Journal,* October 4, 1986, p. 2388.

Buckley, William F. "Avoiding Canada's Problem." *National Review,* October 18, 1985, pp. 62–63.

Burciaga, Jose Antonio. "Beware of the Tall Ones." *Hispanic Link Weekly Report,* April 21, 1986, p. 3.

California. Assembly and Senate. Arturo Madrid Speaking on Proposition 63, Joint Legislative Committee, September 29, 1986 [text distributed by Tomás Rivera Center].

_____. Assembly Office of Research. *Moving Toward Citizenship: Immigration Reform and the English Language Amendment,* 1987.

"California Becomes Seventh State to Declare English Its Official Language in Landslide Election Victory." *Up-date,* November-December 1986, p. 1+.

"California Legislature Holds Hearings on English-Only." *San Francisco Chronicle,* September 30, 1986, p. 8.

Carlin, David R. "Charm and the English Language Amendment." *Christian Century,* September 19, 1984, pp. 822–823.

Castro, Ray. "Shifting the Burden of Bilingualism: The Case for Monolingual Communities." *The Bilingual Review,* 3.1, 1976, pp. 3–28.

Cazden, Courtney B., and David K. Dickinson. "Language in Education: Standardization Versus Cultural Pluralism." In Charles A. Ferguson and Shirley Brice Heath, *Language in the USA,* Cambridge: Cambridge University Press, 1981.

Chambers, Marcia. "California Braces for Change with English as Official Language." *New York Times,* November 26, 1986, p. A20.

Chapman, Stephen. "Make English the Official Language." *Chicago Tribune,* February 22, 1985, p. I15.

"Chávez Begins First Against 4 Propositions." *San Francisco Chronicle,* September 27, 1984, p. 11.

Chaze, William L. "Can Miami Cope with New Flood of Refugees?" *U.S. News and World Report,* May 12, 1980, pp. 55–56.

Church, George J. "The Welcome Wears Thin." *Time,* September 1, 1980, pp. 8–10.

Clines, Francis X. "The Mother Tongue Has a Movement." *New York Times,* June 3, 1984, sec. 4, p. E8.

Cohen, Richard. "English Will Only Get Better." *Washington Post,* Nov. 5, 1986, p. A21.

Combs, Mary Carol. "English-Only Movement Just Adds Insult to Injury." *Atlanta Journal and Constitution,* November 28, 1985, p. A17.

_____, and John Trasviña. "Legal Implications of the English Language Movement." In *The English Plus Project.* Washington, D.C.: The League of United Latin American Citizens, 1986, pp. 24–29.

Conklin, Nancy Faires, and Margaret A. Lourie. *A Host of Tongues: Language Communities in the United States.* New York: The Free Press, 1983.

Cooper, Robert E., and Roxana Ma, et al. *Bilingualism in the Barrio.* Bloomington: Indiana University Press, 1971.

Corwin, Miles. "It's Official: In Fillmore, You Have to Habla Inglés." *Los Angeles Times,* May 6, 1986, part I, pp. 3, 21.

Cox, Gail Diane. "Citizen Movement Seeks to Proclaim English 'Official'." *Los Angeles Daily Journal,* April 25, 1986, p. 1+.

Crawford, James. "Immersion Method Is Fairing Poorly in Bilingual Study." *IDRA* (Intercultural Development Research Association) *Newsletter,* June 1986, pp. 2–3, 7, 9–10, 12.

Crowell, Michael G. "American Traditions of Language Use: Their Relevance Today." *English Journal* **59,** 1970, pp. 109–115.

Dart, John. "Bishops Oppose English-Only Measure." *Los Angeles Times,* September 26, 1986, part I, p. 29.

"Debates Growing on Use of English: Ethnic Groups to Fight Official Language Plan in California." *New York Times,* July 21, 1986, pp. A1, A8.

del Olmo, Frank. "English Only Rules Are Un-American." *Los Angeles Times,* May 16, 1985, part II, p. 7.

————. "Make Something Happen—in Whatever Language." *Los Angeles Times,* January 7, 1985, part II, p. 15.

————. "Se Habla Inglés: Prop 63, A Cruel Joke, Could Cost Us Dearly." *Los Angeles Times,* August 28, 1986, part 2, p. 5.

————. "Ugly Or Polite, It's Racism." *Los Angeles Times,* October 31, 1986, part II, p. 7.

Donahue, Thomas S. "U.S. English: Its Life and Works." *International Journal of the Sociology of Language,* 1985, (56), pp. 99–112.

————. "Proposition 63: English Only." *Los Angeles Times,* September 29, 1986, part II, p. 8.

Drake, Glendon. "American Linguistic Prescriptivism: Its Decline and Revival in the 19th Century." *Language in Society,* 6, 1977, pp. 323–339.

Edwards, Don. "Bilingual Ballots," in *The English Plus Project.* Washington, D.C. The League of United Latin American Citizens, 1986, pp. 1–3.

Eng, Lilly. "Monterey Park Struggles to Speak with One Voice on English Issue." *Los Angeles Times,* November 30, 1986, part IX, p. 1.

————. "Monterey Park Voids Stand for English as Official Language." *Los Angeles Times,* October 29, 1986, part I, p. 35.

"English, a Durable Tongue." Editorial. *Christian Science Monitor,* July 24, 1986, p. 15.

"English Is Our Language Heritage." In Charles A. Ferguson and Shirley Brice Heath, *Language in the USA,* Cambridge: Cambridge University Press, 1981.

"English Isn't the Only Language We Speak (Letters)." *Washington Post,* August 9, 1986.

"The English Language Amendment (Rebuttal)." *English Journal* 77 (March 1988): 83–85.

"The English Language: Out to Conquer the World." *U.S. News and World Report,* February 1985, pp. 49–52.

"English-Only Foes Get Some Legislative Help." *Los Angeles Times,* August 14, 1986, part I, pp. 3, 36.

"English-Only Foes to Press Fillmore Fight." *Los Angeles Times,* March 13, 1986, part II, p. 8.

The English Only Movement: An Agenda for Discrimination. Special Convention Issue. The "English Plus" Project. Washington, D.C.: League of United Latin American Citizens, 1986.

"English Only on Ballot." *Hispanic Link Weekly Report,* July 7, 1985, p. 2.

English-Only: The Threat of Language Restrictions. Washington, D.C.: National Association of Latino Elected Officials, 1989.

"English, Sí; English Only, *No!*" Editorial. *Milwaukee Journal,* August 28, 1985.

"English Spoken Here." *Christian Science Monitor,* August 8, 1986, p. 14.

"English Spoken Here, O.K.? A California Crusade to Stamp Out Bilingualism." *Time,* August 25, 1986, p. 27.

"English, Yes; Zenophobia, No." Editorial. *New York Times,* November 10, 1986, p. 122.

Enríquez, Sam. "Object to Bilingual Program: Columbus Parents Ask for English-Only Classes. *Los Angeles Times,* November 21, 1986, part IX, p. 1.

————. "Parents Seek English-Only Classes." *Los Angeles Times,* November 24, 1985, part II, p. 17.

Estrada, Leobardo F. *California's Non-English Speakers.* Claremont, Calif.: Tomás Rivera Center, [1986].

Fallows, James. "Viva Bilingualism: English Has Nothing to Fear." *New Republic,* November 24, 1986, pp. 18–19.

Faris, Gerald. "U.S. Investigating Bias Complaint Against Bay Harbor Hospital." *Los Angeles Times,* February 2, 1986, part IX, p. 1.

Farr, Marcia, and Harvey Daniels. *Language Diversity and Writing Instruction.* New York: ERIC Clearinghouse on Urban Education, 1986.

Ferguson, Charles A. "Diglossia." In Dell Hymes, *Language in Culture and Society,* New York: Harper and Row, 1964.

Fernandez, Elizabeth. "Long Wait Greets Those Wanting to Learn English." *San Francisco Chronicle*, September 6, 1984, p. 8.

Field, Mervin. "Most Californians Want Ballots in English Only." *San Francisco Chronicle*, September 6, 1984, p. 8.

Foster, Barbara. "Public Libraries in Metropolitan Miami: ¿Aquí Se Habla Español?" *Journal of Ethnic Studies* 17 (1), 1989, 129–135.

Fowler, Roger. "Popular Attitudes to the Use of English." *Studia Neophilologica* 37:2, 1965, pp. 374–381.

Front, Rabbi Henri E. "English-Only: Is It Necessary? Measure Threatens to Divide Us and Tarnish Our Proud Heritage." *Los Angeles Times*, November 2, 1986, part II, p. 16.

García, Dawn. "Language Logjam: Students Swamp English Classes." *San Francisco Chronicle*, November 28, 1986, p. 1+.

Gillam, Jerry. "Initiative Seeks to Make English Official State Language: Campaign Finance Reform Measure Misses, But Toxics Crackdown Could Win a Spot on Ballot." *Los Angeles Times*, June 26, 1986, part I, p. 3.

González, Angelo. "Bilingualism, Pro: The Key to Basic Skills." *New York Times*, November 10, 1985, sec. XII, p. 62.

González, Roseann Duenas. "The English Language Amendment: Examining Myths." *English Journal* 77 (March 1988): pp. 24–30.

Gorney, Cynthia. "Bilingual Education's Dilemmas Persist." *Washington Post*, July 7, 1985, sec. I, p. A1.

Griffin, Bill. "Language Limits." *East Los Angeles Tribune*, October 2, 1985, p. A-10.

Grosjean, Francois. *Life in Two Languages: An Introduction to Bilingualism*, Cambridge: Harvard University Press, 1982.

Gutiérrez, Félix. "A New Language of California Commerce-Spanish." *Los Angeles Herald Examiner*, October 3, 1986, p. A15.

Hanzalek, Astrid T. "Connecticut Opinion: The Proper Role of Bilingual Education." *New York Times*, December 29, 1985, sec. IICN, p. 14.

"Hayakawa Accuses Hispanics of Pursuing a Separatist Agenda." *National Council of La Raza Education Network News*, March/April 1985, pp. 3–4.

Hayakawa, S.I. "A Common Language, So All Can Pursue Common Goals." *Los Angeles Times*, October 29, 1986, part II, p. 13.

_____. "English-Only: Linguistic Focusing . . . Or Fixing a Non-Problem?" *San Diego Union*, October 12, 1986, p. C1.

_____. "English (Only) Spoken Here." *California Magazine*, May 1986, pp. 95–107.

Hays, C.L. "Clamoring for English." *New York Times Education/Life Section*, January 4, 1987, p. 10.

Hefferman, Nancy. "Bill Introduced to Make English California's Official Language." *Los Angeles Times*, January 9, 1985, part I, p. 1.

Henry, William A. "Against a Confusion of Tongues." *Time*, June 13, 1983, p. 30.

Hernández, Antonia. "Let's Define the Agenda." *Hispanic Link Weekly Report*, November 24, 1986, p. 3.

Hernández, Marita. "Abolishment of Bilingual Ballots Sparks Anger." *Los Angeles Times*, August 9, 1984.

Hill, Gladwin. "Everyday Use of Foreign Languages Is Rising in U.S." *New York Times*, May 5, 1981, p. C20.

Hitchens, Robert C. "The Role of Spanish Language Media." In *The English Plus Project*. Washington, D.C.: The League of United Latin American Citizens, 1986, pp. 19–23.

Hockman, Anndee. "Fairfax: 'English and Only English': Educators Point to Test Scores as Proof of ESL's Success." *Washington Post*, July 9, 1985, sec. I, p. A8.

"How Miami Adjusted to Its Bilingual Ban." *San Francisco Chronicle*, October 20, 1986, p. A7.

Hudelson, Sarah. "The Role of Native Language Literacy in the Education of Language Minority Children." *Language Arts* 64 (December 1987): pp. 827–841.

Hughes, John. "English Spoken Here." *Christian Science Monitor*, August 9, 1986, p. 14.
"Ideas and Trends: Is English the Only Language for Government?" *New York Times*, October 26, 1986, sec. 4, p. 6.
In Defense of Our Common Language. Washington, D.C.: U.S. English, 1984.
"In Plain English." Editorial. *Los Angeles Times*, November 7, 1986, p. 14.
Ingram, Carl. "Prop. 63 Backers Aim at Bilingual Education." *Los Angeles Times*, November 24, 1986, p. I:3.
"Jingoism, In Any Language." Editorial. *New York Times*, October 11, 1980, p. A14.
Judd, Elliot L. "The English Language Amendment: A Case Study on Language and Politics." *TESOL Quarterly*, **21** (1), 1987, pp. 113–135.
"Judge Rejects Suit for Translations." *New York Times*, October 24, 1982, p. 149.
Kenji, Hakuta. *Mirror of Language: The Debate on Bilingualism*. New York: Basic Books, 1986.
Krebs, Albin. "Amendment Urged to Make English Official Language." *New York Times*, April 15, 1981, p. 28.
"Language: Issues and Legislation." *Harvard Encyclopedia of American Ethnic Groups*, Cambridge, Mass.: Belknap Press of Harvard University, 1980, pp. 619–629.
Language Loyalty in the United States. The Hague: Mouton, 1966.
"Language Wars in Florida." *Newsweek*, June 30, 1986, p. 24.
"Latinization of the Miami Area Is Showing No Signs of Abating." *New York Times*, April 18, 1973, p. 125.
"Latino, Asian Units Call English-Only Movement 'Un-American'." *Los Angeles Times*, August 21, 1986, part I, p. 23.
"Latinos Hit Firms' English Fluency Rule." *Los Angeles Times*, June 23, 1985, part II, p. 32.
Leibowitz, Arnold H. *Federal Recognition of the Rights of Language Minority Groups*. Rosslyn, Va.: National Clearinghouse for Bilingual Education, 1982.
_____. "The Official Character of Language in the United States: Literacy Requirements for Immigration, Citizenship, and Entrance Into American Life." *Aztlan*, **15** (Spring 1984): pp 27–70.
"Let's Not Speak English Only." Editorial. *Denver Post*, July 25, 1986, p. B6.
"Let's Say Adios to 'Official' English." Editorial. *Business Week*, Nov. 10, 1986, p. 154.
Lewis, Kathy. "Diametrically Opposed Views Surround Language Question." *Houston Post*, November 23, 1986, p. A:24.
Liebowicz, Joseph. "The Proposed English Language Amendment—Shield or Sword?" *Yale Law and Policy Review*, **3**, 1985, pp. 519–550.
Lindsey, Robert. "Debates Growing on Use of English: Ethnic Groups to Fight Official Language Plan in California." *New York Times*, July 21, 1986, part I, p. A1.
Llorente, Elizabeth. "Bilingual Family at Home." *New York Times*, November 10, 1985, sec. XII, p. 52.
Loo, Chalsa M. "The 'Biliterate' Ballot Controversy: Language Acquisition and Cultural Shift Among Immigrants." *International Migration Review* **19.3**, 1985, pp. 493–515.
Mcbee, Susanna. "English Out to Conquer the World." *U.S. News and World Report*, February 18, 1985, pp. 49–52.
McCain, John. "Bilingual Education: The Need for Equity." In *The English Plus Project*. Washington, D.C. The League of United Latin American Citizens, 1986, pp. 4–6.
Macías, Reynaldo. *Are English Language Amendments in the National Interest?* Claremont, Calif.: Tomás Rivera Center, 1989.
_____. "From Language Discrimination to Language Equity." [Claremont, Calif.: Tomás Rivera Center, 1986].
McManus, Walter S. "Labor Market Costs of Language Disparity: An Interpretation of Hispanic Earnings Differences." *American Economic Review* **75**, 1985, pp. 818–827.
Mallea, John R. *Quebec's Language Policies: Background and Reponse*, Quebec: Les Presses de l'Université Laval, 1977.

Malone, Julia. "Hispanic Groups Foresee Backlash, Ease Competition to Immigration Bills." *Christian Science Monitor*, April 2, 1985, p. 1.

Marshall, David F. "The Question of an Official Language: Language Rights and the English Language Amendment." *International Journal of the Sociology of Language* **60**, 1986, pp. 7–75.

Mathews, Jay. "Immigrant Dominance Sparring a Backlash: Town Turns Against Ethnic-American Leaders." *Washington Post*, May 10, 1986, sec. I, p. A3.

_____. "Initiative Seeks to Make English the Civil Tongue: Official Language Law Likely in California." *Washington Post*, October 11, 1986, sec. 1, p. A4.

May, Lee. "Alien Law Puts Strain on English Classes." *Los Angeles Times*, February 25, 1987, p. I16.

_____. "Battle over Bilingualism: Opposition Intensifies to Ads Using Spanish." *Los Angeles Times*, September 8, 1986, part I, p. 21.

_____. "English-Only Foes Line Up Behind U.S. Education Bill." *Los Angeles Times*, June 11, 1986, part I, p. 3.

_____. Latinos Assail Bilingual Education Plans." *Los Angeles Times*, January 25, 1986, part I, p. 3.

_____. "U.S. Faulted on Bilingual Education: GAO Says Misuse of Research Led to Criticism of Programs." *Los Angeles Times*, November 8, 1986, part I, p. 20.

Medley, Richard. "The Tower of Babel and the Winds of Destiny." *Hispanic Link*, October 27, 1985.

"A Melting Pot Heats Up." *Los Angeles Times*, July 18, 1986, part II, p. 10.

Michelson, H. "An English Only Crusade." *Macleans*, October 8, 1984, p. 8.

Mitchell, Henry. "On Speaking the Language." *Washington Post*, September 12, 1986, p. F:3.

"Monterey Park Library Caught in Political Cross-fire." *Library Journal* (December 1988): p. 20.

Murdock, Deroy, and Willie Brown, Jr. "Point Counterpoint: The English Language Amendment." *Point of View*, Fall 1986, pp. 17–19.

"NCLR Opposes Threats to Pluralism." *El Noticiario*, Third Quarter 1985, p. 5.

"N.Y. Caucus Responds to Prop. 63." *Hispanic Link Weekly Report*, November 24, 1986, p. 2.

"No on Proposition 63." Editorial. *San Francisco Chronicle*, October 20, 1986, p. A54.

"Norman Cousins Quits Group for English Language Prop. 63." *Orange County Register*, October 16, 1986, p. C2.

Not English Only, English Plus. Bilingual Education Issue Analysis. Miami, Florida: Spanish-American League Against Discrimination (SALAD) Education Committee, October 15, 1985.

Nunberg, Geoffrey. "An 'Official Language' for California?" *New York Times*, October 2, 1986, sec. A, p. 23.

"The 'Official Language'." Editorial. *Los Angeles Daily Journal*, June 20, 1986, p. 4.

"Outlawing Tongues." *Commonwealth*, December 5, 1986, pp. 648–649.

Pachon, Harry P. "Bilingual Education: A Vital Step in Mastering English." *Christian Science Monitor*, September 24, 1985, p. 15.

"Passage of Proposition 63 (Letters)." *Los Angeles Times*, November 14, 1986.

Pierce, Neil. "Here, Opportunity Speaks English: Will Bilingualism Condemn Immigrants to the Ultimate Racism?" *New York Times*, June 26, 1983, p. D5.

"Proposition 63: Official Language (Letters)." *Los Angeles Times*, October 18, 1986, part II, p. 2.

"_____." *Los Angeles Times*, November 1, 1986, part II, p. 4.

"Proposition 63: Se Habla Inglés (Letters)." *Los Angeles Times*, September 13, 1986, part II, p. 4.

"Quebec's Legislature Again Makes English an Official Language." *Wall Street Journal*, December 17, 1979, p. 9.

Ramírez, J.D. "Comparing Structured English Immersion and Bilingual Education: First Year Results of a National Study." *American Journal Education* 95, 1986, pp. 122–148.

Reese, Michael, and Gerald C. Lubenow. "California Blahs." *Newsweek*, October 20, 1986, p. 35.

Remarks of Hon. Baltasar Corrada Resident Commissioner from Puerto Rico on Senate Joint Resolution 167, Congress of the United States, House of Representatives. Washington, D.C., June 12, 1984.

"Report to the Network." *La Red/The Net: Newsletter of the National Chicano Council on Higher Education.* October 1986, pp. 1–4.

Reyes, David. "Boos Greet Prop. 63 Debator in Barrio: Santa Ana Audience Critical of English Language Measure." *Los Angeles Times*, October 15, 1986, part II, p. 4.

Rodríguez, Richard. "Bilingualism, Con: Outdated and Unrealistic." *New York Times*, November 10, 1985, sec. 12, p. 63.

––––––––. "Prop. 63 Would Betray State's Future." *Los Angeles Times*, October 26, 1986, part IV, pp. 1–2.

––––––––. "S.I.N. Is In." *California Magazine*, April 1986, pp. 79–109.

––––––––. "Unilingual, Not Unilateral." *Wall Street Journal*, June 25, 1985.

Rokyo, Mike. "Stamp of Approval for Native Tongue." *Chicago Tribune*, September 18, 1986, p. I8.

San Miguel, Guadalupe. *One Country, One Language: A Historical Sketch of English Language Movements in the U.S.* Claremont, Calif.: Tomás Rivera Center, 1986.

Sanoff, Alvin P., and Lucía Solorzano. "It's at Home Where Our Language Is in Distress." *U.S. News and World Report*, February 18, 1985, pp. 54–57.

Se Habla (Solamente) Inglés Aguí: English (Only) Spoken Here . . . or Should Be." *California Magazine*, May 1986, pp. 95, 105–107.

"Seeing the Light (Editorial)." *Los Angeles Times*, October 24, 1986, part II, p. 4.

"Senator Torres Supports Efforts to Promote English Proficiency." *News from Senator Art Torres*, (press release #16) April 4, 1986.

Setting the Record Straight: Dispelling the Campaigns Myths Behind Proposition 63. [Oakland, Calif.: Californians United Against Proposition 63, 1986].

Sillas, Herman. "English Is Just a Language." *Hispanic Link*, January 27, 1985.

Simon, Paul. "Expanding Language Horizons: English Plus." In *The English Plus Project*. Washington, D.C.: The League of United Latin American Citizens, 1986, pp. 7–10.

Skelton, George. "Deukmejian Opposes 3 Controversial Propositions." *Los Angeles Times*, September 3, 1986, part I, p. 3.

"Speaking the Legal Language." *Orange County Register*, October 12, 1986, p. L6.

"Special Report: Short Answers to Common Questions About Bilingual Education," *Agenda*, Fourth Quarter, 1981.

Stalker, James C. "Official English or English Only." *English Journal* 77 (March 1988): pp. 18–23.

Stencel, Sandra. "Bilingual Education: Melting Pot vs. Cultural Pluralism." *Editorial Research Reports*, August 19, 1977.

Stewart, Jill. "Challenged English-Only Rule: Panel Rejects Court Clerk Plea." *Los Angeles Times*, January 31, 1985, part IX, p. 1.

––––––––. "Huntington Park Judges 'Incredulous': English-Only Rule Still Creating Uproar." *Los Angeles Times*, April 11, 1985, part IX, p. 1.

"Suit Challenges Court English-Only Rule." *Los Angeles Times*, March 24, 1985, part I, p. 16.

Sundberg, Trudy J. "The Case Against Bilingualism." *English Journal* 77 (March 1988): pp. 16–17.

Tanzer, Andrew. "Little Taipei." *Forbes* (Monterey Park, California), May 8, 1985, p. 88.

"'Temporary' Bilingual Education Lives On." *Washington Times*, August 18, 1983.

Torres, Arnoldo S. "English-Only Movement Fosters Divisiveness." *Interracial Books for Children Bulletin* 17 (3–4) 1986, pp. 18–19.

_____. *Testimony on S.J. Res. 167 English Language Amendment Before the Senate Judiciary Subcommittee on the Constitution.* Washington, D.C.: League of United Latin American Citizens, 1984.

Trasviña, John. "An Unethical Proposition." *Political Review* (Santa Barbara, Calif.), October 7, 1986, pp. 4, 8.

_____. *Official English/English-Only: More Than Meets the Eye.* Washington, D.C.: National Education Association, 1988.

Trasviña, John D. "Official Language Means Discrimination." *USA Today,* July 25, 1986.

Trombley, William. "Assemblyman Vows to Carry the Ball for English-Only Action." *Los Angeles Times,* November 6, 1986, part I, pp. 3, 31.

_____. "California Elections: English-Only Proposition Kindles Minorities' Fears." *Los Angeles Times,* October 12, 1986, part I, pp. 1, 29, 30.

_____. "California Elections: Many Supporters Also Favor Bilingual Education, Ballots: Latino Backing of 'English-Only' a Puzzle." *Los Angeles Times,* October 25, 1986, part II, p. 5.

_____. "Norman Cousins Drops His Support of Prop. 63." *Los Angeles Times,* October 16, 1986, part I, pp. 3, 22.

_____. "Prop. 63 Backer Will Try to Defeat Opposing Candidates." *Los Angeles Times,* October 1, 1986, part I, p. 3.

_____. "Prop. 63 Roots Traced to Small Michigan City: Measure to Make English Official Language of State Sprang from Concern Over Immigration, Population." *Los Angeles Times,* October 20, 1986, part I, p. 3.

_____. "Prop. 63—The Latest Battle in War of Words Over Language." *Los Angeles Times,* October 21, 1986, part I, p. 3.

Trueba, Henry T. "Instructional Effectiveness: English-Only for Speakers of Other Languages?" *Education and Urban Society* 2 (August 1988): pp. 341–62.

Tucker, G. Richard. "Implications of Canadian Research for Promoting a Language Competent American Society." In *The English Plus Project.* Washington, D.C.: The League of United Latin American Citizens, 1986, pp. 11–18.

"Unassimilated Illegal Immigrants Imperil Society, Lamm Tells Panel." *Los Angeles Times,* May 30, 1986, part I, p. 4.

"United States Moving Toward a Bilingual Society?" *English Around the World,* 29.4, 1983, p. 7+.

United States. Congress. Senate. Senator Huddleston speaking to propose an amendment to the Constitution of the United States with respect to the English Language. S.J. Res. 167, 98th Cong., 1st sess., September 19, 1983. *Congressional Record.* vol. 129.

_____. _____. _____. Subcommittee on the Constitution of the Committee on the Judiciary. *Hearings on the English Language Amendment,* 98th Congress, 2nd. sess. SJ Resolution 167. Washington: GPO, 1985.

Veltman, Calvin J. "The Evolution of Ethno-Linguistic Frontiers in the United States and Canada." *Social Science Journal,* 14, No. 1, pp. 47–58.

Ward, Mike. "Language Problem Arises in City: Monterey Park Argues Over English vs. Chinese Signs." *Los Angeles Times,* November 23, 1985, part V, p. 5.

_____. "Language Rift in All American City." *Los Angeles Times,* November 13, 1985, sec. CC, part II.

_____, and Victor Valle. "Attempts to Make English Official Language Set Back." *Los Angeles Times,* November 27, 1985, part II, p. 5.

"We Don't Need Laws to Protect English." *USA Today,* July 25, 1986.

"Why English Is So Easy to Mangle." *U.S. News and World Report,* February 18, 1985, p. 53.

"Why English Should Be Our Official Language." *Education Digest* 50:9, 1987, pp. 36–37.

Will, George F. "In Defense of the Mother Tongue." *Newsweek,* July 8, 1985, p. 78.

"Wilson Backs Initiative for English-Only Law in State." *Los Angeles Times,* August 21, 1986, part I, pp. 3, 23.

Woo, Elaine. "Immigrants: A Rush to the Classrooms." *Los Angeles Times,* September 24, 1986, part I, pp. 1, 28, 29.

"Words of War: Proliferation of Spanish in U.S. Inspires Action Against Bilingualism: Some Even Want to Amend the Constitution to Give English Protected Status." *Wall Street Journal,* July 22, 1985, pp. 1 + .

Worsnop, Richard L. "Bilingualism Controversy." *Editorial Research Reports,* November 10, 1980.

Wright, Guy. "U.S. English." *San Francisco Sunday Examiner and Chronicle,* n.d., p. B-9.

Yardley, Jonathan. "Bilingualism and the Backlash." *Washington Post,* July 28, 1986, sec. D2.

"You'd Be a Nobody If They Didn't Make You Learn English." *Christian Science Monitor,* April 20, 1983, p. 22.

Yzaguirre, Raul. "English Only Amendments: Are They Necessary?" *NCLR Noticiero/News Release,* June 12, 1984.

————. "The Perils of Pandora." *Hispanic Link,* April 20, 1986.

————. "A Positive Response to English-Only Advocates." *Hispanic Link,* April 20, 1986.

————. "Put Up or Shut Up." *National Council of La Raza Education Network News,* March/April 1985, pp. 7–9.

APPENDIX A:

¿Habla usted

ESPAÑOL?

¿Tiene usted una

PREGUNTA?

?

Su biblioteca puede
ayudarle a encontrar
lo que busca

On its fourth page: "This brochure provided by CORE, California Opportunities for Reference Excellence; this project is funded through the Library Services and Construction Act."

145

¿QUÉ, CÓMO, CUÁNDO Y DÓNDE?

La biblioteca provee libros y revistas en español para niños y adultos, así como las respuestas a preguntas específicas que Ud. pueda tener.

Por ejemplo:

• Cómo podría reparar mi automóvil?

• Dóndo podría encontrar discos y cassettes para aprender inglés?

• Cuáles son los requisitos para adquirir ciudadanía de los Estados Unidos?

• Qué es hipertensión?

• Cuándo debo vacunar a mi bebé?

Por el momento, no tenemos disponible ningún empleado que hable español, pero si escribe su pregunta en español en la sección interior, haremos todo lo posible para brindarle la información que desea...

SPANISH LANGUAGE REFERENCE IN-TAKE FORM

Sírvase darnos su nombre, dirección y número de teléfono para así poderlo(a) localizar cuando la respuesta esté lista o en caso que nosotros necesitemos más información para encontrar la respuesta a su pregunta.

En caso que tengamos que enviar su solicitud a otra biblioteca, le estaremos agradecidos si nos indica si necesita la información para una fecha fija; Muchas gracias!

NOMBRE   . FECHA DE LIMITE

CALLE   # DE APTO.   CIUDAD   CODIGO POSTAL

NUMERO DE TELEFONO Y LA MEJOR HORA PARA LLAMARLE*

Por favor escriba su pregunta en español, describiendo lo más claro posible, lo que desea saber:

Otros datos que pudiesen ayudarnos a encontrar el libro o la respuesta que Ud. necesita: (Sírvase encerrar en un círculo la respuesta apropiada).

PARA QUIEN?   CUANTA INFORMACION?   QUE IDIOMA?

-Para niño?   -Breve?   -Sólo español.

-Para adulto?   -Otro _____   -Español y/o Ingles.

   Información Básica?   -Otro _____
            o
   Información Técnica?

POR FAVOR ENTREGUE ESTE PAPEL A LA/EL BIBLIOTECARIA/O. NOS COMPLACE MUCHO EL SERVIRLO(A)!

LIBRARY WORKSPACE:

              Library: _____

              Staff Contact: _____

              Phone No. _____

              Date: _____

Reproduced at 50 percent of original size.

APPENDIX B:
RASD GUIDELINES FOR
LIBRARY SERVICES TO HISPANICS

RASD Committee on Library Services
to the Spanish Speaking*

1. Introduction

In this document the RASD Committee on Library Services to the Spanish Speaking has reached a goal in the articulation of long-awaited Guidelines to reach this important minority community. Provision of library services to Hispanics can prove to be complex: nationality, regional differences and culture provide a myriad of combinations for that single community. As an example, there are significant linguistic and cultural differences reflected in the varieties of Spanish spoken by Mexicans, Puerto Ricans, Cubans and other Hispanic groups. To recognize these differences and to respond correctly to them is a major theme within these Guidelines.

REFORMA, the National Association to Promote Library Services to the Spanish-Speaking, has taken an active role in the production of this document: one committee member served as liaison to REFORMA, and the organization has given input and has reviewed the final document.

Although these guidelines were written by persons with professional interest in service to Hispanics, they were written consciously for all librarians who only now may have begun to require the initiation of service to this population. In that sense, the Guidelines are a basic beginners manual intended for a hypothetical librarian whom we envisioned as an administrator of a medium-to-small institution which has become aware of the needs of an Hispanic community within its service area. As with any guideline, this one is designed to aid in the development of that service and to remind readers of professional concerns regarding the target population and of the staff who work with that population.

Although the committee is aware of numerous terms for his target population, it has chosen the word "Hispanic" as that term has been used in the 1980 Census.†

Reprinted by permission of the American Library Association.
†*U.S. Department of Commerce, Bureau of the Census. 1980 Census of Population, General Social and Economic Characteristics: U.S. Summary, Appendix, pp. B-4, B-5.*

2. *Collection and Selection of Materials*

The Hispanic communities in the United States do not speak and read only Spanish; nor do they speak and read only English; nor are they bilingual. The Hispanic communities have diverse needs, and are entitled to materials and access to those materials diverse enough to meet those needs. As with all activities involving the selection process, there are standard criteria to aid in the selection of library materials.

2.1 *Relevancy*   The selection of library materials for Hispanics should meet the educational and recreational needs of the community by providing relevant and culturally sensitive materials. Stereotypes should be avoided.

2.2 *Language*   The collection should contain materials in English and bilingual materials. Materials selected should reflect the particular linguistic characteristics of the community served. They should also include standard Spanish language titles from Spain and other Hispanic cultures.

2.3 *Physical Access*   If a separate collection of materials for Hispanics is maintained by the library, it should be visible and accessible to the community. In libraries which do not separate these materials, adherence to 2.4 is strongly recommended.

2.4 *Bibliographic Access*   Bibliographic access to the library's collection should include Spanish language subject headings in the public catalog when appropriate for the population served. Locally produced access and identification aids including lists, bibliographies and point of use bibliographic instructional materials should be in Spanish when appropriate.

2.5 *Formats*   Print and non-print materials, whether they be educational or recreational, should be included.

3. *Programs, Services and Community Relations*

Programming, both traditional and non-traditional, is an effective vehicle to attract and meet the needs of the Hispanic community. This is particularly true for those who have recently immigrated and who are unfamiliar with the library services available in the United States. As a result of the potentially limited resources available for service to Hispanics within any given institution, cooperation among all libraries serving the target population is encouraged. Such cooperation may manifest itself in the sharing of costs of programs, cooperative acquisitions or joint borrowing privileges to name but a few.

3.1 *Diversity of Culture*   Because the population served may be composed of several different Hispanic cultures, each specific culture must be considered in the development of programming and should be accurately reflected in its content.

3.2   *Outreach Services*   In order to aid in the planning and delivery of library services to meet community needs, there should be an ongoing process of community analysis and assessment. To further these aims:
   (1)   the library should participate in the work of local community organizations of Hispanics;
   (2)   the library should work with such organizations in the development and presentation of library programs and services.

3.3   *Inter-Cultural Understanding*   As part of its activities in working with local populations in which is represented a multiplicity of cultures, the library should actively promote inter-cultural communication and cooperation among those cultures represented.

3.4   *Service to Non-User*   Attention should be paid to the library non-user. Programs, literature and publicity should be used in non-traditional ways and in settings designed to attract those for whom libraries are not part of the experience of life.

3.5   *Bibliographic Instruction* should be made in Spanish when necessary.

3.6   *Language*   In keeping with the ALA policy in support of multilingual services, the choice of language to be used for programming and services (Spanish, English, bilingual or monolingual) as well as vocabulary, accent and nuance must be carefully selected. Choices should be based upon the characteristics of the local community.

4. *Personnel*

Librarians serving Hispanic communities should be actively recruited. Contact should be made with Hispanic graduates of American Library Association accredited library education programs, and extensive use should be made of hot lines, minority recruiting services and services provided by Hispanic library organizations. Professional staff should be recruited from library education programs accredited by the American Library Association. It is also recommended that in all cases, written personnel procedures and affirmative action programs should be established and fully implemented. See ALA Policy Manual for amplification of these.

4.1   Qualifications—Professional and Support Staff
   (1)   In order to be sensitive to the library and information needs of the Hispanic community, in addition to the standards required of librarians and support staff, bilingualism and biculturalism are qualities that should be sought in order to enhance the service delivery to this large and growing community.
   (2)   Bilingual/bicultural librarians and support staff should be adequately compensated in positions where job specifications or actual conditions require the knowledge of Spanish.

4.2   *Staff Development*
   (1) Librarians and support staff should be provided opportunities to exchange information and ideas as well as the opportunity to participate in continuing education programs which would enhance the services provided to libraries in Hispanic communities. Examples of programs that could be explored include training in: English as a second language, acquisition of Spanish language materials, citizenship requirements and community information services.
   (2) Opportunities for advancement should be provided and encouraged by the library administration.

5. Buildings

The library building, through its location, architecture, or appearance, should be an attraction, not a barrier, to members of the Hispanic community.

5.1   *Interior and Exterior*   While the structure may not be altered in any significant way, interior and exterior decor can be modified by choosing decorations and graphics to create an ambiance suitable to the clientele to be served. Care must be taken that the alterations made will conform to the culture of the community.
5.2   *Signage* in any library serving a bilingual community, signs should be bilingual. Attention must be paid to the particular dialect of Spanish used so that the wording, phraseology and connotation of the language conform to the culture of the community. Signage should be both prominent and visible.
5.3   *Location* when it is possible to control the location of the library within the community to be served, a location should be considered that will induce the target population into the library. When space is allocated within the existing structures, it should be both visible and accessible.

Adopted by the American Library Association in June 1988.

APPENDIX C:
"SAY SÍ" MANUAL

Queens Borough Public Library

This manual has been prepared by the Queens Library's Hispanic Committee to help the Queens Borough Public Library staff assist Spanish-speaking patrons with a limited command of English. Non-Spanish speaking staff should locate the appropriate answer in the manual and point to the Spanish translation for the patron to read. This manual is a project in the library's "Say Sí to Your Library" outreach campaign.

Credits   September 1988

The Queens Borough Public Library's Hispanic Committee thanks the Library Awareness Project of the South Bay Cooperative Library System, California, for permission to adapt its manual published in 1986.

Hispanic Committee, Queens Library

Ronald Alvarez	Amado González
Harriet Benjamin	Diane Guzzo
Zoila Bravo	Ruth Herzberg
Sue Fontaine	Rina Jiménez
	Adriana A. Tandler

María A. Fiol, chair

Lost Library Cards

Patron	**Library Employee**
1) I lost my library card.	1) You will have to pay $1.00 for the replacement of your card and show proper I.D. (driver's license, recent telephone, gas or electric bill).
Perdí mi tarjeta de la biblioteca	Tendrá que pagar $1.00 y mostrar identificación apropiada (licencia de conducir, cuenta reciente de

152

teléfono, gas o electricidad) para reemplazar su tarjeta.

Please give me your name and address so I can check your record and withdraw your lost library card. If you do find it, do not use it because it will not be valid.

Por favor, deme su nombre y dirección para poder buscar su archivo y anular su tarjeta perdida. Si la llega a encontrar no la use, ya que ha quedado anulada.

Patrons Inquiring About Children's Services

Patron

1) Is there a special area in the library for children?

   ¿Hay un área especial para niños en la biblioteca?

2) Is it true that there are special programs for children?

   ¿Es cierto que hay programas especiales para niños?

3) Where are the children's Spanish language books?

   ¿Dónde están los libros en español para niños?

4) Does the library have a children's story hour?

   ¿Tiene la biblioteca hora de cuentos para niños?

Library Employee

1) Yes, let me tell you where it is.

   Sí, déjeme mostrarle donde está.

2) The librarian will tell you about special programs for children.

   La/el bibliotecaria/o le informará sobre los programas especiales para niños.

3) The Spanish language books for children are in the Children's Room.

   Los libros en español para niños están en la sala de niños.

4) Please go the children's room and ask the librarian.

   Por favor vaya a la sala de niños y pregúntele a la/el bibliotecaria/o.

Juvenile Patron Applying for a Library Card

Patron

1) How can I check out books?

   ¿Cómo puedo sacar libros?

Library Employee

1) You need a library card.

   Necesita tener una tarjeta de la biblioteca.

2) I would like to have a library card.

Quisiera tener una tarjeta de la biblioteca.

2) What grade are you in?

¿En que grado estás?

Adult Patron Applying for a Library Card

Patron

1) How can I check out books?

¿Cómo puedo sacar libros?

2) I would like to have a library card.

Me gustaría tener una tarjeta de la biblioteca.

Library Employee

1) You need a library card.

Necesita tener una tarjeta de la biblioteca.

2) a. If you want to take out two books today, you must show me some identification with your name and address, such as a driver's license, recent telephone bill or a recent gas or electric bill.

Si usted quiere dos libros hoy, tiene que mostrarme alguna identificación con su nombre y dirección, por ejemplo una licencia de conducir o una cuenta reciente de teléfono, de gas o de electricidad.

2) b. (If patron provides the proper I.D.) Please fill out this application. Self address and sign this post card. When you receive this post card in the mail, bring it with you to the library, and you will receive your card. You may check out two books today.

(Si el cliente enseña la identificación apropiada) Ahora, por favor, llene esta solicitud, ponga su nombre y dirección en esta tarjeta postal y fírmela. Cuando reciba por correo esta tarjeta postal, tráigala a la biblioteca y le daremos su tarjeta de la biblioteca. Hoy puede sacar dos libros.

2) c. If you do not wish to check out books today, or do not have the proper I.D., please self address and sign this post card. When you receive this post card in the mail,

bring it with you to the library and
you will receive your card.

**Si no quiere sacar libros hoy o si no
tiene la identificación apropiada,
por favor, ponga su nombre y dirección en esta tarjeta postal, y fírmela.
Cuando reciba por correo esta tarjeta postal tráigala a la biblioteca y
le daremos su tarjeta de la biblioteca.**

Miscellaneous Questions

Patron

1) Where is the bathroom?

   ¿Dónde está el baño?

2) Where is the water fountain?

   ¿Dónde está la fuente de agua?

3) Do you have a copy machine?

   **¿Tiene una máquina de hacer
   copias?**

4) Where is the children's library?

   ¿Dónde esta la biblioteca de niños?

5) Where is the film being shown?

   ¿Dónde se exhiben las películus?

6) Where is the Auditorium?

   ¿Dónde está el Auditorium?

Library Employee

1) Let me show you where it is.

   Déjeme mostrarle donde está.

2) We don't have a water fountain.

   No tenemos fuente de agua.

3) Yes, let me show you where it is.

   Sí, déjeme mostrarle donde está.

4) The children's library is on the:
   a—first floor
   b—second floor

   **La biblioteca de niños está en:
   a—el primer piso
   b—el segundo piso**

5) The film is being shown in the
   Auditorium.

   **Las películas se exhiben en el Audi-
   torium.**

6) The Auditorium is in:
   a—the basement
   b—first floor
   c—second floor

   **El Auditorium está en:
   a—el sótano
   b—el primer piso
   c—el segundo piso**

Using the Library

Patron

1) Do I have to buy the books or rent them?

   ¿Tengo que comprar los libros o alquilarlos?

2) I understand the library services are free.

   Tengo entendido que los servicios de la biblioteca son gratis.

3) What if the library is closed when I come to return the books?

   ¿Y si la biblioteca está cerrada cuando venga a devolver los libros?

4) How much is the fine?

   ¿Cuánto es la multa?

5) How long can I have the books?

   ¿Por cuánto tiempo puedo tener los libros?

Library Employee

1) No, the books belong to the library. We lend them free of charge.

   No, los libros pertenecen a la biblioteca. Nosotros los prestamos gratis.

2) Yes, but if you return a book late, you will have to pay a fine.

   Sí, pero si usted devuelve los libros tarde, tendrá que pagar una multa.

3) In the Central Library in Jamaica, you may deposit books in the book slot when the library is closed. In the branches, book slots will not be open overnight or on week-ends.

   En la Biblioteca Central de Jamaica, usted puede depositar los libros en el buzón cuando la biblioteca esté cerrada.
   En las bibliotecas-sucursales que tengan buzones, estos no estarán abiertos de noche, ni durante los fines de semana.

4) The fine is 10¢ a day per adult book, cassette or record, and 2¢ a day for a juvenile book, cassette or record.

   La multa es 10¢ diarios por cada libro, cassette o disco de adultos y 2¢ diarios por cada libro, cassette o disco de ninos.

5) Books are checked out for three weeks (21 days). Some books may only be checked out for one week (7 days). Music records, cassettes and magazines may only be checked out for one week (7 days). Language and book cassettes can be checked out for three weeks (21 days). Some materials are for reference only. They cannot be checked out, but you may use them in the library.

   Los libros se prestan por tres semanas (21 dias). Algunos solamente se pueden sacar por una semana (7 dias). Revistas, discos y cassettes musicales se prestan por solo una semana (7 dias). Los cassettes para estudiar idiomas y los libros en cassette se pueden sacar prestados por tres semanas (21 dias). Algunos materiales son de consulta y estos no se pueden sacar pero los puede usar en la biblioteca.

6) How many books can I take out?

6) You are allowed to take out as many books as you like.

¿Cuántos libros puedo sacar?

Se le permite sacar todos los libros que desee.

7) Is it possible to renew this book?

7) Yes, generally it is possible to renew a book.

¿Podría prorrogar el préstamo de este libro?

Sí, generalmente se permite prorrogar el préstamo de los libros.

Vocabulary—English to Spanish

A

address	la dirección
adult	el adulto
application	la solicitud
around the corner	a la vuelta (de la esquina)
art	el arte
astronomy	la astronomía
auditorium	el auditorio
author/writer	el autor/el escritor
auto repair	reparación de autos
autobiography	la autobiografía

B

bathroom	el baño
bible	la biblia
bibliography	la bibliografía
biology	la biología
book	el libro
bookstack	los estantes de libros
bookstore	la librería

borrow	tomar prestado
branch	la sucursal
building	el edificio
business	el comercio/el negocio

C

car	el carro/el automóvil
card catalog	el catálogo
cassette	el cassette
change	el cambio
to check out	tomar prestado/ sacar
chemistry	la química
children's room	la sala para niños
circulation desk	el escritorio de circulación
citizenship	la ciudadanía
classification number	el número de clasificación
clock	el reloj
closed	cerrado
computer	la computadora

cookbook	el libro de cocina
copy	la copia
copy machine	la máquina foto- statica
	la máquina de copiar
crafts	las artesanías

D

desk	el escritorio
director	el director
downstairs	abajo
driver's license	la licencia para manejar

E

economics	la economía
education	la educación
elevator	el elevador
employee	el empleado
English	el inglés
entrance	la entrada
envelope	el sobre
exit	la salida

F

federal	federal
fiction	ficción
file	el archivo
(to) fill out/fill in	llenar
film	la película
fine	la multa
forms	las planillas
free	gratis

G

gardening	la jardinería
geography	la geografía
geology	la geología
good-bye	adiós
government	el gobierno
government documents	los documentos del gobierno
guide	la guía

H

hello	hola
history	la historia
homework	la tarea
hour	la hora
house	la casa

I

income tax	el impuesto de ingresos
index	el índice
information	la información

K

key	la llave

L

language	la lengua/el idioma
last name	el apellido
law	la ley/el derecho
to the left	a la izquierda
lend	prestar
letter	la carta
librarian	la bibliotecaria el bibliotecario
library	la biblioteca
library card	la tarjeta de la biblioteca
literature	la literatura
location	la localidad/el lugar
(to) look for	buscar

M

magazine	la revista/las revistas
magazine index	el índice de revistas
map	el mapa
math	las matemáticas
medicine	la medicina

microfilm reader	la máquina de microfilm	report	el reporte
microform	la microformata	research	la investigación
music	la música	research paper	el trabajo de investigación
		(to) return	devolver
		right, to the	a la derecha

N

name	el nombre
new books	los libros nuevos
newspaper	el periódico
non-fiction	no-ficción
novel	la novela

S

school	la escuela
science	la ciencia
scrap paper	el papel borrador/ el papel para notas

O

outside	afuera
overdue	vencido

sociology	la sociología
Spanish	el español
Spanish language books	los libros en español
special collection	la colección especial
sports	los deportes
staircase	la escalera
stamp	la estampilla/el sello
state	el estado
story	el cuento/la historia
street	la calle
subject	el tema

P

painting	la pintura
pamphlet	el folleto
paper	el papel
paperback	el libro de bolsillo
parking lot	el estacionamiento
pen	la pluma
pencil	el lápiz
periodical room	la sala de periódicos
photography	la fotografía
physics	la física
please	por favor
poetry	la poesía
program	el programa
psychology	la psicología

T

table	la mesa
taxes	los impuestos
telephone	el teléfono
telephone books	la guía de teléfonos
telephone number	el número de teléfono
thank you	gracias
time	el tiempo/la hora
title	el título/los títulos
travel	el viaje
typewriter	la máquina de escribir

R

records	los discos
reference desk	el escritorio de referencia el escritorio de consulta
religion	la religión
(to) renew	renovar

U

upstairs	arriba

W

water fountain	la fuente de agua
weather	el tiempo

Y

you're welcome	de nada/no hay de que

Z

zip code	la zona postal

Vocabulary — Spanish to English

A

abajo	downstairs
adios	good-bye
adulto	adult
afuera	outside
apellido	last name
archivo	file
arriba	upstairs
arte	art
artesanías	crafts
astronomía	astronomy
auditorio	auditorium
automóvil	car
autor	author
autobiografía	autobiography

B

baño	bathroom
biblia	bible
bibliografía	bibliography
bibliotecario/ bibliotecaria	librarian
biografía	biography
biología	biology
buscar	to look for

C

cambio	change
carro	car
carta	letter
cassettes	cassettes
catálogo	card catalog
cerrado	closed
ciencia	science
cuidadanía	citizenship
colección especial	special collection
comercio	business
computadora	computer
copia	copy
cuento	story

D

de nada	you're welcome
deportes	sports
(a la) derecha	to the right
dirección	address
director	director
discos	records
documentos del gobierno	government documents

E

economía	economics
edificio	building
educación	education
elevador	elevator
empleado	employee
entrada	entrance

escalera	staircase
escritor	writer
escritorio	desk
escritorio de circulación	circulation desk
escritorio de consulta	reference desk
escuela	school
español	Spanish
estacionamiento	parking lot
estado	state
estampilla	stamp
estantes de libros	bookstacks

F

federal	federal
ficción	fiction
física	physics
folleto	pamphlet
fotografía	photography
fuente	fountain

G

geografía	geography
geología	geology
gobierno	government
gracias	thank you
gratis	free
guerra	war
guía	guide
guía de teléfonos	telephone books

H

historia	history
hola	hello
hora	hour/time
hora de cuentos	story hour

I

idioma	language
impuestos	taxes

índice	index
índice de revistas	magazine index
información	information
inglés	English
investigación	research
(a la) izquierda	to the left

J

jardinería	gardening

L

lápiz	pencil
lengua	language
ley	law
librería	bookstore
libro	book
libro de bolsillo	paperback
libro de cocina	cookbook
libros en español	Spanish language books
libros nuevos	new books
licencia para manejar	driver's license
literatura	literature
localidad	location
llave	key
llenar	to fill out/fill in
lugar	location

M

mapa	map
máquina de copiar	copy machine
máquina foto-stática	
máquina de escribir	typewriter
máquina de microfilm	microfilm reader
matemáticas	math
medicina	medicine
mesa	table
microformata	microform

multa	fine	reserva	reserve
música	music	revista	magazine

N

S

negocio	business
no-ficción	non-fiction
nombre	name
novela	novel
número de clasificación	classification number
número de teléfono	telephone number

sala de periodi-cos	periodical room
sacar	take out/check out
sala para niños	children's room
salida	exit
sello	stamp
sobre	envelope
sociología	sociology
solicitud	application
sucursal	branch

P

T

papel	paper
papel borrador	scrap paper
papel para notas	scrap paper
película	film
periódico	newspaper
pintura	painting
planillas	forms
pluma	pen
poesía	poetry
por favor	please
prestar	lend
programa	program
psicología	psychology

tarea	homework
tarjeta de bib-lioteca	library card
teléfono	telephone
tema	subject
tiempo	time/weather
título	title
tomar prestado	to borrow
trabajo	paper
trabajo de in-vestigación	research paper

Q

V

química	chemistry

vencido	overdue
viaje	travel
vuelta de la esquina, (a la)	around the corner

R

Z

religión	religion
reloj	clock
renovar	renew
reparación de autos	auto repair
reporte	report
reprografía	photocopies

zona postal	zip code

Months of the Year
Los Meses del Año

enero	January
febrero	February
marzo	March
abril	April
mayo	May
junio	June
julio	July
agosto	August
septiembre	September
octubre	October
noviembre	November
diciembre	December

Days of the Week
Los Dias de la Semana

lunes	Monday
martes	Tuesday
miércoles	Wednesday
jueves	Thursday
viernes	Friday
sábado	Saturday
domingo	Sunday

Numbers
Los Numeros

uno	one	1
dos	two	2
tres	three	3
cuatro	four	4
cinco	five	5
seis	six	6
siete	seven	7
ocho	eight	8
nueve	nine	9
diez	ten	10
once	eleven	11
doce	twelve	12
trece	thirteen	13
catorce	fourteen	14
quince	fifteen	15

dieciseis	sixteen	16
diecisiete	seventeen	17
dieciocho	eighteen	18
diecinueve	nineteen	19
veinte	twenty	20
treinta	thirty	30
cuarenta	forty	40
cincuenta	fifty	50
sesenta	sixty	60
setenta	seventy	70
ochenta	eighty	80
noventa	ninety	90
cien, ciento	one hundred	100
doscientos	two hundred	200
trescientos	three hundred	300
cuatrocientos	four hundred	400
quinientos	five hundred	500
seiscientos	six hundred	600
setecientos	seven hundred	700
ochocientos	eight hundred	800
novecientos	nine hundred	900
mil	one thousand	1,000
un millón	one million	1,000,000

Basic Subdivisions of the Dewey Decimal Classification
Clasificacion de Dewey

000	Obras Generalas	General Works
100	Filosofía	Philosophy
200	Religión	Religion
300	Ciencias Sociales	Social Sciences
400	Lingüística	Linguistics
500	Ciencias Puras	Pure Sciences
600	Ciencias Aplicadas	Applied Sciences
700	Bellas Artes	Fine Arts
800	Literatura	Literature
900	Historia	History

Key to Pronunciation

The pronunciation of vowels and consonants in Spanish differs from that in English. Here are a few of the most common examples:

Pronunciation of Vowels:

a is pronounced ah
e   eh
i   ee
o   oh
u   u (in bull)
y   ee

Pronunciation of Consonants:

j is pronounced as the English "h"
g in ge is pronounced as the English "h"
g in gi is pronounced as the English "h"
g in ga is pronounced like "garlic"
g in go is pronounced like "garlic"
g in gu is pronounced like "garlic"

APPENDIX D:
SANTA BARBARA PUBLIC
LIBRARY QUESTIONNAIRE

1. How would you identify your ethnic heritage?

   1____ Mexican-American/Chicano
   2____ Mexican
   3____ Other Latino
   4____ Native American
   5____ Black
   6____ Asian—Chinese
   7____ Asian—Japanese
   8____ Asian—Filipino
   9____ Other Asian: _____
   10____ Decline to identify

2. The public library is known as a place where one may check out books, magazines, or borrow records. The library is also a place where one goes or calls for information, and is also a place for special activities for children, cultural programs, and other services.

   Do you know where the nearest library is located?

   1____ Yes
   2____ No

3. Are you aware that all basic library services are free?

   1____ Yes
   2____ No
   3____ Don't know

4. Do you or a member of your family have a library card?

   1____ Yes
   2____ No
   3____ Don't know

5. In the past year have you visited or used any services of the Santa Barbara Public Library?

   1____ Yes
   2____ No (go to #10)
   3____ Don't know (go to #10)

1. **¿De que origen proviene usted?**

   1____ Mexico-Americano/Chicano
   2____ Mexicano
   3____ Otro Latino
   4____ Indio
   5____ Negro
   6____ Asiático—Chino
   7____ Asiático—Japones
   8____ Asiático—Filipino
   9____ Otro Asiático: _____
   10____ Prefiero no contestar

2. **La Biblioteca Pública es conocida como un lugar donde se presta libros, revistas, o discos. La biblioteca tambien es un lugar donde alguien puede llamar para información, y es un lugar para activdades especiales para niños, programas, culturales, y otros servicios. ¿Sabe Ud. donde se encuentra la biblioteca más cercana?**

   1____ Sí
   2____ No

3. **¿Sabe Ud. que los servicios basicos de la biblioteca son gratuitos?**

   1____ Sí
   2____ No
   3____ No sé

4. **¿Tiene Ud. o alguien en su familia una tarjeta de la biblioteca?**

   1____ Sí
   2____ No
   3____ No sé

5. **Durante este ano pasado—¿Ha Ud. visitado o usado qualquier servicio de alguna biblioteca en Santa Barbara?**

   1____ Sí
   2____ No (prosiga al #10)
   3____ No sé (prosiga al #10)

6. Which of the following have you used or are you using? (check as many as apply)
    1 _____ Central Branch (40 E Anapamu)
    2 _____ Eastside Branch (1102 E Montecito)
    3 _____ Goleta Branch (500 N Fairview Av.)
    4 _____ Carpinteria Branch (5141 Carpinteria Av.)
    5 _____ Book Mobile
    6 _____ Other _____
    7 _____ Don't know

7. Who in your household uses the library(s) you mentioned? (check as many as apply)
    1 _____ Self
    2 _____ Spouse
    3 _____ Children
    4 _____ Other household members _____

8. If you have used a Santa Barbara Public Library, what type of materials do you check out the most? (check as many as apply)
    1 _____ Books, magazines, newspapers
    2 _____ Films
    3 _____ Records, cassettes
    4 _____ Art prints
    5 _____ Other _____
    6 _____ Don't know

9. In the past year how often have you used a public library?
    1 _____ At least once a week (go to #12)
    2 _____ At least once a month (go to #12)
    3 _____ At least once every six months
    4 _____ Don't know

10. The following are a number of reasons why some people never or seldom (once every 6 months) use the library. Do you feel that any of them are true for you? (check as many as desirable)
    1_____ Library does not have the material I want
    2_____ I am too busy to go to the library
    3_____ I am not interested in the library
    4_____ I buy my own books or magazines
    5_____ Personal health problems make it difficult for me to use the library
    6_____ I don't know about the library
    7_____ The library is not open during the right hours
    8_____ The library is hard to get to/no transportation
    9_____ The staff at the library is not friendly
    10_____ No one on the staff speaks my language
    11_____ Other _____

11. If you are not using the library, how could the library serve your needs and interests?
    _____
    _____
    _____
    _____

6. ¿Cual de las siguientes a Ud. usado o usa actualmente?

    1 ____ Biblioteca Central (40 E Anapamu)
    2 ____ Biblioteca Pública del Este (1102 E Montecito)
    3 ____ Biblioteca Pública de Goleta (500 N Fairview Av.)
    4 ____ Biblioteca Pública de Carpinteria (5141 Carpinteria Av.)
    5 ____ Biblioteca ambulante
    6 ____ Otra _____
    7 ____ No sé

7. ¿Quién en su hogar usa la biblioteca(s) que Ud. nombro? (marque todos los que apliquen)

    1 ____ Yo solamente
    2 ____ Su esposa/esposo
    3 ____ Los niños
    4 ____ Otros miembros de su hogar _____

8. Si Ud. a usado su tarjeta bibliotecaria — ¿Qué clase de materiales a Ud. preferido?

    1 ____ Libros, revístas y periódicos
    2 ____ Películas
    3 ____ Discos y cintas grabadas
    4 ____ Reproducciónes gráficas de arte
    5 ____ Otro _____
    6 ____ No sé

9. Durante el año pasado — ¿Con qué frequencia ha usted usado alguna biblioteca públia?

    1 ____ Por lo menos una vez por semana (prosiga al #12)
    2 ____ Por lo menos una vez por mes (prosiga al #12)
    3 ____ Por lo menos una vez cada seis meses
    4 ____ No sé

10. Por las siguíentes razones, hay personas que nunca o raramente visitan la biblioteca — ¿Cuales le corresponden a usted? "Raramente" se considera cada 6 meses.

    1____ La biblioteca no tiene los materiales que deseo
    2____ Estoy muy ocupado para usar la biblioteca
    3____ No estoy interesado en usar la biblioteca
    4____ Yo compro mis libros o revistas
    5____ No uso la biblioteca porque no me siento suficiente bien de salud para ir
    6____ No sé de la biblioteca
    7____ La biblioteca no esta abierta durante el tiempo más conveniente para mi
    8____ Es dificil para ir a la biblioteca/hay falta de transportación
    9____ Los que trabajan en la biblioteca no son muy amables conmigo
    10____ Nadie en la biblioteca habla en mi idioma
    11____ Otro _____

11. Si no usa Ud. la biblioteca — ¿Cómo podra la biblioteca servir sus intereses?

_____
_____
_____
_____

12. The following are some of the reasons people use the library. Do you (user)/ Would you (nonuser) use the library for any of these reasons) (check all that apply)

   1_____ Read or borrow newspapers or magazines
   2_____ Read or borrow books
   3_____ Use or borrow materials other than books (films, language tapes, records, etc.)
   4_____ Meet friends/drop off children/pick up children
   5_____ Use the photocopy machine
   6_____ Obtain information about community services
   7_____ School assignments or other study purposes
   8_____ Attend a children's library program
   9_____ Job information
   10_____ For a meeting
   11_____ Reference or to have a question answered
   12_____ Other _____
   13_____ Don't know

13. Which language or languages are spoken in your home? (check one)

   1_____ English
   2_____ Spanish only
   3_____ Both English and Spanish
   4_____ Mostly English
   5_____ Mostly Spanish
   6_____ Asian language
   7_____ Other _____

14a. Do you or anyone in your household read in English, Spanish or in another language?

   1_____ Yes
   2_____ No (go to #18)
   3_____ Don't know (go to #18)

14b. Who reads?

   1_____ Self
   2_____ Other household members

15. In which language do you prefer to read? (check one)

   1_____ English
   2_____ Spanish
   3_____ Both English and Spanish
   4_____ Asian language
   5_____ Other _____
   6_____ Don't know

16. What kinds of material do you prefer to read in your free time? (check as many as apply)

   1_____ Magazines
   2_____ Newspapers
   3_____ Foto novelas
   4_____ Comic books
   5_____ Books

12. **Los siguientes son unos ejemplos por los cuales las personas usan la biblioteca.— ¿Usa usted o usaria la biblioteca para cualquiera de estos? (marque los necesarios)**

    1____ Para leer o pedir prestado libros
    2____ Para leer o pedir prestado periódicos o revistas
    3____ Para usar o pedir prestados otros materiales, ademas de libros, películas, cintas, discos
    4____ Para reunirse con amigos/o dejar a los niños
    5____ Para usar la maquina que hace foto-copias
    6____ Para obtener información de servicios en la comunidad
    7____ Para propósitos de escuela o estudio
    8____ Para asistir a un programa para niños
    9____ Para información de trabajo
    10____ Para una júnta
    11____ Para referencia o contestación de preguntas
    12____ Otra razón _____
    13____ No sé

13. **¿Cuáles idiomas se hablan en su hogar? (marque una)**

    1____ Inglés
    2____ Solamente español
    3____ Inglés y español
    4____ Mayormente inglés
    5____ Mayormente español
    6____ Un idioma asiático
    7____ Otro _____

14a. **¿Leé usted, o alguien en su hogar inglés, español, o en otro idioma?**

    1____ Sí
    2____ No (proceda al #18)
    3____ No sé (proceda al #18)

14b. **Quienes leén dichos idiomas?**

    1____ Yo
    2____ Otros en mi hogar

15. **¿En que idioma prefiere usted leér?**

    1____ Inglés
    2____ Español
    3____ Inglés y español
    4____ Idioma asiático
    5____ Otro _____
    6____ No sé

16. **¿Qué clase de materiales prefiere leer en su tiempo libre?**

    1____ Revistas
    2____ Periódicos
    3____ Fotonovelas
    4____ Libros cómicos
    5____ Libros

17. **If you read books, what kind of books do you most often read?**

    1____ History
    2____ Religion
    3____ Animals
    4____ Crafts
    5____ Home making
    6____ Biographies
    7____ Studying language
          a) English____   b) Spanish____   c) Other_____
    8____ Travel
    9____ Mysteries
    10____ Plays
    11____ Short stories
    12____ Romance
    13____ Translation of U.S. best sellers
    14____ Stories or essays by Latin American authors
    15____ Books about Mexico/Chicanos
    16____ Literature
    17____ Adventure
    18____ Comic books
    19____ Politics
    20____ Other _____

18. **Which of the following newspapers do you read? (check as many as apply)**

    1____ Santa Barbara News Press
    2____ Santa Barbara News and Review
    3____ Los Angeles Times
    4____ Los Angeles Sentinel
    5____ La Opinion
    6____ La Voz del Pueblo
    7____ Excelsior
    8____ Other _____
    9____ Don't know
    10____ Don't read newspapers

19. **How many magazines do the members of your household currently subscribe to? (check one)**

    1____ None (go to #21)
    2____ One to two
    3____ Three to four
    4____ Five or more
    5____ Don't know

20. **Are any of these in Spanish or in another language?**

    1____ Spanish
    2____ Other language
    3____ English only
    4____ Asian
    5____ Don't know

17. Si leé libros—¿Qué clase de libros lee mas a menudo?

1____ Historia
2____ Religión
3____ Animales
4____ Artesania
5____ Hogar
6____ Biografías
7____ Estudio de lenguage
　　　a) inglés____　b) español____　c) otro_____
8____ Viajes
9____ Misterio
10____ Dramas
11____ Cuentos cortos
12____ Romance
13____ Traducciónes de libros populares en inglés
14____ Cuentos o ensayos por autores Latino Americanos
15____ Libros sobre México/Chicanos
16____ Literatura
17____ Aventura
18____ Libros cómicos
19____ Política
20____ Otro _____

18. ¿Cuál de los siguientes periódicos leé usted? (marque todos los qué lea)

1____ Santa Barbara News Press
2____ Santa Barbara News and Review
3____ Los Angeles Times
4____ Los Angeles Sentinel
5____ La Opinion
6____ La Voz del Pueblo
7____ Excelsior
8____ Otro _____
9____ No sé
10____ No leo periódicos

19. ¿A cuantas revistas se subscriben los miembros de su familia, actualmente? (marque uno)

1____ Ninguna (proceda al #21)
2____ Uno a dos
3____ Tres a cuatro
4____ Cinco o mas
5____ No sé

20. ¿Son algunas en español, inglés, o en otro idioma?

1____ Español
2____ Otro idioma
3____ Solamente en inglés
4____ Idioma asiático
5____ No sé

21. **What are your major sources of information?**

    1____ Radio
          ε) Santa Barbara stations:_____
          b) Oxnard stations:_____
          c) Los Angeles stations:_____
          d) Other _____
    2____ Television
          a) Local station KEYT (channel 3 or 6) ____
          b) Los Angeles KMEX (channel 34 or 8) ____
          c) Other _____
    3____ Newspapers and magazines
    4____ Books
    5____ Family and friends
    5a____ Identify _____   Relationship _____

    6____ Public library
    7____ Social service agencies
    8____ Other _____

22. **Which one of the above do you rely on most?**

    1____ Radio
          a) Santa Barbara stations ____
          b) Oxnard stations ____
          c) Los Angeles stations ____
          d) Other _____
    2____ Television
          a) Local station KEYT (channel 3 or 6) ____
          b) Los Angeles KMEX (channel 34 or 8) ____
          c) Other _____
    3____ Newspapers and magazines
    4____ Books
    5____ Family and friends
    5a____ Identify _____   Relationship _____

    6____ Public library
    7____ Social service agencies
    8____ Other _____

23. **Are there times when you or someone in your household needs information on government services, health, or social services?**

    1____ Yes
    2____ No
    3____ Don't know

24. **In your opinion, what kinds of social service information are needed by you or those in your household? (check as many as apply)**

    1____ Information about schools and education
    2____ Information about job openings
    3____ Information on drugs and alcohol
    4____ Personal or family counseling
    5____ Where to get emergency food, clothes, money

21. ¿Cuáles son sus mayores recursos de información?

   1____ Rádio
       a) Estaciónes de Santa Barbara:_____
       b) Estaciónes de Oxnard:_____
       c) Estaciónes de Los Angeles:_____
       d) Otros _____
   2____ Televisión
       a) Estación local KEYT (canal 3 o 6) ____
       b) Los Angeles KMEX (canal 34 o 8) ____
       c) Otros _____
   3____ Periódicos y revistas
   4____ Libros
   5____ Familia y amigos
   5a____ Identifique _____   Relación _____
       _____   _____

   6____ Biblioteca pública
   7____ Agencia de servicios sociales
   8____ Otros _____

22. De los nombres ya mencionados— ¿De cual depende usted más?

   1____ Rádio
       a) Estaciónes de Santa Barbara ____
       b) Estaciónes de Oxnard ____
       c) Estaciónes de Los Angeles ____
       d) Otros _____
   2____ Televisión
       a) Estación local KEYT (canal 3 or 6) ____
       b) Los Angeles KMEX (canal 34 o 8) ____
       c) Otros _____
   3____ Periódicos y revistas
   4____ Libros
   5____ Familia y amigos
   5a____ Identifique _____   Relación _____
       _____   _____

   6____ Biblioteca pública
   7____ Agencia de servicios sociales
   8____ Otros _____

23. ¿Existen ocasiones cuando Ud. o alguien en su casa necesita información acerca de los servicios del govierno, salud o servicios sociales?

   1____ Sí
   2____ No
   3____ No sé

24. En su opinion— ¿Que clase de información de servicios sociales son los que se nesecitan en su hogar? (marque los necesarios)

   1____ Información escolar y educacional
   2____ Información acerca de oportunidades de trabajo
   3____ Información acerca de drogas y alcohol
   4____ Consultas personales y familiares
   5____ Donde conseguir en caso de emergencia, alimentos, ropa o dinero

    6___ Information on housing and landlord-tenant problems
    7___ Information on immigration and citizenship
    8___ Legal counseling or assistance
    9___ Information on low cost medical or health services
    10___ Translations
    11___ Information on recreational facilities or programs
    12___ Transportation
    13___ Where to get help in emergency or crisis situation
    14___ Assistance in dealing with agencies
    15___ Information on welfare
    16___ Consumer information
    17___ Other _____

25. **Are you aware that the library can provide you information, or refer you to agencies that offer information on these services?**

    1___ Yes
    2___ No
    3___ Don't know

26. **Given your choice, what language would you prefer to use when asking for help at the library? (check one)**

    1___ English
    2___ Spanish
    3___ Asian
    4___ Other _____
    5___ Don't know

(Everyone must answer #27)

27. **Which of the following services offered by the Santa Barbara Public Library have you heard of? (check as many as apply)**

1___ Books	17___ Periodical index
2___ Story hours for children	18___ Telephone ref/services
3___ Magazines and newspapers	19___ Reserves and interlibrary loans
4___ Records and cassettes	20___ Microfilm and microfiche
5___ Films	21___ Large type books
6___ Paperbacks	22___ Civil service exam books
7___ Children's books	23___ College catalogs
8___ Reference books and services	24___ Community resource directory
9___ Young adult books	25___ Genealogy material
10___ Business reference section	26___ Government documents
11___ Service to shut-ins	27___ Local history files
12___ Books in Spanish	28___ Maps
13___ Black studies books	29___ Telephone books
14___ Chicano studies books	30___ Community room
15___ Art prints	31___ Member of Black Gold Cooperative Library System
16___ Pamphlets	32___ Spanish films
	33___ Spanish records
	34___ Don't know

6____ Información sobre vivienda y problemas propietario e inquilino
7____ Información referente con ciudadania e immigración
8____ Información sobre el bajo costo de servicios médicos y de salud
9____ Consulta y asistencia legal
10____ Traducciónes
11____ Información acerca de las facilidades de programas recreativos
12____ Transportación
13____ Donde conseguir ayuda en caso critico de emergencia
14____ Asistencia relacionada con agencias
15____ Información acerca del "Welfare"
16____ Información para el consumidor
17____ Otro _____

25. ¿Sabe Ud. que la biblioteca le provee información, o lo pone en contacto con las agencias que le ofrecen información en estos servicios?

1____ Sí
2____ No
3____ No sé

26. De acuerdo a su gusto—¿Que idioma preferiría usted cuando pregunta por asistencia en la biblioteca?

1____ Inglés
2____ Español
3____ Asiático
4____ Otro idioma _____
5____ No sé

(Todos deben contestar #27)

27. ¿Cuáles servicios ofrecidos por la biblioteca conoce Ud.? (marque los qué sean necesarios)

1____ Libros
2____ Hora de cuentos infantiles
3____ Periódicos y revístas
4____ Discos y cassettes
5____ Películas
6____ Libros en rústica
7____ Libros infantiles
8____ Libros sobre referencias y servicios
9____ Libros para adultos
10____ Sección referente a negocios
11____ Servicios para personas recluidas
12____ Libros en español
13____ Libros de estudio de la raza negra
14____ Libros de estudios chicanos
15____ Reproducciónes gráficas sobre arte
16____ Folletos
17____ Indice de periódicos
18____ Servicio de información por teléfono
19____ Préstamo de libros entre bibliotecas, y reservas
20____ Microfilm y microfiche
21____ Libros impresos con tipo grande
22____ Libros para exámenes de servicios civiles
23____ Catálogos colegiales
24____ Directorio de recursos de la comunidad
25____ Material geneológico
26____ Documentos del gobierno
27____ Archivos de historia local
28____ Mapas
29____ Directorios telefónicos
30____ Salón de la comunidad
31____ Miembro de la cooperativa bibliotecaria "Black Gold"
32____ Películas en español
33____ Discos en español
34____ No sé

(Nonusers, go to #34)

28. **Have you used this service? (check as many as apply)**

1____ Books
2____ Story hours for chil-
       dren
3____ Magazines and news-
       papers
4____ Records and cassettes
5____ Films
6____ Paperbacks
7____ Children's books
8____ Reference books and
       services
9____ Young adult books
10____ Business reference sec-
        tion
11____ Service to shut-ins
12____ Books in Spanish
13____ Black studies books
14____ Chicano studies books
15____ Art prints
16____ Pamphlets

17____ Periodical index
18____ Telephone ref/services
19____ Reserves and interlibrary
       loans
20____ Microfilm and microfiche
21____ Large type books
22____ Civil service exam books
23____ College catalogs
24____ Community resource directory
25____ Genealogy material
26____ Government documents
27____ Local history files
28____ Maps
29____ Telephone books
30____ Community room
31____ Member of Black Gold Coop-
       erative Library System
32____ Spanish films
33____ Spanish records
34____ Don't know

29. **What do you feel are the four best things about the library? (check 4)**

1____ Book collection
2____ Films, tapes, records,
       art prints
3____ Spanish-language collec-
       tion
4____ Newspapers and maga-
       zines
5____ Reference services/
       collection
6____ Children's material

7____ Young adult materials
8____ Hours of service
9____ Staff
10____ Quiet atmosphere
11____ Library building
12____ Shelving arrangement
13____ Services in Spanish
14____ Adult material
15____ Other _____
16____ Don't know

30. **Of these services, do any of these need improvement?**

1____ Book collection
2____ Films, tapes, records,
       art prints
3____ Spanish-language collec-
       tion
4____ Newspapers and maga-
       zines
5____ Reference services/
       collection
6____ Children's material

7____ Young adult materials
8____ Hours of service
9____ Staff
10____ Quiet atmosphere
11____ Library building
12____ Shelving arrangement
13____ Services in Spanish
14____ Adult material
15____ Other _____
16____ Don't know

(Si no han usado la biblioteca pasar al #34)

28. **¿Ha hecho Ud. uso de estos servicios? (marque los que sean necesarios)**

1____ Libros
2____ Hora de cuentos infantiles
3____ Periódicos y revístas
4____ Discos y cassettes
5____ Películas
6____ Libros en rústica
7____ Libros infantiles
8____ Libros sobre referencias y servicios
9____ Libros para adultos
10____ Sección referente a negocios
11____ Servicios para personas recluidas
12____ Libros en español
13____ Libros de estudio de la raza negra
14____ Libros de estudios chicanos
15____ Reproducciónes gráficas sobre arte
16____ Folletos
17____ Indice de periódicos
18____ Servicio de información por teléfono
19____ Préstamo de libros entre bibliotecas, y reservas
20____ Microfilm y microfiche
21____ Libros impresos con tipo grande
22____ Libros para exámenes de servicios civiles
23____ Catálogos colegiales
24____ Directorio de recursos de la comunidad
25____ Material geneológico
26____ Documentos del gobierno
27____ Archivos de historia local
28____ Mapas
29____ Directorios telefónicos
30____ Salón de la comunidad
31____ Miembro de la cooperativa bibliotecaria "Black Gold"
32____ Películas en español
33____ Discos en español
34____ No sé

29. **¿Cuáles son los cuatro servicios mejores de la biblioteca?**

1____ Colección de libros
2____ Películas, cintas grabadas, discos
3____ Colección en idioma español
4____ Periódicos y revistas
5____ Colección de servicios de referencia
6____ Material infantil
7____ Material para jóvenes
adultos
8____ Horas de servicio
9____ Personal administrativo
10____ Ambiente silencioso
11____ Edificio bibliotecario
12____ Arreglo de la colección
13____ Servicios en español
14____ Material para adultos
15____ Otro _____
16____ No sé

30. **De estos servicios—¿Cuáles cree Ud. necesitan mejorar?**

1____ Colección de libros
2____ Películas, cintas grabadas, discos
3____ Colección en idioma español
4____ Periódicos y revistas
5____ Colección de servicios de referencia
6____ Material infantil
7____ Material para jóvenes
adultos
8____ Horas de servicio
9____ Personal administrativo
10____ Ambiente silencioso
11____ Edificio bibliotecario
12____ Arreglo de la colección
13____ Servicios en español
14____ Material para adultos
15____ Otro _____
16____ No sé

31. **If you use or have used the library, which of the following do you feel is most needed to meet your needs? (check as many as apply)**

1____ Larger book collections
2____ Larger nonbook collections (records, cassettes, films, etc.)
3____ More newspapers and magazines
4____ Better reference service/materials
5____ Adult programs
6____ Children's books
7____ Longer hours
8____ More materials in Spanish
9____ More materials on the Mexican-Americans and their history
10____ More materials on the black experience
11____ More materials on the Asian experience
12____ More materials on the Native American experience
13____ Spanish-language programs and services
14____ Library displays
15____ Bilingual/bicultural staff
16____ Other _____
17____ Don't know

32. **In general, the library staff seems to be:**

1____ Helpful
2____ Somewhat helpful
3____ Occasionally helpful
4____ Never willing to be of any help
5____ Other _____
6____ Don't know

33a. **If you use, or have used the library, on a scale of one to ten, do you consider the service of the Santa Barbara Public Library to be: (circle one)**

poor		inadequate		adequate		good		excellent	
1	2	3	4	5	6	7	8	9	10

33b. **If 4 or below marked, why?**

_____

_____

34a. **Have you moved into Santa Barbara within the past year?**

1____ Yes
2____ No
3____ Don't know

34b. **How long have you lived in this neighborhood?**

1____ More than one year
2____ Less than one year
3____ Other

31. Si Ud. usa o a usado la biblioteca—¿Cuáles de estos servicios, cree Ud. satisfacen sus necesidades? (marque las necesarias)

1____ Engrandecer la colección de libros
2____ Engrandecer la colección de discos, cintas, películas, etc.
3____ Más periódicos y revistas
4____ Mejorar el servicio de referencia de materiales
5____ Programas para adultos
6____ Libros infantiles
7____ Extención del horario
8____ Más materiales en español
9____ Más materiales sobre el México-Americano y su historia
10____ Más materiales acerca de la experiencia de la raza negra
11____ Más materiales acerca de la experiencia asiática
12____ Más materiales acerca de la experiencia de los indigenas de norte america
13____ Servicios y programas en idioma español
14____ Exposiciónes bibliotecarias
15____ Miembros del personal bilingues y biculturales
16____ Otro _____
17____ No sé

32. ¿En general, como considera nuestro personal?

1____ De mucha ayuda
2____ Algo de ayuda
3____ Ocacionalmente de ayuda
4____ Nunca dispuestos a ayudar
5____ Otro _____
6____ No sé

33a. Si Ud. usa, o ha usado la biblioteca, en la escala del uno al diez, en qué posición considera Ud. los servicios bibliotecarios públicos?

pobres	inadecuados	adecuados	buenos	excelente

1	2	3	4	5	6	7	8	9	10

33b. Si marcó menos que cuatro en la escala—¿Nos podría usted explicar brevemente por que?

_____

_____

34a. ¿Se ha usted mudado a Santa Bárbara durante el año pasado?

1____ Sí
2____ No
3____ No sé

34b. ¿Por cuánto tiempo a Ud. vivido en esta vecindad?

1____ Más de 1 año
2____ Menos de 1 año
3____ Otro

35. **Which of the following best describes your current employment? (check one)**

1____ Manufacturing or other industry
2____ Other blue collar positions
3____ Military
4____ Retired
5____ Not working at all
6____ Unemployed
7____ Professional – Educational
8____ Professional – Management
9____ Professional – Government
10____ Professional – Trades
11____ Professional – Sales
12____ Other _____
13____ Don't know

36. **How many people are living in your home?**

1____ 1 to 2
2____ 3 to 5
3____ 6 to 8
4____ 9 or more

37. **What was your approximate total household income last year?**

A 1____   *[These letters were keyed to a governmental form.]*
B 2____
C 3____
D 4____
E 5____
F 6____
G 7____
H 8____
I 9____ Decline to state

38. **How much education have you completed?**

1____ 1 to 6 years
2____ 7 to 9 years
3____ 10 to 12 years
4____ 2 years of college (AA degree)
5____ 4 years of college (BA degree)
6____ Graduate school
7____ Vocational school
8____ Adult education
9____ GED completion
10____ ESL

39. **What is your approximate age?**

1____ Under 15
2____ 16 to 19
3____ 20 to 24
4____ 25 to 34
5____ 35 to 49
6____ 50 to 59
7____ 60 and over
8____ Don't know

35. **¿Cuál de los siguientes describe mejor su ocupación? (actualmente)**
  1____ Manufacturero u otra industria
  2____ Otra técnica o vocacional
  3____ Ejército militar
  4____ Retirado
  5____ Desempleado
  6____ Actualmente sin trabajo
  7____ Profeción educativa
  8____ Profeción administrativa
  9____ Profeción gubernamental
  10____ Profeción comercial
  11____ Profeción de ventas
  12____ Otro _____
  13____ No sé

36. **¿Cuántas personas viven actualmente en su hogar?**
  1____ 1 a 2
  2____ 3 a 5
  3____ 6 a 8
  4____ 9 o más

37. **¿Cuál fué aproximadamente su ingreso total el año próximo pasádo?**
  A 1____
  B 2____
  C 3____
  D 4____
  E 5____
  F 6____
  G 7____
  H 8____
  I 9____ Prefiero no contestar

38. **¿Cuál fue su educación total?**
  1____ 1–6 años
  2____ 7–9 años
  3____ 10–12 años
  4____ Dos años de universidad
  5____ Cuatro años de universidad
  6____ Escuela universitaria de graduados
  7____ Escuela vocacional
  8____ Educación adulta
  9____ Certificado de estudios generales
  10____ ESL

39. **¿Cuál es su edad aproximadamente?**
  1____ Menos de 15
  2____ 16 a 19
  3____ 20 a 24
  4____ 25 a 34
  5____ 35 a 49
  6____ 50 a 59
  7____ 60 o más
  8____ No sé

40. In order to verify that I have conducted this interview, may I please have your name, address, and telephone number? We could also put your name on a mailing list to send you information about library programs.

Thank you very much for your time and cooperation. You have been very helpful.

Name _____ (optional)
Address _____
City _____
Telephone _____ ( ) No phone

Interviewer's signature
_____

Date _____

41. Respondent is:

1____ Male
2____ Female

42. Census tract in which interview took place: _____
Block number: _____
Time started _____ Time finished _____

40. Para poder verificar que yo personalmente he conducido esta entrevista, — ¿Por favor me podria Ud. dar su nombre, dirección, y teléfono? Tambien podriamos poner su nombre en una lista de correo para enviarle información sobre los programas de la biblioteca.

Muchisimas gracias por habernos brindado su tiempo y cooperación, ha sido Ud. de muy gran ayuda para esta encuesta.

Nombre _____ (opcional)
Dirección _____
Ciudad _____
Teléfono _____ ( ) no tengo

Firma del entrevistador
_____

Fecha _____

41. **Respondiente:**

1____ Masculino
2____ Femenino

42. **Area censada:** _____

Numero de cuadra: _____
Tiempo de comienzo _____ **Tiempo final** _____

INDEX